Your Deaf Child's Speech and Language

Mary Courtman-Davies, FCST

THE BODLEY HEAD
LONDON SYDNEY
TORONTO

To Alexandra
and all the other children
who showed the way – this book
is affectionately dedicated

British Library Cataloguing
in Publication Data
Courtman-Davies, Mary
Your deaf child's speech and language.
1. Children, Deaf-Language
I. Title
401'.9   HV2483
ISBN 0-370-30149-8

Printed in Great Britain for
The Bodley Head Ltd
9 Bow Street London WC2E 7AL
by Redwood Burn Ltd, Trowbridge
set in Monotype Imprint 101
by Gloucester Typesetting Co. Ltd
First published 1979

CONTENTS

CONTENTS

FOREWORD

Tell me   –   I forget
Show me   –   I remember
Involve me   –   I understand
(*Ancient Chinese proverb*)

It is clear that much of a child's development of basic communication skills is acquired in the home and that the parents are his natural teachers. Whether they intend to or not, they manipulate the conditions of learning that will determine the child's acquisition of language. If, however, they encounter difficulties in this task because their child's language development is delayed or deviant, then it is the professional's role to consider how best to help them in this prodigious task.

The greatest need for a hearing-handicapped child is a parent who can understand the problem and adjust to it. He also needs parents who, as a result of this understanding, will be able to foresee what his needs will be. The involvement of the parents must encompass more than being a recipient of information – it must aim towards increasing their understanding and developing their competence in dealing with the problem. Parents of such children can be helped to undertake the task and they are eager for information and advice on how to become active participants in the treatment of their child.

It is with a keen understanding of the parents' need for involvement that Mary Courtman-Davies handles her subject. She writes not only as an experienced speech therapist but also as a parent. Throughout her subject, she anticipates parents' questions and helps them to develop strategies appropriate to their child to assist him in learning to listen, to communicate and to learn. Her objectives are intended to lead to their active participation rather than passive understanding. She recognises that parents of hearing-handicapped children are like other parents, experiencing periods of confusion and discouragement and having many questions to ask. She also recognises, however, that they can experience success and satisfaction if given sufficient information and the opportunity to be involved in the total management of the problem of their child's handicap.

JEAN M. COOPER
Principal, The National Hospitals College of
Speech Sciences, London

ACKNOWLEDGEMENTS

I would like to give grateful thanks to the following for their invaluable help in compiling this book:

My husband for painstakingly typing and retyping the manuscript, for drawing charts and diagrams, for checking and putting in alphabetical order word lists, for generally ordering the manuscript and for endless discussions about the content and format of the book; Joan Reinhardt for her continued suggestions, support and encouragement; Geoffrey Ivimey of the Institute of Education for his invaluable guidance, inspiration and help and for reading the manuscript; Monty Shulberg, audiologist, who by his sympathetic and expert handling of children's hearing aids has contributed so greatly to my work with hearing-impaired children: he also read part of the manuscript and offered suggestions; Mrs Paber, of the Children's Bookshop, Muswell Hill, for her continued guidance and patient discussion of children's books; Jay Young, of the National Children's Deaf Society, and the staff of the Royal National Institute of the Deaf library, who obtained books and articles; William Heinemann Medical Books Ltd for permission to base Figure 3, page 44, on a chart which appears in *The Deaf Child* by E. Whetnall and D. Fry; my family who at times endured uncomplainingly an uncomfortable home life whilst the book was being written.

Last, but certainly not least, to the many parents who gave me insights into the problems of hearing-impaired children and particularly to those parents who allowed their children's case histories to be incorporated into this book. Passing references to children are based on an amalgam of children encountered in thirty years' clinical work and do not necessarily refer to any particular child.

YOUR DEAF CHILD'S
SPEECH AND LANGUAGE

I

Hearing, Understanding and Communication

At birth, every human baby shares with animals, birds and reptiles an ability to respond to sound. The baby alone has the potential ability to organise the speech sounds it hears into words and sentences with meaning. This interpretation of groups of speech sounds (or comprehension) is performed by the brain which, in the case of the baby, is capable of analysing, storing and later reproducing the sounds heard. As Edith Whetnall said in *The Deaf Child*: 'The main use of hearing in man is to enable him to comprehend, store and reproduce articulate speech.'

The normal baby responds to sounds from the first hours of his life. Up to the age of three months, a loud sound such as a bang may make the baby blink, or react with a generalised jerk of his whole body. Quiet sounds (like someone tip-toeing to his crib) will, if he is awake, result in a cessation of general movement. As he grows older and more physically mature, the baby will begin to lift and turn his head to familiar sounds. By eight months, when he is sitting up, he will definitely show by a vigorous turn of the head that he can locate familiar sounds such as running bath water, or the click of a spoon on a cup. During these months the baby perpetually hears his mother's voice, and he responds strongly to her intonation and vocal qualities at feeding and bathing times. He is, at this stage, rather like a stranger in a foreign country; he hears, but has not yet learned to understand what he hears.

As well as listening intently, infants make a variety of noises during their first year and though it is difficult to say when babbling begins, this reiteration of consonants (ba ba ba, ma ma ma, etc.) is usually very noticeable in babies of about eight months. The child makes a variety of sounds; some of these belong to the language he will use later, others will never be used at all. At this stage, the mother often repeats the child's babble to him, and his hearing her stimulates him to further babble. He also hears his own babble and this feeding back of his own voice to his ears further stimulates his babbling. Babbling seems to be a sort of 'try-out' of the organs of speech; the infant learns to control the breath force coming from the lungs and to co-ordinate it with the muscles of his lips, tongue and soft palate.

During his first year, the baby's hearing is highly sensitive – more sensitive than it will ever be again in his life – and he uses this sensitivity gradually to distinguish between the various speech sounds.

This is a considerable task since there are twenty-four consonants and twenty vowels in the English language* making no allowance for variations in accent. The phrase 'Look at the car' contains nine separate vowel and consonant sounds; the phrase 'Drink your milk' ten sounds.

By constant listening to his mother, the baby distinguishes an oft-repeated word, becomes able to recognise it again and associates it with an object. Thus, when his mother says, 'Show me your shoe,' he looks down at it, while 'Play pat-a-cake' results, at last, in his voluntarily attempting to clap his hands because his mother has often accompanied these words with the same action. This association of sounds heard with meaning occurs towards the end of the first year of the baby's life.

During the second year of life, the baby's hearing is still very acute and this is also a period when he is likely to begin to use recognisable words himself. The baby starts to speak by imitating some word that is often said to him. His first imitations may not be accurate, but his mother, in perpetually repeating words to him, gives him a pattern, and his hearing her, and hearing himself, helps him to approximate more and more nearly to the adult model. He also *feels* how a word is said (a good example is the buzzing of the lips when 'mama' is said) and these tactile sensations, like the sound of words, help him to build up a memory of words which is stored in the brain for later use.

Each word stands for an idea – thus in being able to understand 'teddy', 'shoe' or 'pat-a-cake', the baby shows that his ideas or concepts are developing. A great step forward is taken when the baby realises that by saying a word (i.e. voicing an idea) he can cause something to happen. When he spontaneously says 'Teddy' and his

* *Sounds* that make up a word that is heard should not be confused with the *letters* that are used when a word is written down.

mother passes his teddy to him, he realises that speech is a means of altering and controlling his environment.

Language development is a very complicated subject and a description of it must be limited here to saying that considerable numbers of words are distinguished by listening and stored in the brain. Not all these early words are names of objects, and some belong to categories that cause things to happen, like 'off', 'want', 'open', but there is none the less a pronounced noun growth between one and two years old. There is also an increasing tendency to use a word when an object is not present – thereby illustrating that the 'idea' is becoming more detached from the object. The young child does not always differentiate between objects that seem the same – thus eighteen-month-old Amanda embarrassingly hailed every man in the park as 'Daddy'!

At eighteen months or perhaps two years of age, the baby attempts to join words or, more accurately, to join ideas, since he makes combinations such as 'Open door,' 'Off chair,' 'Baby apple.' Phrases gradually lengthen, e.g. 'Give Johnny apple,' but it will be some time before a sentence is complete with articles, conjunctions and 'little' verbs such as 'is' and 'are'. It seems, however, that a child possesses an innate faculty for forming correct grammatical patterns – provided he hears enough language from adults. The mistakes and omissions he makes early on, 'I didid it,' 'I going to park,' are gradually corrected as he listens to the correct patterns of adults. Though random mistakes continue throughout childhood, the main rules of sentence construction have been mastered by four years of age. The vowel system is complete by three years of age and the consonant system between five and eight years.

All this is possible because the brain, primed by the ear, functions like a great computer. From the moment of birth it is learning to differentiate between sounds, to discard those that are meaningless, to store those that are meaningful in their correct sound sequence, e.g. 'lollipop' and not 'poppilol'. Sentence sequences are also stored, or rather the rules that govern sentence formation, so that the child recognises 'I am jumping over the log' as correct, but 'I is jumped the over log' as nonsense. The more material stored, the stronger becomes auditory recall so that the three-year-old able to repeat 'Twinkle, twinkle little star' becomes the six-year-old who remembers correctly his words in the school play.

Since listening plays so vital a role in learning to talk, this seems a good point at which to discuss the human ear (Figure 1). This is divided into three parts. The outer ear comprises the pinna or the part which is visible on the outside, together with a canal which terminates at the ear drum, and it is from this canal that wax is often syringed. The middle ear is a tiny cavity on the other side of the ear drum, crossed by three bones called ossicles. A tube leads from the middle ear to the throat. (The feeling of discomfort in the ears experienced in an aircraft is due to unequal pressure between the air in the middle ear and the air surrounding the body; pressure is relieved by swallowing because this admits more air to the middle ear.) The inner ear is a small system of cavities in the bones of the skull. One cavity, which looks like a minute snail's shell, is called the cochlea and contains a delicate membrane, the basilar membrane, which connects with the central nervous system. The fibres of the auditory nerve transport impulses to the brain.

Since air is an elastic medium, any sound we make disturbs it and sets up sound waves. The vowels and consonants uttered by the human mouth also create sound waves. If a mother says, 'Where's teddy?' these sound waves travel through the air and, provided the child is near enough, set his ear drum vibrating. The drum, in turn, transfers the vibrations to the ossicles, so carrying the sound waves across the cavity of the middle ear to the inner ear. Here the vibrations of the basilar membrane are converted into electrical impulses and carried by the auditory nerve to the brain. It is not until a message has reached the brain that it is fully interpreted, that is, meaning is given to it.

It will be seen that the full process of hearing does not merely mean that a sound is audible, but describes the whole skill of detection, recognition and interpretation of the meaning of the sound. We *hear* a foreign language like Chinese or Zulu but it is most unlikely that we understand it. If the child responds to 'Where's teddy?' by picking up the toy, the sound waves have not merely travelled to the child's ears, but his brain has also detected, recognised and interpreted the meaning of the sounds, so causing him to act upon it.

The further language develops, the more it is used in conjunction with the mental processes. This begins to be noticeable at about three years old, when the child is fond of observing that

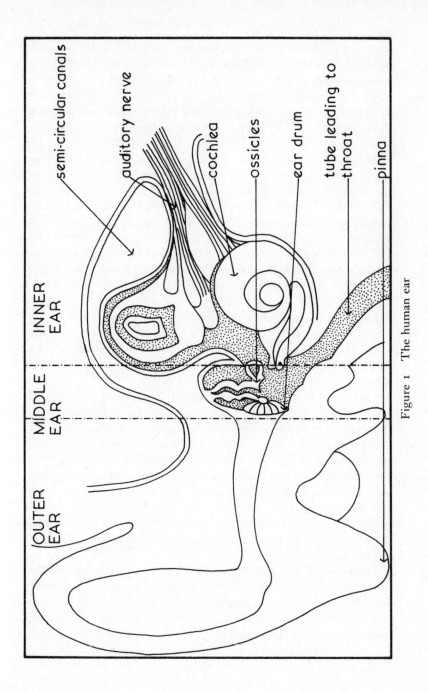

Figure 1   The human ear

objects are 'the same' and commenting upon this. Soon he begins to comment upon objects that are 'not the same'. The three-year-old who, on being shown a small elastic band, announced, 'It's not a ring,' had noticed differences in colour, texture and size but also a similarity in shape. As development continues, the child assembles in his mind objects that are 'the same in some ways' so that categories are formed. 'Green', 'blue', 'red', and 'yellow' all belong to the category 'colour'. 'Cow', 'horse', 'rabbit', 'sheep' all belong to the category 'animal'. This ordering of the child's mental material extends into all fields so that he recognises groups of objects that fly, groups of objects that are round, groups of objects that are useful, groups of objects that are dangerous. This firm internal structure enables the child to add quickly to existing information. 'What is a gerbil?' he asks and when his mother replies, 'It's an animal rather like a rat,' this is only meaningful if he already knows the class word 'animal' and if the word 'rat' evokes some mental image.

Language is thus the instrument by which the child's ideas begin to grow. The intensive questioning of the three- or four-year-old is not a search for information so much as a practice of the mechanics of questioning, but later questioning seeks to fit new information into the matrix already formed.

Closely related to this is reasoning. A five-year-old who remarked, 'All mammals have milk. A mummy has milk so a mummy is a mammal,' was a little precocious but displayed excellent classification which enabled him to place his mother in a particular category without aid from an adult. This is one way of manipulating facts; they are regrouped to produce a logical answer. Imagination consists of taking known material and regrouping it, so that a new configuration that is creative rather than logical appears. Both reasoning and imagination require a considerable fund of verbal knowledge, as well as practice in manipulating this knowledge in a flexible way.

Language is also the means by which the child himself can describe objects, places and events. 'Why didn't you collect me from that horrible house sooner? I was unhappy!' said four-year-old Geraldine to her mother after a visit. The mother was left in no doubt as to the exact category in which Geraldine, at any rate, placed her hosts and also her own feelings.

The growth of language is also, then, connected with the maturation of feeling.

A two-year-old may kick and scream instead of communicating, but by three years old a child is beginning to have the power to explain *why* an object is so important to him or *what* has frightened him. At three years old Geraldine requested her mother to check under the curtains, then in the cupboard and finally under the bed for a lurking alligator. On being assured that her mother could detect no alligator, the child went calmly to sleep. As well as allaying fears, the power of the child to exchange ideas with his mother modifies his primitive responses to other people; on her advice he controls his desire to snatch toys or hit his friend and so works towards becoming a more mature person.

A hearing-impaired child has difficulty in understanding language, in expressing himself, in forming words clearly and in all the ramifications of language development because part of the ear or nervous system is not functioning and his brain is consequently deprived of the information provided by listening under normal conditions.

It is important, at this stage, to distinguish between conductive and perceptive deafness. Conductive deafness is due occasionally to a condition of the outer, but more usually of the middle ear which prevents sound waves being carried to the inner ear. Heavy catarrh and suppurative conditions of the middle ear can cause conductive deafness in childhood, though modern medicine has decreased their frequency. Perceptive deafness is due to damage in the intricate mechanism of the inner ear or to the fibres of the auditory nerve. Most children suffering from perceptive deafness are born that way; of every 1,000 births one child has hearing impaired before, at or just after birth. A few children are born normally but suffer damage to the inner ear or auditory nerve due to severe illness in early childhood.

The result of perceptive deafness is that, depending upon its degree, the child misses many or most of the vital listening experiences of the first years of life. Without this listening, at worst he cannot identify words or associate words with objects or build up a store of words. The words used by other people remain meaningless to him and he consequently does not produce words of his own. To begin with his mother, not realising that he has a hearing loss, probably talks normally to him but gradually, as he does not respond as she had expected, or because she knows he is deaf, she ceases to talk to him. When this happens the child is doubly deprived. Not only is his hearing impaired but he is probably receiving less stimulus than a normally-hearing child and he cannot possibly learn as a normal child does. Thus arises the lack of speech or the defective speech and language of the hearing-impaired child.

Yet, if we consider, the *brain* of the hearing-impaired child is perfectly normal.* In some cases it may even be an unusually good brain. That normal brain is as capable as any other brain of organising into meaningful patterns the messages it receives from the outside world. It can store these patterns, sequence them and recall them. If only messages can reach it in the first place the hearing-impaired child can learn to comprehend, to express himself, and to develop in thought and feeling as other children do.

If he is to develop, the hearing-impaired child must be given, first of all, loud sounds; that is, he must be provided as early as possible in life with hearing aids. He must hear sounds not as often as the hearing child, but even more often. A hearing child of five years old has had approximately 5,000 hours' practice in listening to speech. Instead of receiving less, as he often does, the hearing-impaired child must receive *more* listening hours. If his parents truly wish him to talk, they must speak to him most of his waking hours, being careful to stay close to him so that he can pick up all the sound he possibly can. The child must be encouraged to watch his mother's face and so supplement the auditory messages he receives by visual ones. Most important of all, if they want their hearing-impaired child to talk, the parents must make their communication both lively and rewarding. A child who sees dreary, expressionless faces cannot be as motivated to watch them as the child who sees animated faces and is rewarded for his own efforts by love and enthusiasm.

Last of all, parents must be prepared to make special efforts to teach their hearing-impaired child to talk. A normal child talks

* There are, of course, children with multiple handicap of whom this is unfortunately not true, but for the great majority of hearing-impaired children it is true.

because he hears his parents talk. Provided he is given enough experience, a hearing-impaired child will do the same, but considerably later than usual. Unless deliberate and consistent efforts are made to speed up his progress, he will remain behind his contemporaries and consequently experience difficulty, both socially and educationally. The parents must therefore, if they wish him to keep up with his peers, make extra efforts to carry out definite teaching with him from the earliest possible time, to continue this teaching and make it a regular part of their lives. Many disappointments with hearing-impaired children come from lack of realisation of the need for continued special attention. The child is given hearing aids, the parent talks conscientiously, and then is disappointed that the child is still well behind his peers in speech development.

It is as though the child who does not hear is a garden on which rain (sound) rarely falls. The owner of the garden painstakingly carries water in a watering-can, and is rewarded with some rather stunted growth. Who is surprised if a sprinkler (special teaching) turned on the whole garden for a number of hours each day makes the garden almost as normal as if rain fell regularly?

Whether or not the hearing-impaired child talks is the decision of his parents. With the right hearing aids, enough sound, enough looking and enough teaching he can learn to do so, but only his parents, and in particular his mother, can provide him with these things.

2

The Effects of
Hearing Loss upon the
Child's Development

The child whose hearing loss is detected early, who is fitted with hearing aids and receives the maximum auditory and visual input is at a great advantage compared to the hearing-impaired child who has not had these things. The quicker and more efficient the action by the adults in the environment, the fewer problems there are likely to be. However, hearing-impaired children who have had every advantage from birth are rare, and we must consider the problems that are, unfortunately, the common lot of many of them. In discussing these, I would like to stress that I have known numbers of hearing-impaired children who have suffered from these problems and were helped to overcome them, so that they became almost as normal as other human beings.

The most obvious problem is speech and language and we must now be more specific about these terms:

*Language** This implies the acquired use of symbols, usually audible (speech) or visible (writing), for the purpose of communication. These symbols are conventional and specific to a community of individuals, geographical or social. Communication, therefore, is usually through the spoken or written word but it is possible in a limited form without the use of verbal symbols when sounds, gestures or primitive inarticulate sounds can be indicative of feelings and desires and can convey information.

Speech This is the audible expression of language, consisting of organised patterns of articulation. When arranged with an agreed (a conventional) symbolic meaning, these constitute spoken language.

* *Terminology for Speech Pathology*, authorised by the College of Speech Therapists.

Articulation   The process of producing the sounds used in speech by movements of the lips, jaw and tongue and palate pharyngeal mechanism in co-ordination with respiration and phonation. A recognised number of such sounds is used in combination in the spoken language of each particular social and geographical group.

We have already said that because the deaf child is deprived of normal listening, he does not learn to understand his own language. The fitting of hearing aids makes sounds much louder and more definite but does not automatically teach him to interpret those sounds. Lip-reading is slowly acquired and the hearing-impaired child consequently understands much less than a normal child. How little he understands depends upon many factors, but hearing-impaired children usually have less comprehension of the spoken language than is generally attributed to them, and have difficulty in following simple, spoken instructions and explanations. They cannot follow a story without pictures and it is a considerable time before they can enjoy being read aloud to. One teacher commented to me, 'Would you have thought that Dora would have understood *The Magician's Nephew* which I'm reading aloud to the class?' I would have been most surprised if Dora, though she spoke quite well, understood a word of it. Because of his lack of understanding and because adults do not understand his lack of verbal comprehension, the world can be a very confusing place to the hearing-impaired child.

Because the child has not had a normal number of listening hours, his memory for words is not built up in a normal way. Many parents protest when told that their child's auditory memory is poor, and cite instances of his responsiveness when revisiting a place, or even his good memory for the route a car should take. These are, however, examples of visual memory – often excellent in a hearing-impaired child – but it is auditory memory that is essential in gaining speech. The test of auditory memory is whether a child can remember the names of objects, actions or qualities and whether he can repeat a sentence with the words said in the correct order. The auditory memory of a hearing-impaired child who speaks little is poor; not because there is anything intrinsically faulty in it but because it has never been exercised by the storing and linking of words that goes on perpetually in normal children. Parents often wonder why their deaf child cannot learn 'Baa baa black sheep' or 'Away in a manger'. In the first place the piece has much less meaning to a deaf child than to a normal child, and in the second his memory is far too weak to contain the chain of words.

A child reproduces what has been said to him, but in the case of the hearing-impaired child it is what he *thinks* has been said. A child with perceptive deafness picks up very little of even a short sentence when he first begins to talk and the 'communicating by one word' stage may last a considerable time. Many profoundly deaf children are still at this stage when they are six years old. As the child learns to listen and to lip-read, words cohere, but much of the sentence is missing to the deaf child and he produces language according to his perception of it. Thus 'Mary is going to Ann's home' is perceived as 'Mary go Ann home' and reproduced in just that way. It may take several years and much practice before the hearing-impaired child can produce a sentence grammatically. Children deliberately taught to write correct sentences rather than being simply exposed to plenty of spoken language tend to produce written word combinations like 'My brother and me was went in a swimming by Mummy car.' They feel that numbers of words should be present, but have insufficient memory of appropriate tense and word sequence. Vocabulary is also restricted. It has been said that a normal young child must hear a word thirty times before that child can use it. The deaf child misses hearing a word so often that he takes much longer to acquire vocabulary.

Articulation is likely to be poor in those with severe hearing loss or in those whose audiogram shows sudden drops or sharp peaks. A severely or profoundly deaf child may hear only vowel sounds and even those not clearly. He will produce what he has heard combined with what he is able to lip-read, so that many consonant sounds are omitted or replaced by other sounds. A partially deaf child may receive a distorted pattern of consonants and says them poorly or not at all. For hearing-impaired children, the consonants 's', 'z', 'sh', 'ch', 'j', 't', 'k' are particularly difficult for reasons that will be explained later, and the final consonants of words, difficult to hear, are likely to be left off. Voice, the clarity and intonation of which are normally monitored by the child's auditory feedback, is frequently affected so that the voice of a very deaf child may be deep and gruff, or shrill, or monotonous. The voice of a partially-hearing child is comparatively normal in pitch, but may be flat and lacking in musicality.

Such problems are more or less obvious to anyone dealing with a hearing-impaired child. The problems concerned with the workings of the thought processes are more subtle. These are not obvious when the child is in the early stages of learning to communicate, because his inability to speak conceals his lack of thought, but the more he begins to use speech and to attempt to exchange thoughts with other people, the more obvious it becomes that his brain has not been normally 'programmed'. Therefore stages reached early in life by a hearing child are reached much later by a hearing-impaired child.

An obvious example of this is the limitation of the child's concepts or ideas. I have already mentioned the eighteen-month-old child who hails all men as 'Daddy'. He has learned one label which he applies to a large class of people who seem to him to have the same characteristics. Soon he learns the word 'man' which he later divides into 'grandpa', 'postman', 'milkman', etc. A hearing-impaired child takes much longer to reach this stage of differentiation. Thus, at five and three-quarter years profoundly deaf Mary classed the girls at school as 'girl' and herself as 'girl' but her eighteen-month-old baby sister as 'baby'. When told, 'Baby is a girl,' she shook her head and laughed. Baby was a baby and could not have two labels! This over-simplification, normal in hearing young children, is very typical of hearing-impaired older children and a great effort is needed to show them that a person or object may have several labels, and also that specific objects each have a label. Thus objects in the bedroom (pillow, duvet, bed, nightdress, sheet, etc.) each have a name and are not all 'sleep'. Lacking such basic concepts, it is not surprising that later ideas are also limited and that the hearing-impaired child lacks the childhood general knowledge taken for granted in the normal child. As one mother said, 'My hearing-impaired son has no idea that the child who lives with us is his *brother*.'

Basically, the hearing-impaired child lacks the firm internal thought-structure founded on past experience that enables the hearing child to assimilate new knowledge easily. Thus he may seem very slow to take in something told to him. One effect of this is that while a hearing town-dwelling child can learn from books about country objects like barns, cowsheds and stiles, these lack any reality to a deaf child. He has to see to believe and even having seen, he assimilates more slowly. Even when he has apparent knowledge of a subject and considerable spoken language, this slow assimilation is obvious. Thus a child may question: 'Who put the fish in the pond?'

Adult:	'I put the fish in the pond.'
Child:	'Where did you got them?'
Adult:	'I bought them in the village.'
Child:	'Did you bought them in the shop?'
Adult:	'Yes, I bought the fish in the shop.'
Child:	'Did you put the fish in the pond?'
Adult:	'Yes, I put them in the pond.'
Child:	'Who put the fish in the pond?'

This type of exchange is maddening and makes the adult wonder whether anything at all is being achieved. In fact, a hearing-impaired child who questions thus is very far on the road to communication and trying hard to get information into his slowly maturing framework. It is as though he had to practise and practise, asking questions and receiving information, however paltry.

It must be seen, from what has been said, how very unready to assimilate the new ideas presented in formal school study a hearing-impaired child will be unless, of course, he has gained considerable spoken language. To benefit from schooling a child needs at the very least to be able to understand what his teacher says, e.g. 'Copy out *everything above* the line,' 'Add the *top* number to the *bottom* number,' 'Make your writing *bigger*,' 'Write *on* the line.' Many of these words, frequently used in school, represent a quite advanced level of childhood language and are rarely understood by hearing-impaired children at the normal age. How much understanding is needed to follow a basic nature lesson, say, about a daffodil in which the words 'bulb', 'autumn', 'plant', 'earth', 'roots', 'spring', 'shoot', 'grow', 'bloom' are likely to be used and whose meaning must be appreciated for the lesson to have any value at all! Yet many parents believe that if only they can get their child to school, education will miraculously solve his problem. As the headmistress of a normal school containing a nearly speechless seven-year-old said to me when I started to help the child: 'I always thought Lucy needed something very special done to help her!' The school instruction given to this child had meant nothing whatsoever to her, since her existing level of comprehension was less than that of a three-year-old.

The judgement of hearing-impaired children is also immature – once again due to lack of information and practice. A hearing-impaired child's judgement is as sound as anyone else's when the situation is visible. He will not, for instance, run into a busy road. He is immature in his assessment of what to say and when to say it, and once again this is typical of the child who is doing well in acquiring speech at a much later age than usual. We all overlook the verbal indiscretions of a very tiny child and think it under-standable when a two-and-a-half-year-old announces to the company, 'I was a naughty boy. I did pooh in my pants.' It is merely embarrassing when a six-year-old blurts out, 'You're fat,' or 'My mummy says your house is cold.' Eight-year-old Eliza, who had had little spoken language but was learning fast, seemed, once she had acquired words, to say whatever came into her head. Luckily, her family was broad-minded, but even they were embarrassed when she announced loudly at tea-time in the presence of an elderly aunt, 'I can see Aunt Jane's pink knickers.' It is, of course, up to the parents to try to convince the child of the unwisdom of such remarks.

Untruthfulness comes into much the same category. Once they have learned the power of the spoken word, some hearing-impaired children believe that it can achieve anything. This seems alarming, but is again a normal part of development and will pass. A child who has developed far enough to tell an untruth is capable of understanding 'true' and 'not true'* and can usually be trained, as any other child can be, to be truthful.

The ability to think is linked to the ability to imagine. Imagi-nation consists of having a basic fund of experience which is rearranged to show a new configuration. Thus a normal seven-year-old, having never seen a witch, has heard enough stories about witches to write a short piece of his own when his teacher says, 'Write a story about a witch.' He manages to incorporate in his story ideas relevant to witches – pointed hat, broomstick, dark cave, black cat, magic, etc. Most hearing-impaired children of this age

* cf. Bloom, F., *Our Deaf Children*.

find it difficult to write about subjects outside their immediate experience. They stick to what they know from their own lives. Thus one highly intelligent child of seven with severe high-tone hearing loss wrote, 'The witch got up, she got dressed, she had breakfast, she went to school, she had lunch, she played, she came home'! A story she wrote about a rabbit was identical. Not only did the child lack the fund of knowledge normal to seven-year-old children, she was incapable of assembling the little knowledge she had in order to write something more appropriate. Similarly, in the playground, the hearing-impaired child may be admired because he is a skilful climber or football player, but if a group of children are playing make-believe games he can neither follow their fantasy nor contribute his own. Sometimes a child will learn a set formula for, say, a game of schools and will, if allowed to choose a game, always play this game rather than venture on something new. This is not to say that many hearing-impaired children do not become imaginative once they have acquired enough ideas, and if they are given the right encouragement.

The normal child relies heavily upon vision but whilst he is busy using his eyes (cutting out or doing a puzzle, for example) his ears are constantly bringing information to his brain in a way that makes the environment meaningful. Certain behaviour in hearing-impaired children occurs because environmental sound is much reduced and they are deprived of valuable information. Vision is of the utmost importance to the hearing-impaired child, but the next most important senses to him, in this order, are sense of touch, sense of smell and sense of taste. The greater the degree of hearing loss, the less the importance of hearing to him. (This does not mean that, with training, sound cannot in time increase in importance, but we must consider the child in his original state.)

Most parents realise that their hearing-impaired child is sharp-eyed; he will detect slight changes in a room or minute flaws in an object. It is not always also realised that visual messages without attendant auditory clues can be a terrifying experience. A hearing-impaired child may be startled as a shadow falls over his cot because he has not heard accompanying footsteps. One child screamed without apparent reason at night – until her parents realised that she was frightened by the reflections of car lights passing over the bedroom ceiling. The lack of car noise made the lights meaningless and terrifying to her.

Hearing-impaired children vary in the degree to which they use tactile sense, but it is fairly common for the fairly deaf child persistently to stroke someone's dress or the smooth arm of a chair. One child of seven had 'a thing' about fur. If there was fur in the room, she felt compelled to finger it and she even referred to fur a great deal when no fur was present! A four-year-old was 'mad about hair' – her own or that of anyone else. Andrew, discouraged from having his dog on his bed, could often be found asleep with his fingers in the dog's beautiful, thick coat. Hearing-impaired children frequently love swimming – the sea with waves that bounce against their bodies being preferred to a calm swimmng pool.

Some very deaf children can be seen to cup their hands around objects in order to smell them and so discover more about their nature. They are alert to scents of all kinds and girls may be unable to leave scent bottles alone!

Some deaf children are either faddy or greedy over food, but since this is also true of normal children this is not so striking as licking, which occurs sometimes in very deaf children. The licking of a window pane seems to be a combination of tactile and gustatory sensation. Some parents do not object to touching, licking and smelling behaviour; others are irritated by it. It is well to remember that such behaviour springs from a normal desire on the part of the child to learn from his environment. The wise parent will try to increase the child's information by other means rather than admonish him for something he is doing to compensate for lack of normal stimulus.*

Some hearing-impaired children are extremely active. Again, since the auditory channel is denied them, they try to find out about their environment by running up to something, rummaging, handling and looking. Many enjoy vibration and will jump on a shaky floor or slam a door because they enjoy the physical sensa-

* It seems as though the average human being *needs* a certain amount of sensation: if one channel of communication is blocked, others are overused. This happens with many adults who suddenly lose their hearing; they become very fidgety, as if extra physical movement (which is accompanied by physical sensation) compensated for the loss of auditory sensation.

tion. Since we all of us normally learn to control the noise we emit through listening to ourselves, some deaf children drag their feet when they walk, make noises with their feet when seated and are noisy breathers when they have a head cold.

What has been said above tends to be more characteristic of the severely and profoundly deaf than of the partially hearing, but what follows may be common to all hearing-impaired children.

Young hearing-impaired children are often difficult to handle. They are wayward, demanding, restless and active. The child's behaviour is understandable, since his normal 'in' and 'out' channels to other people are impaired and he cannot understand what is happening to him or express his frustrations verbally. Since his mother is the person closest to him and usually understands his needs and communications, he clings to her and may create noisy scenes if she tries to leave him with someone else. He understands much less than a normal child of the same age that she will return in time. This clinging behaviour can be very trying. Ruth, for instance, at six years old, would make protesting noises and start to pursue her mother if the mother merely wanted to go to the bathroom! Milly, at the same age, could not for a long time adapt to a special teacher or a therapist. If her mother was in the room, Milly clung and sucked her thumb. If her mother left her, Milly would scream for an apparently unlimited length of time.

Normal children become independent of the mother because they understand what is required of them and because they understand her explanations of a situation that involves her leaving them. They also have confidence in their ability to ask for what they need in her absence. The hearing-impaired child's limitations make him much more dependent and therefore immature in his reactions.

If a child has frequent tantrums that are not related to being left, parents should try to see what provokes these and avoid situations in which tantrums are likely to occur. Some children, for instance, become very tired by long shopping trips on which they mustn't touch the goods on show. If this evokes tantrums it is better to avoid the situation. If tantrums do occur at home despite precautions, the child should not be threatened, bribed or cajoled since attention tends to prolong the tantrum. A display of anger by adults accompanied by shouting or smacking is inclined to set a bad example to the child rather than arrest the tantrum. A violent child must be restrained, but since most tantrums are merely noisy, the wisest course of action is to sit quietly near the child without touching him until the storm is over.

The important thing to remember is that lack of communication plays an important part in the trying behaviour of young hearing-impaired children. If understanding and expression can be built up, the child will mature and his behaviour will improve.

Young hearing-impaired children frequently have bad nights. There are difficulties at bedtime, further difficulties about the mother leaving for the night and the child may then appear at regular intervals downstairs during the evening. Sleep hours may be short, the child not falling asleep until ten or eleven p.m. and waking at five or five-thirty a.m. Naturally, the child and his family live in a state of exhaustion that adds to the difficulties of the following day.

It has already been pointed out that random lights tend to frighten a child. The normal fears of childhood tend also to be increased at night because, with light reduced, the hearing-impaired child feels even more cut off from people. It is obvious that parents should make sure there are no random lights and offer some kind of nightlight or keep the landing light on.

Some bad nights undoubtedly occur because, although the child is physically tired, he has not had the mental activity that tires the normal three- or four-year-old. At this age the child's brain should be kept busy by endless questions, stories and conversations with his mother. Without this necessary formative mental activity, the partially-hearing child (though perhaps exhausted and exhausting) is not tired in the way he should be. If this *is* the cause of bad nights, once again, the child will become better when he is under-standing and speaking more. On the other hand, one mother found that her three-year-old son slept better if he was taken for a good run in the park rather late in the afternoon. He was a very physic-ally active child who had obviously taken a surplus of physical energy to bed with him.

Unless he is obviously frightened, an effort should be made to keep the hearing-impaired child in bed. His wants should be sup-plied *before* he is put down and if he appears downstairs he should not be given drinks, biscuits or a look at the television. Equally, he should not be allowed to sleep in his parents' bed. The worst 'night bird' ever known to me undoubtedly felt very isolated when his nocturnal wanderings started at two or three years old. Since he was permitted to come down at intervals and join in the family life and also to sleep in his parents' bed, he was nine before he acquired good sleeping habits and slept a night through in his own bed.

A hearing-impaired child who is being educated in a partially-hearing unit or school for the deaf is likely to have fewer problems with his peer group than a child who is the only one in his group with a hearing problem. Hearing-impaired children together develop a feeling of 'sameness'; they play games suited to their disability and have less consciousness of their shortcomings. In the early years, at three and four, when children engage in many physical games, splashing, balancing and running, there are fewer difficulties between the hearing-impaired child and his hearing peers than there are at five and six years old. At this age, when children communicate together and speech is used in games, the hearing-impaired child is often at a loss. When imaginative games are played and he has nothing to contribute he may be assigned a dull or 'baddie' role. He also finds it impossible to understand the punning jokes beloved by seven- and eight-year-olds.*

If the hearing-impaired child goes to normal school and is wisely handled, he may ultimately make a place for himself with the hearing group. His parents should, however, understand the strain imposed upon a normal child who spends a day with a hearing-impaired friend. Hearing-impaired children, even when they have gained a considerable amount of speech, are slow to grasp the rules of a new game and tend to want to play known games over and over again. It is wise, therefore, not to expect the span of play and conversation that may engage two normal children, but to offer some outdoor activity such as a trip to the park and also for an adult to play some organised games with the children for part of the day.

At about six years old, the child will probably realise that he is deaf. There are numerous ways in which that realisation dawns,

* Understanding of the riddle:
'When is a cook bad?'
'When he beats an egg!'
requires not only knowledge of the verb 'beat', unlikely in a hearing-impaired child, but also the verbal sophistication and mental flexibility to perceive its double meaning.

but it is bound to come. The more speech he has, the more questions the child will ask and it is best to answer these questions truthfully. It is usually helpful to point out that so-and-so wears glasses for his eyes – hearing aids are rather the same things for ears. Some children ask whether they will always be deaf; it is wise to give a candid answer, but to point out that if the child works hard, his speech will improve. At an older level, some children protest at the unfairness of being born deaf. One of the most stalwart mothers I have known replied to her eleven-year-old daughter, 'But life is *not* fair – you must realise this.' This mother was not callous; she had done everything in her power to help her daughter and the child knew it. But in showing her acceptance of the burden thrust upon them both, she set her child the example of realistic adjustment. Basically, the degree to which the parent can accept the child's handicap conditions the child's own adjustment to it.

Difficulties, or hopefully lack of difficulties, will always be increased by the innate personality of the child and by his parents' attitude to him. One professional worker, after years with hearing-impaired children, said she thought they had to try to be 'extra nice people' in order to be accepted in the hearing world. Pauline, for instance, had been allowed to be selfish and arrogant in the home, to feel that she was a 'special' person, with particular rights and privileges. She spoke well and it was not so much her handicap as her poor emotional control and demands to be always first that made her unpopular with her normal peers. She did learn, under considerable pressure from other children, to take her place with them and to be nicer to them, but it was a hard lesson for her to learn.

Dora, who was admitted to a normal girls' school at seven, had been very sheltered at home and had never experienced unkindness. Though her communication and school work were quite good, the other children picked out flaws in her speech and called her 'baby'. Dora was not accustomed, either, to being pushed and jostled and she frequently shed tears. Her parents wanted to complain to the school, but since her teachers were known to be good and understanding, it was suggested to the parents that Dora should be left to fight her own battles. She survived in the school world and was a stronger person for her experiences.

Hearing-impaired people find it very frustrating not to know what is being said, and children often clamour, at table, for example, to know what the visitor is saying to Daddy, etc. This is understandable, but very irritating and not likely, once again, to win the child friends. The hearing-impaired child has to learn that a group conversation is often too difficult for him to follow. While he is at home with his parents, they should make it their job to give him a brief resumé of what is being said at intervals if it concerns him. The parents should not be afraid, on the other hand, to say, 'What is being said at the moment is grown-up talk – not for you. Eat your lunch.' It is said that deaf people are suspicious and feel, if they cannot understand what is being said, they must be under discussion. Some normal people are, of course, more naturally suspicious and sensitive than others, but often it is the self-centred child, normal or hearing-impaired, who has these feelings of being talked about. It may be helpful to say, 'Why do you think we are talking about you? Do you think you are very interesting? We are speaking of something else!'

Parents should also be firm about interrupting at other times. Unable to utilise auditory clues easily, the hearing-impaired child is prone to speak when he feels like it and parents are not inclined to stop him, perhaps because they are so happy that he speaks at all. They should try to realise how unattractive an interrupting child is and to curb him. As he matures and becomes more used to utilising auditory and visual clues, he will realise when it is his turn to speak.

If I have seemed to dwell on some rather depressing aspects of hearing-impaired children, it is because I want to reassure parents that they are not alone in the problems they face with their particular child. Many of the problems will vanish as the environment becomes more meaningful to the child; others are a sign that great progress is being made. Any child who has enough speech to make personal remarks, tell untruths, clamour for information and interrupt has recognised that oral communication is worth having, and is well on the way to acquiring it!

3

The Effects of Hearing
Loss upon Parents and Family

It is useless to deny that it is a grievous blow to parents when they are told that they have produced a handicapped child. Every normal parent wishes his child to be 'all right', to grow to normal manhood or womanhood and to take his place in the world. If we are honest, most of us, as parents, want a bit more. We are inclined to want *our* child to be better looking, more advanced in school or more popular than others, according to what our values are. When a child is born with a handicap, the parent no longer feels a joyous 'What will he become?' but a frightened 'Whatever will become of him?' As one father of a profoundly deaf four-year-old said bitterly, 'What sort of future is there for someone like him?'

To anxiety about hearing are often added worries as to whether the child is really normally intelligent. Perhaps he is mentally backward or brain-damaged? Those fears are often reinforced by the unwitting comments of friends and neighbours who know nothing about hearing-impaired children.

Though parents of a hearing-impaired child, if they are normally sensitive human beings, feel deep sorrow at their child's condition, ways of coping with these feelings vary according to the sort of personalities the parents have had before the intervention of the handicapped child. It is not so much that, initially, the parents are changed by the traumatic thing that has happened to them as that they react to their child's hearing loss in a manner typical of their general reaction to life.

Some people, for instance, habitually find it very hard to face reality, since reality contains some unpleasant features. Mrs A had had many pointers during her daughter's three and a half years that Emily was not hearing normally; these she always pushed aside with the excuse that the child 'wasn't interested' or 'wasn't concentrating'. When partial hearing loss was finally diagnosed, Mrs A could still never bring herself to admit its implications. She did not help the child to learn to communicate because 'Mothers

(33)

should not be teachers'. She denied the extent of the hearing loss, telling people, when it had to be mentioned, that Emily was 'a little hard of hearing'. When anyone pointed out the child's increasing failures, the mother became defensive, finally falling back on 'Emily has such a lovely personality – I know she'll be all right.' Not only did the mother's inability to face the unpleasant fact of the hearing loss and its implications prevent her from helping Emily, but it also barred Emily from accepting help or helping herself. As an older child she usually denied that she had a hearing problem and frequently placed herself at the back of the classroom to show that she was 'normal'.

Mrs B had apparently accepted her daughter's severe hearing loss from infancy, but was so grieved by it that she could not mention the child to her friends. When compelled by circumstances to refer to her daughter (an almost totally non-communicating eight-year-old) she would say, 'She's so independent, she's sure to manage.' This girl too had great difficulty in accepting her handicap.

In the case of both Mrs A and Mrs B it was as though they sought compensation for the handicap by attributing to their children remarkable powers of survival. The reality of the situation was not faced at all.

Some parents, equally unaccepting, seek a magic outside the child and go the weary round of faith healers, or cling to false hopes in other ways. One mother who, after years of perseverance, taught her daughter to speak normally described how, before she took practical measures, she 'always expected Kate to wake up one morning speaking normally'.

Other parents admit the fact of the hearing loss and its implications but give way, understandably, to despair. Mrs C wept intermittently through her son's early years and could think of no practical ways to help him except by teaching him colours. Not surprisingly, the child wept a great deal too. However, weeping may be no bad thing – it is, at least, an acknowledgement and release of natural grief; such weeping often ceases, too, when practical help is offered. Defensiveness or lack of realistic thinking are much harder to help.

A mother who was able to voice her grief said, 'It's terrible, terrible, when you are told your child is deaf. You feel useless. You can't even make a baby properly.' This opens up the question of guilt. Many mothers feel a deep guilt because their child is hearing-impaired and saddled with a lifelong handicap. The mother feels she has 'made a bad child' – a sort of 'second' or 'reject'. This guilt is intensified if the child's hearing loss is due to *rubella*, since the mother often feels 'responsible' for catching German measles.

One such mother was convinced that she would never have given birth to her deaf baby had she troubled to have an injection after she had caught the disease. Such an injection is by no means a guaranteed safeguard, but to tell Mrs D so was only to relieve her guilt slightly. She still felt that she was responsible for producing a faulty child.

Many parents, while accepting their child's handicap, are intensely protective of him. Such protectiveness may take many forms. Mr and Mrs E were quick to tell professional workers how very shy and sensitive their child was. Teachers had, in these parents' estimation, to work extra hard to interest Rose and to win her affection. To demand that Rose make an effort to be pleasing and friendly to her teacher was not part of the parental scheme at all. In their eyes, Rose was a handicapped creature whose sensitivity must be respected. Naturally, Rose made little effort with her work; she had come to be amused – let the teacher amuse her!

Over-protection may take the form of falling in with the child's wishes over many small things in the home. Parents may feel that it is a 'shame' for the child to have to work at learning to talk when other children learn naturally, and they allow him to watch television or to engage in aimless play when it would be kinder to make him do something more constructive.

Inability to deny treats and material things to a handicapped child is also commonplace. Unable to make him normal, the parents attempt to compensate the child by giving him constant new toys, and by rarely denying his requests for sweets and ice cream. As one father said, 'He's going to have a wretched life, let's make him happy while he is young.'

Yet another group of parents are misled by absence of speech into allowing the hearing-impaired child to behave as though he were much younger than his years. Certainly, hearing-impaired children are often immature for their years but there is no need to support this immaturity. Even though the child cannot communicate, he can be taught to dress himself, to play quietly for periods on his own, not to interrupt adult conversation and not to disrupt a room by obstreperous behaviour.

Fortunately, as well as being over-protective, parents may also have many positive qualities that emerge as they face their child's situation. Once Mrs F had grasped that her child was severely deaf but could be helped to learn to talk, she worked regularly and steadily to help her. On one occasion she remarked cheerfully, 'I don't want to do all this work, you know, but Sally is *my child* and I want to do the best I can for her.' This mother was rewarded by seeing Sally take her place in a normal school and also in the hearing world.

Some hearing-impaired children can be maddening – their lack of understanding coupled with, perhaps, wilfulness and bad nights has driven some parents to more violent feelings than they would like to acknowledge. Many parents have wished on occasion that their child had never been born. Again, parents driven to these lengths feel very guilty and there is seldom anyone to tell them that it is natural for them to feel furious and resentful at the burden placed upon them. It is also well to remember that many parents of normal children have also wished on occasion that they had remained childless – indeed that they had never married, even never been born themselves!

Many problems arise because child and parent lack basic communication. The older the child grows without speech, the harder it becomes for some parents to establish *rapport* with him. One such mother watched with a sort of frozen horror while her four-and-a-half-year-old daughter rushed about the room making unintelligible noises. Even physical communication between the two seemed to have been impaired and the mother could have been interpreted as a hard, rejecting woman. Actually, when she was able to voice some of her feelings, she showed that there were many basic things about her child's condition that she simply couldn't understand. Once she understood, for instance, that the rushing about was a substitute for verbal communication, her child became less of a strange and terrifying creature to her. As aspects of her child's condition were explained and she was shown how to help the child, the two began to develop a warm relationship.

The advent of a hearing-impaired child places a strain upon a whole family and shows up weak places that have been there before. If the mother has always been a poorly organised person, she is not likely to improve as a result of the extra burden placed upon her. The father comes home later and later to avoid the chaos at home and the marital relationship is placed under considerable strain.

The over-protective attitudes of one parent may irritate the other, whilst in some homes the child has the parents well trained. They dare not go out together lest he is displeased, and so sacrifice any personal life of their own.

Siblings of a hearing-impaired child tend to reflect parental attitudes towards him – if his parents cannot accept him as he is, how can his brothers and sisters? In one home where the parental relationship was poor and the handicapped child poorly accepted, her brother referred to her in public as 'my little mentally defected [sic] sister'. He was never really reproved for this or for other cruel teasing. Sometimes, on the other hand, an older sister becomes almost a second mother, reinforcing the mother's protective and defensive attitudes. At other times there is indifference and a lack of real caring for the welfare of the handicapped child.

The positioning of the hearing-impaired child in the family may be important. The birth of a new baby is recognised as being psychologically important for older children. When the newcomer is also handicapped and the mother is often taking him to clinics or special lessons, jealousy of him may be increased. A child born after the handicapped child may equally be left to 'take his chance' whilst the handicapped child receives help. It is worth while mentioning here that some younger siblings of hearing-impaired children pick up some remarkable gestures and noises from the elder child – alarming to the parent, but gradually outgrown. The first word of one such younger normal sibling was 'mine' accompanied by fierce gestures of pointing to herself; the second was 'don't' again with an admonishing finger!

The reaction of other relatives should also be considered. Many are positive, supportive and genuinely helpful, but even grandparents can be destructive. One grandmother 'couldn't bear ill people' while another insisted that 'it was just like her son's wife to have a deaf child'. Yet a third constantly protested against her daughter-in-law's gallant efforts to teach her severely deaf daughter to talk. 'Too much time and money is being spent on that child,' she reiterated.

It is said that a handicapped child brings love into a home, but it is more true to say that a handicapped child brings out love that is already there. I have been fortunate in seeing many loving homes containing a hearing-impaired child. One of the most remarkable was that of David who, although severely deaf, spoke normally by the time he was six. The youngest, when his hearing loss was diagnosed, of four children under seven years old, how easily could this little boy have been pushed aside. So firm was the relationship between David's parents, so sure were they of their priorities, however, that David received the benefit of five willing and interested helpers. When the goal of normal communication was finally achieved, his eldest sister commented, 'Well, Mummy, he was always sweet, but it's even nicer now he talks properly.' There is no doubt at all that loving homes provide the greatest number of successes.

People are mortal and mortals change slowly. If a parent is helped by anything that is said in this book, perhaps it is because he or she was on the verge of change anyway. But if direct advice should be given it is this: do not be ashamed if you feel grief or resentment that you have a hearing-impaired child. These feelings are normal – talk to some trained person about them if you can. Try to accept that your child has a hearing problem and that the way to help him is through practical measures and hard work. Try not to protect and indulge him. Let him lead as normal a life as possible and don't make the mistake of sacrificing the corporate life of your family on his behalf.

4

Diagnosis and Audiometry

The first three chapters of this book will have been readily understandable to parents, particularly since many will have had first-
hand experience of the things described. This one deals with
technical matters which may be more difficult to understand. I
have made every effort to simplify the material as far as possible, but
parents should not be surprised if it is necessary to read parts of the
chapter several times before fully comprehending them. This is
particularly true of the consonant and vowel chart and the explanations relating to it. Parents who do find this material difficult are
urged to read it slowly and to study the chart at length since their
comprehension is vital to their understanding of the nature of the
difficulties of their hearing-impaired child.

The last thirty years have seen an enormous advance in the early
detection of hearing loss. Screening tests by health visitors, testing
in maternity and child welfare clinics and gradually increased
awareness of child development by parents have led to hearing
impairment being suspected in the first or second year of life. The
proportion of diagnoses delayed for some reason until the third,
fourth or even fifth year of life are now considered outstandingly
late. There are places like the Nuffield Centre* where children
are sent from many parts of the country for diagnosis by experts
once hearing loss has been suspected.

The importance of early diagnosis is that the type and extent of
hearing loss can be measured, hearing aids fitted and parents put in
touch with professional people who will help them. So important
are the early fitting and regular use of correct hearing aids that we
speak of a child's 'listening age'. Thus, if a child of four has had
hearing aids fitted when he was three, his listening age is said to be
one year. It is thus obvious that time lived by the child without

---

* The Nuffield Centre for Hearing and Speech, Royal National
Hospital for Throat, Nose and Ears, Gray's Inn Road, London WC1.

correct hearing aids is likely to be largely wasted time as far as learning to speak is concerned. This is particularly serious when one remembers that acuity of hearing and a natural propensity to learn to speak are at their height in the first two years of life, after which there is a gradual diminution of the child's natural ability to listen and to copy sounds and words. It may also be difficult to induce an older child to wear hearing aids.

In the case of babies and young children, diagnosis is made by various tests which involve the child's response to drums, pitch pipes or the human voice, or other even more complicated measures, and it is not intended to discuss these testing procedures here. By the time he is about three years old, a skilled audiologist can encourage a child to co-operate in obtaining an audiogram. The older the child, the better he will be able to co-operate and the more reliable the audiogram is likely to be.

An audiogram is a chart showing in visual form the extent of a child's hearing loss (see Figure 2). The audiologist obtains it by using a machine called an audiometer which emits pure tones – that is, a series of notes, low, medium or high, to which the child is asked to respond by giving some sort of signal when he hears. This signal may be tapping on a drum, holding up his hand or taking a ring off a pyramid. At one time the child wore headphones for pure tone audiometry, but increasingly the tones are emitted by speakers stationed round the room, and the child is not required to wear headphones. This makes a much freer, more acceptable situation for the child and is known as free field audiometry.

The figures down the left-hand side of the audiogram refer to decibels or, in very simple terms, loudness; 10 decibels represents a very soft sound and loudness gradually increases through 20, 30, etc. to 110 decibels which is extremely loud. We obtain some idea of loudness if we think of the following:

> 0 decibels – the softest sound the majority of
>   adults can hear
> 30 decibels – a whisper
> 65 decibels – average conversation
> 70 decibels – a very loud voice
> 85 decibels – a busy road
> 110 decibels – a large aircraft taking off at 100 feet (30
>   metres) distance from the listener

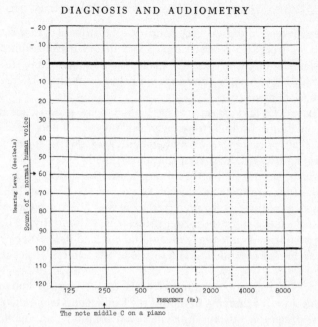

Figure 2 Frequencies tested vary slightly from audiometer to audiometer. Sometimes 125 cycles per second (125 Hz) is not included. Sometimes 6,000 cycles per second (6KHz) is included and 8,000 cycles per second (8KHz) omitted since it is above the speech range.

The figures along the bottom of the audiogram refer to high and low sounds and are perhaps best understood if compared to a musical scale, low at one extreme, high at the other. This highness and lowness is expressed as cycles per second (cps) or more currently Hertz (Hz).* The greater the number of cycles per second, the higher the sound.

4,000 cycles per second (or 4KHz) a high-pitched note		
2,000	,,	(2KHz)
1,000	,,	(1KHz)
520/580	,,	(520 Hz) middle C
250	,,	(250Hz) a low note

Becoming higher ▲   Becoming lower ▼

* Hertz (Hz) is the international unit for the measure of frequency. 1 cps equals 1 Hertz (Hz); 1 KiloHertz (1 KHz) equals 1000 Hz.

This is intended to be a very simple explanation of a very complicated subject. If a more technical and detailed discussion of the physics of sound is needed, the reader is recommended to read *The Deaf Child* by Whetnall and Fry, published by William Heinemann Medical Books Ltd.

The vowels and consonants of English, being sounds, are also of low, medium and high frequency, but they are much more complex than pure tones. To understand why this is so, we must realise a little of how speech sounds are made.

Breath, produced by the lungs, causes the vocal folds – two bands of tissue situated in the larynx – to vibrate. (Part of the larynx is formed by the cartilage referred to as the 'Adam's apple', which will make it easier for the reader to locate it anatomically.) The note thus produced is called *the fundamental note* and its average pitch is 125 cycles per second (125 Hz) in a man and 250 cycles per second (250 Hz) in a woman.

Vowels are made by various parts of the mouth, chiefly the tongue and lips, moving to mould the fundamental note in various ways. (There are twelve English vowel sounds; combinations of these vowel sounds form diphthongs.) All vowel sounds, therefore, contain the fundamental note as well as other notes or tones depending upon the individual characteristics imposed upon them by mouth movements. Thus any vowel contains notes of differing frequencies. A few vowels are of high frequency (e.g. 'ee' as in tr*ee*, 'i' as in *i*t, 'a' as in c*a*t, 'e' as in *e*gg) but the majority of the twelve English vowel sounds are of medium to low frequency. Because vowel sounds are made up of notes of different frequencies most vowels are shown twice on the chart on page 44 (Figure 3) to give visual representation of their components.

Consonants are made by an obstruction to the breath flow as it comes from the lungs. Thus the various parts of the mouth shape the breath flow by, for instance, compressing the air behind closed lips and releasing it to make 'b', or narrowing the airway between the tongue and teeth ridge to form 's'. While some consonants, like all the vowels, have laryngeal vibration, many do not. This is particularly so when they are uttered as part of the speech flow and not as separate words.

Figure 3 shows the vowels and consonants of English in relation to frequency in cycles per second. It is very hard for anyone to depict these things visually with complete accuracy, but visual representation does help understanding to some extent. It will be seen from the chart that the consonants 'm', 'n', 'ng', 'l', 'd', 'b', 'j', voiced 'th', 'z' and 'v' all have low-frequency components, though they also contain high tones which are critical to their intelligibility; 'm', 'n' and 'ng' also contain medium tones. The unvoiced consonants 's', 'f', 't', 'p , 'k', 'sh', 'ch' and breathed 'th' have no elements below 1,500 cycles per second (1.5 KHz). Of these 't' and 'f' are over 3,000 cycles per second (3.0 KHz), while 's' and breathed 'th' are the highest consonants of English. Though the normal ear can hear higher sounds than 's' and breathed 'th', no speech sounds are higher than these. The range of audible frequencies extends in numbers from approximately 15 cycles per second (15 Hz) to 20,000 cycles per second (20 KHz), though neither limit is very precise. The ear is most sensitive to sounds in the frequency range of 500 cycles per second to 4,000 cycles per second, that is, where the majority of speech sounds fall.

It will be seen from Figure 3 that some sounds are depicted high up on the chart, some lower down. This denotes the intensity or strength of a sound and it will be noticed that on the whole vowel sounds have greater intensity than consonant sounds. The degree of intensity is measured by the figures on the left-hand side, breathed 'th' as in ba*th* having the least intensity and the vowel 'or' as in h*or*se being nearly thirty times more intense than breathed 'th'. Intensity or strength of vowels and consonants is complicated by people's individual accents, emphasis and speech differences, but if we remember that very often consonants are 10 or 15 decibels weaker than vowels or diphthongs* we shall have learned something that will be valuable in understanding the problems of the hearing-impaired child. Vowels have not only, then, the advantage of greater intensity than consonants, but are also mostly of low tone, low tones usually being less affected by nerve deafness than medium and high tones.

This type of chart is designed for use in conjunction with the phonetic alphabet. It is not considered practicable to teach this alphabet here and the symbols on the chart have accordingly been changed to 'ordinary letters'.

* Dale, D. M. C., *Applied Audiology for Children.*

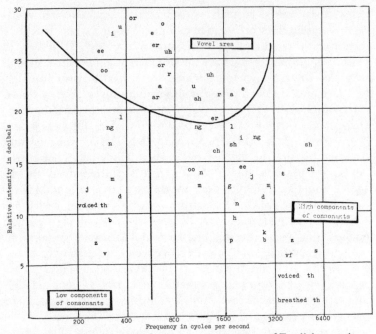

Figure 3   The principal frequency components of English sounds

Consonants present little problem.

1. The 'k' sound in *k*ey, *k*ing and li*k*e is the same from the point of view of sound as that in *c*ome, *c*at and ar*c*. On the chart and throughout this book the symbol 'k' is used.
2. There are two varieties of 'th': breathed 'th' as in *th*in, *th*ick, *th*imble; voiced 'th' as in *th*en, *th*em, *th*ere.
3. 's' as in *s*ee, i*c*e, *c*ircle and 'sh' as in *sh*oe, wa*sh*, *s*ugar are quite different sounds. Though we write two letters, 'sh' is a single sound.
4. 'ng' though represented by two letters is a single sound as in ha*ng*, ba*ng*.

Vowels are more complicated.

In writing English we use five alphabet symbols – 'a', 'e', 'i', 'o' 'u' – and combine these in various ways to denote the twelve vowel sounds of English as well as a number of diphthongs. Our spelling is not however at all consistent. For instance, the vowel sound 'ee'

(44)

may be spelt as 'ee' in tree; 'e' in be; 'ea' in leaf; 'ie' in field; 'ey' in key; 'i' in machine.*

This has been dealt with on the chart by writing a symbol as nearly as possible representative of the sound of a vowel and giving a key to what has been written. The same letters have been used to denote the same sound throughout this book.

Short vowels		Long vowels	
'a'	as in ant	'ah'	as in arm
'e'	as in egg	'ee'	as in eat
'i'	as in it	'or'	as in ought
'o'	as in ox	'er'	as in earnest
'u'	as in look	'oo'	as in hoot
'uh'	as in up		

Diphthongs, being a combination of two vowels, are obviously not portrayed on the chart.

Some Sample Audiograms

When hearing is tested by asking a child to respond to the pure tones emitted by an audiometer and a graph is plotted, we receive some general idea of what a child is likely to hear in terms of consonant and vowel sounds. It is never wise to interpret an audiogram in terms of 'He will be able to hear this' or 'He can't possibly hear that.' Tests of audibility of words should also be carried out and all sorts of responses will then be discovered that do not seem to 'fit' exactly with the pure tone audiogram. None the less, an audiogram provides a broad guide and we should now consider some audiograms and what they may imply in terms of ability of the child to receive speech sounds.

Figure 4 is the audiogram of a normal young child. In practical terms this means that when pure tones are put through the headphones or speakers, the child responds to each frequency in turn and at a certain level of intensity which is then marked on the chart. The marks indicating the intensity, that is the 'softest' sound at any one frequency that the child can hear, are joined together to make the graph. It should be noted that when headphones are placed on a person, each ear can be tested separately – therefore

* Gimson, A. C., *An Introduction to the Pronunciation of English.*

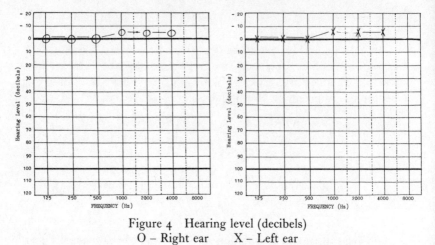

Figure 4   Hearing level (decibels)
O – Right ear   X – Left ear

a graph is given for each ear. When sound is emitted from speakers placed round the room, the person being tested responds using both ears simultaneously and therefore a single line is penned on the audiogram. Figure 5 is an example of the free field response of a normally-hearing child.

Now let us look at the audiogram of a hearing-impaired child (Figure 6) and we see that the intensity of sound has to be raised considerably before he is able to respond to the pure tones. The lines on the audiogram represent threshold, as we have explained,

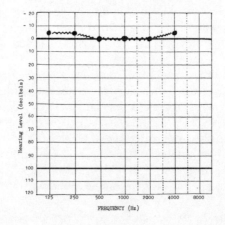

Figure 5   Audiogram showing free field response
of a normally-hearing child

the softest sound he can hear. To appreciate the extent of his deaf-ness we have to consider how much louder the low, medium and high tones have to be than they are for the normal person (Figure 4) if they are to be heard at all. This is often brought home to parents for the first time when they sit with a child who is having an audiogram taken. Some sounds emitted by the audiometer are so loud that they are audible to those in the room not wearing headphones. Yet the child wearing the headphones and having notes fed right into the ear does not respond. In terms of hearing speech, a child with this type of audiogram is likely to hear next to nothing at ordinary conversational level. With the correct hearing aids, of course, he should hear considerably more. This type of audiogram is often referred to as 'flat loss' because of the fairly straight line of the graph. Many workers, including myself, have found that children with this type of hearing loss respond very well to amplification and speech teaching.

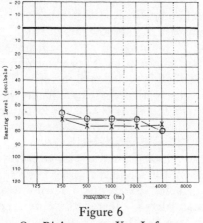

Figure 6

O – Right ear   X – Left ear

A child with the audiogram in Figure 7 has normal hearing for low tones and he will respond to the noise of an aeroplane overhead by saying 'What that?' He also hears the fundamental note, i.e. voice, so he turns when called and often picks up patterns that show a marked rise and fall of voice. He may copy these and his saying, 'Where Daddy?', 'Where you going?', 'What you doing?' convinces people that he must be able to hear. In fact, hearing for consonants

(47)

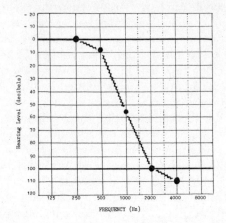

Figure 7   Audiogram showing free field response
of a hearing-impaired child

is poor. Such a child hears vowel sounds and receives, in distorted form, consonants that contain low tones. The consonants 'p', 'k', 't', 'sh', 'ch', 's', 'f' and breathed 'th' (which are high tone) he does not receive. When someone speaks to this child, he will receive a jumble of unintelligible sound and because of these confused messages, he will experience great difficulty in understanding language. A sentence such as 'Is the cat in the basket?' becomes something like '– the - a - - n the b–', and equally 'The cat is in the basket' becomes 'The - a - - - n the b–'.

Because of the missing sounds, apart from rhythmic patterns, question and statement sound the same. If such a child receives good help in developing speech, he will learn – through the hearing he has for tonal patterns – to tell the difference between such apparently ambiguous sentences. Lip-reading and an ability to read books will also help him to fill in the missing sounds so that, in time, he forms a meaningful pattern by synthesising auditory and visual messages. He will have great difficulty in using consonant sounds in his own speech. Not only will word endings be missing, and many high tone sounds omitted, but because of missing high tone elements even 'j', 'd' and 'l' will probably be difficult to reproduce.

A child with an audiogram such as shown in Figure 8 receives

(48)

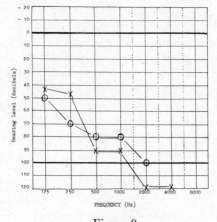

Figure 8
O – Right ear   X – Left ear

low tones poorly, and medium and high tones hardly at all. Because he does not hear low tones well he presents a less confusing picture than the child whose audiogram is shown in Figure 6 and is more likely to be diagnosed early.

The child whose audiogram is shown in Figure 9 is severely deaf. Unaided, he will hear voice if it is spoken very loudly near the ear. He will probably be able to discriminate between vowel sounds and low tone consonants when they are said in isolation, but his reception of speech will consist of intonation patterns and vowel sounds. Because most consonants are inaudible to him there will

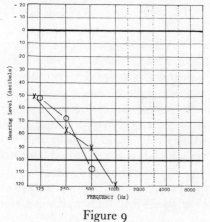

Figure 9
O – Right ear   X – Left ear

be great difficulty in the reception of language and its interpretation, and the production of consonants in the child's own speech will present extreme difficulties.

We now have to consider what is meant by the terms 'partially hearing', 'severely deaf' and 'profoundly deaf' which are still often used in speaking to parents of hearing-impaired children.

In times past, a person who showed a hearing loss between 50 or 60 and 90 decibels was said to be 'partially hearing'. Nowadays, a partially-hearing child is one 'with a hearing loss sufficient to warrant special educational treatment, but with naturally acquired language'.

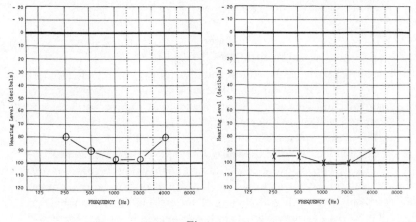

Figure 10
O – Right ear   X – Left ear

The children with the audiograms shown in Figures 9 and 10 were said by consultants to be 'severely deaf'. Though the appearance of their audiograms is quite different, there is certainly a severe hearing problem in each case.

The owner of the audiogram in Figure 11 would be considered 'profoundly deaf'. Figure 9, though intelligent, was quite unable to cope in an ordinary school and was educated in schools for the deaf. Meeting her, one felt she was indeed 'severely deaf'. Figure 10 was well on the way to normality by her sixth year, spoke well and kept up with her peers in a normal school. Figure 11, the deafest of the three, spoke extremely well using all the consonants

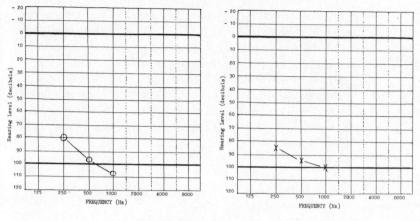

Figure 11

O – Right ear   X – Left ear

of English and was frequently thought, by people meeting her, to be 'just a little hard of hearing'.

The owner of the audiogram shown in Figure 12 was pronounced 'partially hearing', but since little use was made of her residual hearing and other assets, she was once described by her teacher of the deaf as 'resembling a much deafer child'. Certainly, as far as 'naturally acquired language' went, great efforts had to be made to teach her words.

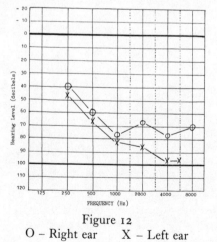

Figure 12

O – Right ear   X – Left ear

Such examples could be repeated many times. Though degree of deafness is, of course, important there are many other factors involved and it should never be decided on the basis of pure tone audiograms alone how well a child will ultimately communicate.

Unilateral deafness should be mentioned. This means there is no hearing at all in one ear. If the other ear is normal, there should be no problems in speech development though there may be problems in the location of sound, particularly in circumstances where there is background noise.

5

Factors beyond Degree of Deafness that Influence Speech and Language Development in the Hearing-Impaired Child

It has been pointed out that while, of course, degree of hearing loss is important, a partially-hearing child may not speak as well as he ought, while some profoundly deaf children speak excellently. It has also been stated that early diagnosis and the correct fitting of efficient hearing aids are key factors.

There are also other very important factors that go to create a child who, though hearing-impaired, understands conversation well, has well developed-concepts and general knowledge, and speaks well himself, a child who, in fact, takes his place with other people in the hearing community.

Edith Whetnall, the otologist whose genius achieved so much for the hearing-impaired child, used to say that, when considering a deaf child, she wished to know first of all about his mother, secondly about the child's intelligence and lastly to look at his audiogram. (Frequently Miss Whetnall refused to allow speech therapists working with a child even to see his audiogram, lest they be adversely influenced by the degree of deafness.)

The mother, then, is the main factor in the child's ability to learn to talk. First of all, she needs to have made up her mind that her child *will talk*. This implies not an unrealistic 'He'll get along all right' or 'They say he's getting on fine,' but a determination and an acceptance that she herself will need to work hard with him at home, and also to take him on numerous tiring journeys to doctors and clinics. The mother needs, therefore, to be strong physically herself and also unselfish. Most of us would rather pursue our particular hobby than spend time helping a child who may not be initially at all enthusiastic!

Though parents should try to understand as much as possible about their child's condition, a highly-intelligent mother is not

necessarily the most successful in teaching her child to talk. It can happen that such mothers become too interested in deafness as an academic problem, and are lacking in the practicality that is necessary for day-to-day living. Common sense *is* essential and also a realistic sense of values. Teaching a hearing-impaired youngster takes time – better to spend that time with him than to have a spotlessly clean house with every cupboard immaculate.

Sometimes, 'mother' and 'home' are spoken of as though they are much the same thing. In fact, they are not. The person a mother is goes quite a long way in creating a home, but the home also shapes the development of woman into mother. For the mother is not a separate entity. She is, first and foremost, her husband's wife and her capacity to be a good mother is partly the outcome of the relationship between herself and the man she has married. A woman is more likely to be a good mother if she and her husband have settled down to a life together, if they have the same objectives and have accepted that, in producing children, they have put behind them the less responsible life that each led before those children were born. Though some social life of their own is essential for parents, constant social activity in the home and haste to put the children to bed so that the parents can go out or entertain is frequently coupled with the failure of the hearing-impaired child to develop spoken language. Successful parents are family-orientated. They are content with their home life and interested in their children. They accept the handicapped child for what he is, and try to give him a good start in life. The mother does not yearn for a job outside the home to give her stimulus, nor does her husband spend evenings and weekends in pursuits that keep him well outside the orbit of his children. The parents are united in enjoyment, of their children and family life. Parents who are positive, lively, outgoing and communicative, and who enjoy speaking to their children are at an advantage. Some parents have imagination and are particularly good at seeing an object or situation from fresh angles, so that they can teach their child something new even though the daily routine is not particularly exciting. As Ian's mother said to him as she lifted in the milk bottles, 'Look! It's a wet day. The milk bottles have made two dry *circles* on the step.'

Parents must keep their sense of proportion. Their handicapped child is important to them, but so are their other children. Mothers,

particularly, can become so eaten up with ambition for the handicapped child's success that he receives too much attention whilst his siblings are neglected.

It usually devolves upon the mother to actually organise the running of the home and mothers of successful hearing-impaired children invariably have the knack of running their homes smoothly. They are responsible people who do not attempt to fit too much into a day, who keep specialist appointments regularly and punctually and do not mislay their children's work material. They keep hearing aids in good working order, use the correct type of hearing aid battery and, above all, they work regularly with the child, not spasmodically as the mood takes them.

While the mother's task is to organise the running of the home, the father is the breadwinner and has to do his job properly. None the less, he should be supportive and interested; able to hear a little each day from his wife of the child's triumphs and failures. He does not grudge the time his wife spends with the child or wish that the money needed to help the child could be spent on some private hobby of his own. He may come home from work too late in the evening to see much of the child, but he takes a turn at working with him during the weekend, or at least spends time in activity with him. (After the weekend, five-and-a-half-year-old Catherine could invariably record in her diary 'I helped Daddy in the loft' or 'Daddy and I talked about my snowman'.)

All the parents I have ever known who reared a hearing-impaired child successfully, possessed these virtues in common – yet all were different and very human people.

David's mother and father regarded David as a joint challenge. His mother was a bright, cheerful person who, though she can hardly have enjoyed the six months she spent going from clinic to clinic until David's hearing loss was finally diagnosed, yet managed to keep the appointments faithfully. She then worked with him each morning before he went to school and kept his work material systematically. David and his father were keen gardeners and at weekends the two were inseparable. It has already been said that David spoke normally by the time he was six years old and though his mother, looking back on the previous four years remarked, 'It was a dreadful time; I don't know how we managed,' she looked as bright and attractive as ever, and even took a part-time job!

A home such as this has a marked pattern of orderly living that provides a basis for the child's learning. Lip-reading is understanding a pattern on the face; listening leads to understanding a pattern that comes into the ear. The child learns these most speedily when his whole life has a predictable pattern. Tom's was a sadder story. His mother was a widow of scant means and without any form of training that would enable her to earn her living. With minimal help, this mother not only taught Tom to speak and helped him adjust to normal school but, when he was established, she obtained a training for herself that enabled her to support them both.

To consider Edith Whetnall's next criterion, the child's intelligence, there is no doubt that a good or even high intelligence is a help. An intelligent child picks up words and ideas more quickly, retains them securely, and fits them better into his existing thought structure. Elspeth, who had severe high tone deafness, had learned to speak very little by the time she was six years of age. Once Elspeth's mother had been taught how to help her, the mother worked hard and well and not only achieved good understanding for Elspeth, but also a place in a normal school where Elspeth was, at eight and a half years old, rated as 'low average for the class'. Without high intelligence, Elspeth might have developed speech, but never as well as she in fact did, while normal schooling would have been quite out of the question.

High intelligence, therefore, may gain some advantage educationally for the hearing-impaired child who speaks well and works hard; in this respect he is no different from a hearing child.

Higher intelligence may also offset other disadvantages. Some hearing-impaired children, like some normal children, have poor health; high intelligence may compensate to some extent for resources that are perpetually drained by coughs and colds. Some children, particularly those whose hearing loss is related to maternal *rubella*, are hyperactive and present great problems in teaching. A hyperactive child is perpetually on the move either from place to place or, if sitting, fingers, feet and eyes are eternally restless. Behaviour becomes much calmer as the child nears adolescence, but lack of concentration in the early years is likely to slow up learning considerably. High intelligence is likely to compensate to some extent for early hyperactivity, since when the child's attention is caught, he will probably remember what is taught to him.

What high intelligence cannot do is to compensate for poor parenting. Even a child with a brilliant mind cannot overcome the disadvantage of parents who perpetually put off getting down to solid work. (It is noticeable that even regular and determined speech therapy sessions are lost on a bright child whose parents are uncooperative.) Two thirds of hearing-impaired children are of average intelligence and well able to learn to communicate if provided by their parents with the right environment in which to do so. There is very little correlation between high intelligence and linguistic ability.

Financial resources matter, of course,* but are negligible in comparison with the good parental qualities already described. Of course, money can purchase sophisticated hearing aids; sometimes it can buy expert help, but fundamentally it is the quality of parent and child that brings success. I have seen excellent results come out of modest homes, and comparatively poor results emerge from affluent homes – perhaps poorer people are more accustomed to making the personal effort that, in the long run, brings about the desired effect.

One mother, the wife of a factory worker, had a profoundly deaf child of average intelligence who spoke beautifully by ten years old, despite a minimum of outside help. When asked how she had achieved it, this mother replied, 'I told myself she just *had* to talk, and I just *had* to teach her.'

The facilities available in the district where a family lives count a lot. Good hearing aids, knowledgeably fitted at a crucial time, a dedicated peripatetic teacher of the deaf who sees the young child regularly and gives positive guidance to the mother, a specialised course such as that for mothers and children run by the Nuffield Centre at Ealing: these things, coming at the right time, may make a considerable difference.

---

* A hearing-impaired child is a handicapped person and, as such, his parents are sometimes eligible for an 'attendance allowance'. This allowance is made at the discretion of an examining doctor, but if granted can be a considerable help. Application is made initially to the Ministry of Health and Social Security.

Basically, however, the corner-stone remains the mother and the home background: on his parents' determination that he *shall* speak whatever the negative factors and whatever the inconvenience to themselves and their child, rests his future speech development.

6

Listening and Looking

Bearing in mind what has previously been said about the hearing-impaired child's inability to hear consonants, we must consider the sensory channels through which we try to build his understanding of speech. Do we rely on his eyes, that is, teach him to lip-read, or do we also try to make use of whatever hearing is left to him, that is, residual hearing?

For many years it was thought useless to try to use hearing at all, on the grounds that if the child was deaf his hearing was useless. If he was to try to understand speech, he must learn to lip-read. It is now realised that skilled and knowledgeable fitting of hearing aids can raise the threshold of the partially-hearing child. The sounds he hears may not be the sounds a normal person hears, but since he hears the same sounds consistently he can learn to interpret them, as a normal person does.

When a normal person uses the telephone, no speech sounds above 1·5 KHz (1,500 cps) are transmitted, yet the brain is so used to interpreting the telephone message and filling in the missing sounds that, unless we dwell on what is missing and distorted, we believe that we are receiving every sound in the message. The benefit a partially-hearing child receives from a hearing aid can be compared to this. The severely deaf child cannot receive as much benefit, but an appropriate hearing aid can bring certain valuable sound messages to him. Whenever possible, therefore, a child's residual hearing should be trained by giving the child the type of exercises in listening described in this book; this is only realistic if he wears efficient hearing aids.

A hearing aid is basically an arrangement of transistors which amplifies sound and makes what its wearer previously heard faintly or not at all, audible. There are many different kinds of hearing aid, each with an individual potential, and each with an individual way of increasing sound. Internally, a hearing aid may be adjusted to give, say, more sound in the high range and less in the low. Unfortunately, many hearing aids increase not only valuable environmental sounds, like rain on the windows, but also extraneous noises that are largely valueless – the best example of this is the scrape of clothing against a body aid, and the rubbing of hands against a desk very near to the aid. (It must also be remembered that hearing-impaired children, though unable to hear well, are often extra sensitive to loud noise. Thus, tipping a bowl of plastic counters on to a polished surface, six inches from a body aid, for instance, may be a quite painful experience to the child and one to be guarded against.)

A hearing aid has an ear mould and, in the case of a body aid, a lead to a microphone which is worn on the chest. This microphone should not be worn lower than the chest or the wearer will be unable to hear his own voice correctly. It should never be submerged under layers of clothing for the sake of concealment. A head-worn aid (also called a post-aural or behind the ear aid) has the advantage of picking up sound at head level and it is freer from the extraneous noises that occur at chest level. Most patients would like their child to wear post-aural aids because, with the aid concealed behind his hair, the child 'looks like everyone else'. Whether body- or head-worn aids are used depends to some degree upon the type and extent of a child's hearing loss. Post-aural aids have become considerably more sophisticated and powerful in recent years and can now be worn by children with severe and profound hearing loss. The decision is, however, one for skilled people and post-aural aids should never be worn for cosmetic reasons at the expense of amplification.

It is most important that every aspect of a hearing aid is correct. To start with the simplest part, the ear mould should fit comfortably and securely. If the child complains of discomfort from a mould, listen to him and have the mould checked. Some children have a particularly sensitive lining to the ear and require moulds made of a soft, not a hard plastic. A mould that falls out is too small – your child grows. You see that he has larger shoes, see that he also obtains larger moulds as he needs them. A persistent whistling noise, even when the aid is at the correct setting, may also be a sign that the mould is too loose. Moulds should be kept free from wax – the hole can be cleaned out carefully with the blunt end of a large darning needle, and the surface of the mould wiped with a soft, damp cloth.

The hearing aids themselves should be checked daily to make sure that the setting is correct and that they are in working order. The batteries should be changed on the same day each week *and the old batteries thrown away*. As the child grows older, he should be taught to do these things for himself rather than be dependent upon other people. (Thirteen-year-old Kate, a practical girl, parcelled up a broken hearing aid on her own initiative and posted it to her audiologist with the plea that he should mend it quickly since she needed it badly!)

A tiny child must be introduced gently to hearing aids and allowed to enjoy some pleasant experience while he wears them for a short time – perhaps sitting on Daddy's lap looking at a book and eating a few smarties. If he associates the aids with pleasurable experience, he will gradually become aware of the advantages of the aids themselves. Unless he is very old when an aid is fitted for the first time, and has objections to it on psychological grounds, a child should want, after the initial strangeness has worn off, to wear his hearing aids. (If you are long-sighted, think how much your reading spectacles mean to you; if you are short-sighted, think of watching television without your spectacles.) Continued protests that aids are 'loud', 'funny', 'naughty' should lead parents to ask themselves whether the aids the child is wearing are the correct ones. Some children do not protest, but are unenthusiastic about their aids and remove them at every possible opportunity, which can be another warning sign that the aids are inappropriate.

Beyond their suitability and good working order is the very important factor of how well the child can be taught to use his aids. People sometimes say, 'If the aids help him to hear so much, why doesn't he learn to speak like other people?' The speech heard through hearing aids, however good the aids, is not of the same quality that normally hearing people receive. There is distortion of speech sounds and it is almost impossible to compensate completely for the falls and rises of the original audiogram. Though hearing aids make speech much louder to the child, the sounds he hears at first have no meaning. He must learn to identify them and to accustom his mind to their order in words, phrases and sentences. It is only as he is gradually trained by exercises such as those described in Chapters 9–14 that he begins to ascribe meaning to sounds, to understand them and reproduce them. It may take many months for this to happen. When the child is making more use of his residual hearing in this way, his pure tone audiogram will often show a rise in threshold. Ultimately, of course, optimum listening is reached; the child is making the best use of his residual hearing and no further development of threshold is possible. The process of learning to *interpret* speech sounds, however, is one that may continue to develop for many years.

For the partially-hearing child, good training of useful residual hearing means not only better voice and articulation, but also better memory for new words, faster progress and greater mobility. He can, for instance, eventually listen to an explanation by his school teacher whilst she points to his work. He can often hear her whilst she is writing, or when she has temporarily turned away from him, provided she is near. It is interesting to consider the following examples.

Carola, partially-hearing and fitted with excellent hearing aids, was none the less trained from the beginning to interpret language through her eyes and was an excellent lip-reader by ten years of age, with completely normal language of her own. Her voice, however, was high and monotonous, and sounded as though she had a perpetual cold. Not trained to listen to the voices of others, Carola could not hear the poor quality of her own and made no improvement in it. Attempts to help her to listen at this late stage of her development failed. Carola could understand language through her eyes, she could communicate, but she was too set in her ways to alter from looking to listening. A further unfortunate factor was that when she was addressed, but was not looking at the speaker, Carola would always have to ask for a repetition – very irritating to other people and not helpful in conversational flow.

Julie, with less hearing than Carola, also had efficient hearing aids, was trained from the beginning to use her residual hearing, and always received speech through this channel. An excellent speaker by the time she was seven, with good understanding, vocabulary and language, Julie was quite able to converse about a play activity whilst her eyes were upon her toys. She would sometimes, as a game, take out her hearing aids and ask her mother to speak to her behind her back. 'Yes,' she would say, 'I can still just hear you, Mummy, but I hear better with my aids.'

The amount of help a severely deaf child derives from listening depends, even with the best possible hearing aids, upon the nature of his residual hearing. Even severely deaf children can, however, learn to ascribe meaning to the sound clues that are fed into their ears. Even profoundly deaf children may make use of the minimal sound clues they receive. They may become aware of voice pitch, of number and length of syllables. Above all, they may feel more in touch with their loved ones through hearing even a little sound from them.

However, it is unrealistic to expect a profoundly deaf child who is not receiving the complete range of speech sounds through his aids to understand speech only through listening. The visual channel probably has high meaning for him, and we have to consider that even normally-hearing people decipher the utterances of others by observing minute changes in facial expressions. We also have to consider that normal children usually have a learning bias – some learn more easily by visual, others by auditory channels. Some adults who become deaf in middle life learn to lip-read very easily, whilst others, who may be equally intelligent, fail to learn at all. We must allow then for some grossly hearing-impaired children being 'natural lip-readers'. The movements of other people's lips make a naturally meaningful pattern to them and are a most valuable channel.

If a general rule can be made, it is to amplify residual hearing as far as possible, to train that hearing to the full and not to teach lip-reading specifically by asking the child, 'Watch me. Look,' before he has had a chance to listen. None the less, lip-reading is a natural and useful channel. A partially-hearing child, for instance, not looking at a speaker's face, may repeat a word wrongly three or four times. In this case if the adult then says, 'Look!' and says the word yet again, the child will probably repeat the word correctly. Equally, it is unwise with a severely deaf child to carry on a piece of work using listening only until he becomes worried and frustrated. Repeat the work, letting him see the face, and then, on the basis of his performance, decide whether or not to have another attempt by ear alone.

It is frequently difficult to decide without a trial teaching period of considerable length just how much benefit a child will derive from listening and how much from lip-reading. Andrew and Mary were both deemed to be profoundly deaf and of the two, judging by audiometry from headphones, Mary appeared to have more residual hearing than Andrew. Andrew had worn the same body-worn hearing aids for most of his life. He wore them when he went to school because he knew he would be in trouble if he went without them, but he removed them the moment he arrived home and never wore them at the weekend. As his mother said, Andrew had never 'got the hang of lip-reading' and at nine and a half was still barely in touch with the speech of other people. At this age he was fitted with specific power post-aural aids which he wore happily all day and never removed until bedtime. Old though Andrew was, intensive auditory training and teaching were begun and eighteen months later Andrew was able to answer varied questions about a previously unknown picture *without watching the speaker's face*. He had also begun to communicate extensively himself and, as verbal communication between Andrew and his family developed, the patterns made by speakers' lips also at last began to have meaning to him, so that his comprehension of daily language improved still further. This boy obviously had useful residual hearing which, when properly amplified, formed the basis for his interpretation of speech, with lip-reading as a useful adjunct.

Mary, who was without understanding or speech, was fitted with powerful body aids at four and a half and was immediately willing to wear these. When given intensive training, her response to sound improved and she learned to select known words by listening alone. However, she found people's faces highly meaningful and became, in two years, a skilled lip-reader, often picking up from adult conversation information not intended for her! For Mary, lip-reading was the primary channel through which she understood speech, though she obviously derived secondary support from her hearing aids.

An older child like Andrew can tell us whether his hearing aids are helpful to him. A young, speechless child cannot do this, yet it is essential to know whether he is fitted with the best possible hearing aids and that the internal mechanism of the aids are rightly adjusted so that they are suited to his needs. The only reliable way of telling this is to have the aids checked by an experienced audiologist who specialises in testing and aiding children.* The ampli-

* 'Despite the emphasis that is placed on hearing aids by all those con-

fication over the frequencies of which an aid is capable can be established by testing it with a special kind of machine. One of the most reliable ways to discover whether one type of aid and aid setting is better for your child than another is by aided audiometry. Already well recognised in parts of the United States of America, aided audiometry is beginning to be carried out in parts of this country, but is still quite difficult to obtain. As with free field audiometry already described, speakers emit pure tones to which the child responds by giving a pre-arranged signal, but he wears his hearing aids to do so. The audiologist traces his response on a graph. The child is then fitted with another hearing aid or aids and the procedure is repeated. The lines on the graph indicate which aids are producing the best threshold, and therefore which aids the child should wear.

Expert hearing aiding can make a world of difference to what a child hears. He can, to some extent, be given more amplification in areas where he has little hearing, and less amplification in areas where he has more hearing. Thus a 'jagged' line on an audiogram (which has already been pointed out as very confusing) can to some extent be levelled or biased towards a better level. His general threshold can be raised so that the world of sound exists for him. As one profoundly deaf child wrote immediately after the fitting of her new post-aural aids, 'I heard the rain go "plop, plop, plop" against the window.' Another girl of seventeen and a half years with excellent speech and language found that for the first time in her life, with new 'directional' post-aural aids, she was able to join in conversation around the dinner table effectively. Previously, she had never been able to locate a new speaker or interpret his opening remarks quickly enough to keep track of new trends in conversation.

It sometimes happens that older children who are good lip-readers are fitted with new hearing aids and that they and their parents are disappointed with the results. A period of auditory

cerned with the hearing-impaired, deaf children are not receiving the maximum benefit from their aids and from the developments that have been carried out in this field. We believe that this is primarily due to the lack of training given to those involved with prescribing and fitting hearing aids. Fitting is carried out on a very ad hoc basis and is not good enough.' *Deaf Children and their Hearing Aids* - A Report by the National Deaf Children's Society. Published May 1978.

training will often result in improved listening, as with a thirteen-year-old boy, a great football fan, who gradually found that with the new aids he could hear loudspeaker announcements at football matches. To obtain the maximum benefit from his new aid it had been necessary for him to have renewed auditory training.

Amplification has, of course, limits. Some children are so enchanted with the world of sound opened up to them by increased amplification that they try to increase it still more by turning up the hearing aids. This is confusing loudness with clarity. Not only does it increase distortion of speech sounds, but it is very bad for the ear and parents should be on the alert; loud whistling may be a sign that the volume is turned up too high.

Your child's hearing aids are not just boxes on his chest, or bulges behind his ears. They are a vital part of his learning to talk. Make sure that he has the most efficient aids you can provide for him and that they are always in good working order.

A great deal has been said about the audibility of vowels and consonants, and their visibility should now be considered. One of the most important things to recognise is that, quite apart from the actual patterns made by vowels and consonants on the lips, we all of us understand a great deal about people and what they are communicating to us by their facial expression. Smiling tells us that a person is pleased or happy, worried lines denote anxiety. We are quick to sense the change in a person's attitude to us by minute alterations in his facial expression and most of us feel we 'don't know where we are' if we meet a person who, for some reason, has an expressionless face. Facial expression is one of the background features of communication, and one reason for the popularity of television is that it communicates to us through not one, but two sensory channels. If vision is important to a hearing person, it is much more so for one to whom sound is reduced, and watching the face is an important part of the hearing-impaired child being in touch with the communication of other people.

In considering lip-reading more specifically, it should be realised that some consonants and vowels are more visible than others. The following is a list of consonants arranged in order of visibility:

Visible Consonants	p b	Made by placing the lips together and then allowing the air to escape from between them with pop or plosion.
	m	The lips are placed together and the air escapes through the nose.
	f v	The upper teeth are placed on the lower lip and the air escapes with friction.
	th (as in thin) th (as in them)	The tongue is placed slightly between the teeth and the air escapes with friction.
	w	The lips are rounded ('w' is not included in Figure 3 on page 44 since phonetically it is a semi-vowel, not a consonant).
Moderately Visible	t d	The tongue tip is raised to touch the ridge behind the teeth and the air allowed to escape with plosion.
	s z	The tongue tip is raised to the teeth ridge and the air allowed to escape with friction.
	l	The tongue is raised to touch the teeth ridge and the air allowed to escape at the sides of the tongue.
	n	The tongue is raised to touch the teeth ridge and the air allowed to escape down the nose.
	sh	The tongue is raised behind the teeth ridge, the lips are protruded and the air escapes with friction.
	ch j	Made like 'sh' but with slight plosion before the friction.

	r	The tongue is raised towards the hard palate and the tip retracted. The air escapes with friction.
Difficult or impossible to see	k or c g	The back of the tongue is raised to touch the back of the palate. The air escapes with plosion.
	ng	The back of the tongue is raised to touch the back of the palate. The air escapes down the nose.
	h	A puff of air before a vowel.
	y	Another semi-vowel which starts with the unremarkable vowel sound 'ee'.

Vowel differences are made by the speaker's tongue height, by lip shaping and width of opening between the jaws; vowels are also of different lengths. While experienced lip-readers pick up the more subtle clues of length and tongue height, it is usually lip shaping and width of jaw opening that give the earliest and easiest vowel clues.

A diphthong is a combination of two vowels, and clues also arise from the movement from one vowel to another.

lip rounding is present and the vowel or diphthong is visible	o	as in	*ox*
	oo	as in	h*oo*p
	u	as in	co*u*ld
	or	as in	*ou*ght
	*oh	as in	*o*pen
	*oi	as in	*oi*l
	*ow	as in	*ow*l
jaw opening aids visibility	a	as in	*a*nt
	uh	as in	*u*p
	ah	as in	*ar*m
	*y	as in	*i*ce
lack of either lip rounding or jaw opening makes these less visible	er	as in	*ur*ge
	ee	as in	*ea*t
	i	as in	*i*t
	e	as in	*e*gg
	*ay	as in	*a*te

*diphthongs

It will be understood why the hearing-impaired child who lip-reads understands a command like '*F*ind the *f*ish' or '*P*ut the *b*aby in the *b*ath.' They contain a proportion of readily visible consonants, while sentences like '*G*et the *k*ey' or 'The ri*ng* is in the si*nk*' are not nearly so readily visible.

Parents may find it enlightening to look in the mirror and repeat the following phrases and sentences for their own observation:

p	*p*op's *p*ink *p*aper
b	*b*ath *b*ig *b*aby
m	*m*ummy *m*ust *m*ean it
f	*f*ind the *f*unny *f*ish
v	*v*ery, *v*ery *v*ain
breathed th	a *th*in, *th*in *th*imble
voiced th	*th*ese and *th*ose
w	*w*here is *W*endy's *w*heel?
t	*t*en *t*iny *t*oes
d	*d*oes *d*addy *d*ig?
s	*s*ee *S*ammy'*s* *s*ocks
z	the *z*ebra i*s* in the *z*oo
l	*l*ook, a *l*ong *l*adder
n	*n*o, *n*one *n*ow
sh	a *sh*ort, *sh*arp *sh*riek
ch	*ch*ange the *ch*airs in the *ch*urch
j	*j*olly *J*ohn the *j*eweller
r	*r*un *r*abbit *r*un
k	*c*ut the *c*a*k*e
g	*g*o and *g*et the *g*un
ng	si*ng* a lo*ng* so*ng*
h	*h*elp *h*im *h*urry
y	*y*es, *y*ou are *y*awning

o	*o*n and *o*ff
oo	wh*o* are y*ou*?
u	l*oo*k at the b*oo*k
or	l*aw* and *or*der
oh	*o*pen your *ow*n
ou	r*ou*nd and r*ou*nd
oi	b*oy*s like t*oy*s
ow	h*ow* n*ow* br*ow*n c*ow*

a	he s*a*t on the c*a*t
uh	come *u*p with *u*s
ah	*a*re you an *au*nt?
y	*i* l*i*ke *i*ce

er	ret*ur*n h*er* b*ir*d
ee	s*ee* m*e* *ea*t
i	*i*t *i*s *i*n
e	*e*gg is *e*xtra
ay	th*ey* *a*te *ei*ght

Some speakers are much more easily lip-read by hearing-impaired people than others and it is usually those who are easy to listen to who are also easy to lip-read. This does not mean that exaggerated lip movements are made, but that the speaker enunciates clearly with just the right amount of mouth action. One of the disadvantages of lip-reading is that not all people speak clearly, that the light may be bad, that the speaker turns away.

A further disadvantage is that some sentences of quite different meaning look identical: 'I meant the drain,' 'I met the train.'

Though the conversational topic gives clues, even deaf people who are skilled lip-readers sometimes show confusion if ideas are closely allied. Thus, speaking to a severely deaf young adult with excellent communication, I said, 'My friend, who is also a *speech therapist*, lives in Dorking.' 'What did you say about *talking*?' rejoined the girl.

From the foregoing the reader will be able to appreciate that both listening and looking as means of understanding speech have their advantages and disadvantages. Luckily, they are often complimentary. Thus a hearing-impaired person may be unable to hear high-tone 'f' and breathed 'th', but will find them readily visible. On the other hand, ambiguities implicit in lip-reading may be cleared up by listening to intonation patterns and other auditory clues. For the hearing-impaired child, learning to interpret and reproduce speech must always involve for him a skilled synthesis of listening and looking.

One eminent and successful teacher of the deaf remarked, 'I don't care what channel you use as long as you talk to the deaf child and talk a lot!'

7

Early Words

It seems natural to the parents of a normally-hearing child to talk to him for one, or even two years, without his saying a recognisable word. The parents of a hearing-impaired child must talk more, louder, and above all for a far longer period of time before the results of their efforts become obvious. They must also, when they talk, make sure that they do so under conditions that make their talking most beneficial to the child.

A great deal that is valuable has already been said and written about the early stages of training a hearing-impaired child. The National Deaf Children's Society produces excellent literature to guide parents. Peripatetic teachers of the deaf go to the child's home to start his early training and advise his parents. Courses are run to teach parents how to handle their young child throughout the day. More guidance is probably given to parents at this stage of their hearing-impaired child's life than at any other time, and it is not intended to try to re-do in this book what others have already done. The earliest stages will be mentioned briefly only to show how they may relate to later developments.

First of all, the young hearing-impaired child needs more contact with environmental sound and with people's voices than a hearing child. One mother placed her partially-hearing baby's pram just outside the kitchen window so that he could hear both kitchen sounds and her voice as she worked in the house. Another mother, whose seven-month-old daughter was always awake during the morning, moved the child from room to room as she cleaned the flat. Exposure to sound of all kinds is vital, and since the baby may not know the source of the sounds he hears, his mother should hold him close to objects that emit sound, such as the telephone, so that he connects sound with source. The mother should go out of her way to produce sound herself, particularly sound that is rewarding to the baby. When the baby's food is ready, for instance, she should tap the bowl with the spoon and call his name. The bath should be prepared within the baby's sight with loud splashing noises; the pram made ready for outings with plenty of sound. If the baby reacts to these sounds, his reaction should be greeted with enthusiasm. He is learning important lessons; sound has a source, sound has a meaning. Whenever possible the baby should be warned by sound (and if not, then by vision) that an adult is coming. It is frightening to him to be suddenly swooped upon and picked up without warning.

These days many mothers seem to be over-eager to place their child, normal or hearing-impaired, in a play group or nursery school. When he is only two, the child may be expected to separate from his mother and integrate with a group, the justification apparently being that 'He loves other children' or 'He is bored at home.' Sometimes the mother is honest enough to say that she simply must have a rest from the child, but often one senses a fear on the part of the parent that the child will 'miss something' or 'get behind' if he does not jump on to the educational band-wagon early. Trained nursery school teachers themselves would, in fact, be the first people to say just how much the child learns about the environment from being closely in contact with his mother and his home during the early years. Valuable lessons about temperature, moisture, weight and texture are learned, the use of objects, the functions of people such as the milkman and the postman. Visits to the shops are packed with colour and incident and, most of all, the child enjoys a one-to-one relationship with his mother that involves, or should involve, speech.

Many mothers, however, seem to believe that there is some sort of magic in placing a child in a group at an early age. They do not seem to realise how much is learned in the home, or that very early nursery placement is most valuable for children who, for one reason or another, are deprived of home learning. If a normal child should remain with the mother, how much greater is the need of the hearing-impaired child! Occasionally, a nursery department of a school for the deaf offers a high ratio of adults to children and very structured language teaching, but there is a tendency among parents to place their child in any nursery or play group for normal children 'to do it good' – without the parents realising that in fact the hearing-impaired child in such a group must share adult attention with perhaps ten or more other children. Though a hearing-impaired child needs playmates, he needs most of all to learn to talk and at this stage, his mother's verbal output is likely to be more structured to his learning needs than the random output of other children. When I am helping a pre-school child, I always dread the onset of compulsory school age – the child is always far more tired than he was at home, and fitting in the necessary work on speech is a problem. To create these problems earlier than need be is wasteful of the valuable pre-school years. Ideally, unless he attends a nursery school that offers him specialised training and a high proportion of adult attention, a hearing-impaired child should be placed in a play group or nursery for two hours on three days each week at the most. If the child has siblings who are near him in age, or if there are plenty of neighbourhood children with whom he can mix, he may not require placement in a group at all.

The whole of a small child's routine in the home, properly used, offers opportunities to stimulate his interest in making contact with people, by learning to listen and look. The parent should talk to the child throughout the day in a relaxed normal voice, commenting upon current activities and using short sentences, not single words. Here again I must mention the virtues of a settled routine. If a child is sure that getting up, washing, dressing and eating breakfast always occur in that order and at roughly the same time, his mind will be more prepared to receive the words his mother says in connection with events. The mother may say at dressing time, 'Here's your vest – put it on – boo!' (as the child's head pops out), 'Put on your pants, one foot, the other foot,' etc. The child is far more prepared to receive this if he has gone to sleep early the previous night and if dressing occurs at a regular time. Some mothers are far more able than others to engage in such simple repetitive talk and some obviously have more time in which to do so. One mother who was honest enough to admit that this sort of talking bored her was actually magnificent once she began to see what it could achieve for her partially-hearing son. Because it took so much effort, she put thought into what she was saying, and became quick to see opportunities for using language.

It should be remembered that normal small children use a great deal of gesture before speech develops and are, indeed, encouraged to do so by games such as peep-bo, pat-a-cake, waving bye-bye. These games are a necessary step to spoken language; the hearing-impaired child needs them as much as the normal child, and his parents should not be afraid, when he plays them, that he is 'starting to sign'. Parents should avoid gesturing extensively to the child themselves when not playing deliberate games, but even if they are careful about this the child may develop an amount of gesture simply because he is short of words. Rather than tell him he is 'naughty' the parents should supply the words the child is trying to express.

A child with sufficient residual hearing and good hearing aids will gradually learn a great deal of language from the parent speaking to him throughout the day.* It has already been said that lip-reading is valuable and indeed essential to some children, but the child does not at first connect watching his mother's face with receiving information. Some children do begin to lip-read naturally but it is obvious to anyone who has seen children and adolescents who cannot understand speech, that lip-reading does not always develop spontaneously. Babies of about six months old are fascinated by faces. Older children look at the mother's face regularly for approbation, permission or affection. When the hearing-impaired child looks at his mother, she should say something short and meaningful about a present object:** 'Here's the ball,' 'Mind, the water's hot,' 'Who's coming?' 'Open the door.'

If he finds relevant information there, the child will look at his mother's face more and for longer periods. The adult should be three to four feet away and in a good light (avoid sitting so that the adult's back is to the window and the incoming light dazzling the child). It is important to be on eye level with the child, so if the mother is trying to speak to the child she should squat. (Similarly,

* If a child has, for some reason, no hearing aids or is wearing aids for only part of each day, the advantages of the mother speaking loudly, near the ear, should not be overlooked. Comments about whatever activity is going on can be made in this way – then repeated, still in a loud voice, in front of the child so that he can lip-read.

** The John Tracey Clinic Correspondence Course for Parents of Pre-School Deaf Children gives excellent guidance on training young children. The course is available free of cost to parents of deaf and hard-of-hearing children aged five and under anywhere in the world. Write to: The John Tracey Clinic, 806 West Adams Boulevard, Los Angeles, California 90007, USA.

he will listen better at ear level and will gain here if he is carried on a hip, though this cuts out lip-reading.) The adult should keep still whilst the child tries to receive information and should use natural, not exaggerated, lip movements. When the hearing-impaired child uses vocalisation, it should be greeted with pleasure by the adult. When he babbles 'da ga, da ga, ba ba ba' the mother should join in enthusiastically, keeping as near the baby as possible. A point occurs in normal child development, usually about the age of eleven months, when, if the mother has noticed some of the sounds that comprise her baby's babble, she can stimulate the baby by using some of these. The mother of a hearing-impaired child should make a point of doing this and of evoking and prolonging the child's natural noise whenever possible. Normal babies make some ugly noises at times so the mother of the hearing-impaired child should not be too quick to assume that her child's less attractive vocalisations are in any way abnormal. Older hearing-impaired children who are just beginning to speak will produce babble and jargon (a sort of nonsense talk) and are sometimes told by their parents 'Don't make that noise.' 'That noise' is an essential part of speech development and the child cannot pass on to 'proper speech' until the earlier stages are worked through. At whatever age, then, babble and jargon appear, they should be greeted with enthusiasm. Recognisable words are more likely to be greeted with joy. When the child says 'duck' the mother should not just repeat 'Yes, duck,' but should amplify the word so that its interest is increased and the child's auditory and visual span lengthened.

> 'Duck – throw bread to the duck.'
> or 'Duck – the duck says "quack, quack".'
> or 'Duck – the duck can swim.'

Most parents put aside some part of the day in which to play with a baby or toddler, the games varying with the age of the child. A baby in a play-pen is delighted if Teddy is repeatedly pushed off the corner of the pen to the accompaniment of 'Teddy's fallen off.' Even if a toddler is inept, he is pleased to play with a large ball and this involves repetitions of one word yet variations in speech pattern:

'Throw the ball.'
'Kick the ball.'
'Roll the ball.'
'Give Mummy the ball.'

The best playthings are often household objects or packaging, such as yogurt pots, ice-cream boxes, tissue boxes and 'squeezey' bottles. Often something bought very cheaply can give great pleasure and teach a lot. For instance, six ping-pong balls rolled across a table, one at a time, delighted one little boy. Each time a ball was rolled his mother said, 'Here comes the ball,' caught it and fitted it into one of six indentations in a plastic chocolate packet. The excellent *Parent's Guide* published by the National Deaf Children's Society outlines the sort of playthings that are suitable between the ages of six months and five years, and the uses that can be made of them. A child usually possesses some toys bought in shops as well as ready-to-hand playthings and, since good toys are expensive, it is important to see that what is bought will give a maximum of wear and use. Bricks are an example of this – versatile and indestructible, plain wooden bricks are the best investment. Posting boxes with holes through which various shapes can be posted, stacking beakers and baskets, stacking rings and nesting barrels or nesting wooden dolls are likely to retain interest. Abbatt Giant Picture Snap and Abbatt Giant Picture Lotto are designed for floor games. Jigsaws of the 'pick up a piece and see the picture' variety provide something to talk about and handle at the same time. A short list of toys is given in Appendix 1. These should by no means be regarded as essential, but as suggestions of what to choose if a new toy is to be bought.

A child's ability to use his residual hearing should be trained from the beginning of life. Even if he has no hearing aids a baby who is rocked and sung to with strong rhythm close to the ear will hear something. His toys should include rattles, drums and a musical box that can be operated by turning a handle. As he grows older, the child will be able to play games that involve response to sound:

1. *Musical Bumps*

   Music from a tape recorder or transistor radio is played at a level the child can hear and he is required to move to it and sit down when the music stops. For the purpose of training hearing the

(77)

child should play this game without other, hearing, children since he will be quick to imitate their sitting down rather than listen to the music.

2. *Hide the Music*

A mechanical music box or transistor radio is well hidden in a place where it can be located only by sound – light, cardboard grocery boxes may be used to enlarge the number of places. The child, who has been asked to go out of the room, is then brought back and asked to hunt by listening.

3. *Matching Sounds*

This requires pairs of objects – two identical rattles, two small toy bells, two hand musical boxes, two drums (yogurt pots with spoons will do). The child sits with his back to the adult, who then 'plays' one instrument. The child must listen and respond by playing the same instrument.

4. *Knock for Knock*

This requires some number sense on the part of the child. The adult and child hold a small block each and the adult gives one, two or three taps. The child, sitting out of sight, responds with the same number of taps. Care must be taken not to tap, say, on the floor where the child is sitting, so giving the child tactile and not auditory clues.

5. *Where did it come from?*

This requires at least three responsible helpers and is recommended as a family game. Using appropriate pictures, the mother says, 'The cow says –' There is a pause and one of the helpers who are seated near the child and two or three feet away, with hand over mouth, says a loud 'Moo'. The child must correctly detect the direction the sound is coming from. The mother then selects another animal, saying very quietly behind her hand who is to make the appropriate noise.

6. *What sounds can you hear?*

It is frequently reported by parents that a child wearing efficient hearing aids for the first time will begin to comment upon sounds he has never heard before – the rain on the window pane, the door bell, aeroplane noise. The child's recognition of these sounds should be greeted with pleasure. The parents may also contrive environmental sounds – knocking at the door, ringing the bell, footsteps, running the tap. The child is asked to listen and his identification of sounds greeted with pleasure. If the child's face lights up to indicate that he can hear something but does not know, or cannot say what, the parent should say, 'You can hear the door bell. Listen! The door bell is ringing.' Then show him the source of the sound.

7. As concentration span lengthens and the child grows a little older, he may be trained to listen through his hearing aids and to respond to speech sounds.

The child is, to begin with, allowed to see the speaker's face while vowel sound 'or' (a most audible vowel) is said loudly and clearly. At the same time, some action is performed: for instance, an empty cotton reel is dropped into a deep tissue box. 'Or' is repeated and the adult directs the child's hand to drop another reel into the box. The child usually soon understands that he must respond, when 'or' is said, by action, and when this idea is well established, the adult produces the sound with the lips covered.* If the child again drops an empty cotton reel into the box, other vowel sounds listed on page 68 should be said, omitting 'ee', 'oo' and 'i', since these contain high tone elements which may be difficult to hear. Consonants may then be introduced, starting with those containing low tones – 'm', 'n', 'ng', 'b', 'd', 'l' – gradually introducing those which are high tone – 'ch', 'sh', 'p', 't', 'k', 'f', 's'. It must be realised that the process described should be a very gradual one. Sounds should be introduced slowly; a child has done well if he has heard 'or' twice and dropped his cotton reels into his box. The game should be played for very short periods – about two minutes even when the child becomes accustomed to it and it should always be abandoned *before* he becomes tired and bored. It is a help to change the child's response – to offer a pile of beakers to be stacked instead of using cotton reels. The parent must be careful to space his production of sounds irregularly, lest the child make a mechanical response based on his expectations instead of

---

* 'Covering the lips' means that the parent places a hand lightly above the upper lip and below the nose so that the lips cannot be seen. The index finger should rest just below the nose, but the hand should be held well clear of the lips so that sound is in no way muffled, with the thumb stretched outwards along the jaw bone. In right-handed people the left hand is used to cover the mouth, leaving the right free to manipulate equipment, etc.

listening. When a high tone consonant such as 's' is introduced, it should be said between vowels and consonants to which a child reliably responds. If the child does not hear it, he is then not aware of the fact. Parents should not be despondent if a child does not, to begin with, respond to high tone sounds. With practice and an appropriate hearing aid, ability to hear often begins to develop, and a child may suddenly 'hear' a consonant to which there has previously been no response. In saying consonants, parents should be careful to *make the sound, not the letter*. With vowel sounds, this is easy, but consonants require consideration. Thus 'm' is not 'muh' or 'em', but a humming noise 'mmm'; 'n' is not 'nuh' nor 'en' but 'nnn'. The nearest parallel is to think how a child is taught to 'sound' letters when he builds words in an early reading book: 's – t – o – p' and not 'es – tee – oh – pee'.

Once the child knows the names of a few everyday objects, he should be asked to select one when there is no possibility of his lip-reading. If his mother says to him casually 'Where's Teddy?' and the child indicates Teddy, his mother should respond in some interesting way – by making Teddy clap hands or turn a somersault. The child will not realise that anything unusual has been asked of him and is more likely to respond when asked to locate another object. Other listening games can be played with simple jigsaw puzzles. It is natural for mother and child to search for puzzle pieces together, and for the child not to be watching the mother's face. The mother may say, 'Where's the car? We're looking for the car,' and pretend to search hard whilst in reality giving the child plenty of time to locate the car. Good listening habits established in these early years are very productive in terms of later speech development. The quality of speech particularly depends upon the degree to which the child is trained to listen to his own speech and that of others.

One aspect of speech development that is often neglected is the training of the muscles responsible for producing speech sounds. The development of these muscles is partly controlled by sucking and chewing, but they are also exercised by the babble and jargon the child produces. Since hearing-impaired children frequently fail to make enough speech noise, the muscles of their mouths are often lax and flabby, and held in unattractive ways – for instance, open with the tongue protruding. It is important, therefore, to give the mouth as much exercise as possible. Hard foods such as carrot and apple which require vigorous chewing help, and the child should be encouraged to close his mouth when not eating or speaking. Drinking through a straw requires lip rounding and tension of cheek muscles. Babbling exercises should be practised:

bah bah bah
dah dah dah
gah gah gah
mah mah mah
nah nah nah
lah lah lah
bor bor bor
dor dor dor
gor gor gor
mor mor mor
lor lor lor
boh boh boh
doh doh doh
goh goh goh
moh moh moh
noh noh noh
loh loh loh

These require vigorous movement of the tongue and lips and increase muscle tone.

All sorts of blowing games are excellent for encouraging breath control and lip rounding – blowing bubbles, blowing a ping-pong ball across a table into a goal, blowing a toy bird that warbles when filled with water, blowing a row of light objects such as yogurt pots off a low wall made of toy bricks.

All these activities – talking to the child, playing games with him, teaching him to listen and to exercise the muscles of his mouth – entail spending time with him and mean that the mother completes the daily routine more slowly and is more tired at the end of it. None the less, time spent at this early stage is well employed and lays down good basic patterns that will be hard to achieve later on if no early work has been done. The chief thing for the parents to remember is that though they may seem to be expending an enormous amount of energy for small immediate return, the efforts made are meaningful and will ultimately show reward. The child's listening and watching, his listening without watching, gradually train him to realise that objects and actions have names and he begins more and more to act upon what is said to him. When this process has developed far enough, and not before, he will say his first words.

8

Maturing in Years
— Still Young in Speech
and Language Development

It frequently happens that despite his parents' efforts to help him in his early years, and their willingness to consult people who specialise in various aspects of hearing loss, the hearing-impaired child falls further and further behind his hearing peers in speech and language development. Dr Conrad, after evaluating the speech, lip-reading and reading age of all deaf children who left school during 1975–6 reported his findings in relation to 360 children as follows: 'When these children leave school, half of them have a reading age of less than seven and a half years; half of them lip-read worse than the average hearing child . . . 70% of them have speech which is difficult to understand and only 10% have speech which is easy' (to understand).*

So concerned was the Deaf Children's Society by this state of affairs that, in February 1977, it organised in London a symposium entitled 'What Went Wrong?' While the symposium showed that in certain sectors hearing-impaired children are being taught to speak well, it is useless to deny that many children have little speech, or speech that is very difficult to understand.

Parents of hearing-impaired children have been encountered who elect for their child not to speak but to acquire a sign language. This is understandable. The child is the responsibility of those who gave him life and they must take decisions for him. But such cases are in the minority. Most parents want their child to learn to speak, and start by believing that he will do so. What, indeed, 'goes wrong'?

Anyone dealing with hearing-impaired children cannot fail to notice that the early stages of speech development proceed fairly well. Despite the difficulties and the delay, the parents, helped and

* Conrad, R., Research carried out on behalf of the Department of Experimental Psychology, University of Oxford, and reported to the R.N.I.D. Conference.

encouraged by professional workers, do succeed in developing some speech in their child and in establishing verbal links with him. It is equally noticeable that it is when the child should be developing more complex speech that he fails to do so, and that it is then that someone often becomes concerned about him. It becomes obvious that not only is the child not catching up in speech development but that he is steadily falling further behind his hearing peers.

I have found in clinical work that many of the hearing-impaired children from four to eleven years of age who are brought for help have speech levels appropriate to a child of between two and three. They are usually said to be improving in their ability to speak, but very slowly, and it is obvious that the gap between them and their hearing peers is steadily widening. The older the child, the more serious is his lack of ability to speak and the harder it will be to remedy it. Ultimately, there comes a point when the child is too old to learn the skills involved in communicating and must remain a person with minimal speech for the rest of his life.

Before going any further, we should consider briefly what level of speech development is to be expected of a normal two-year-old and what further developments take place before the third birthday. This particular year is, in terms of speech development, a very important one containing many changes and no claim is made to go into the developments in detail.

Children of twenty-four months vary a great deal in their individual ability to actually speak: Johnny holds a simple conversation whilst Jimmy says nothing at all. Understanding of the spoken word is, however, present at a very simple level, quite separated from gesture. The child is able to indicate familiar objects, to command, and to understand instructions involving two objects: 'Put the book on the table,' 'Give the cup to Daddy,' 'Give your coat to Mummy.' He may not be accurate every time, but there is a definite acting upon the spoken word. The presence of spontaneous single words and simple word combinations is characteristic of the speech of the average two-year-old: 'Open door,' 'Johnny apple,' 'Where ball?', 'Me good girl.'

At two years six months the child is more reliable in carrying out simple instructions: 'Give the flower to Granny.' He understands by words something of the use of objects. That is, if he is presented with several common objects he can select, when asked, which object he would put on his foot. He can enjoy his mother speaking simply about pictures in a book. At two and a half years the child speaks using a vocabulary of about 400 to 500 words and he builds small sentences like 'Give cake to Tommy,' 'Tommy like chocolate pudding,' 'Tommy gave bread to ducks.' Though he may be talkative, he is often still confused about pronouns and his use of verb tense is unreliable.

During the second half of the third year, he understands much more of what his mother says to him about the house: 'Would you like fish fingers for tea?' 'Don't touch that doggie,' 'Tell Daddy lunch is ready,' 'Go upstairs and fetch me your sponge.'

His own speech shows great increase in vocabulary, particularly in the use of descriptive words such as 'round', 'square', 'sticky', 'tall', 'fat' and his sentence structure is becoming more complicated. He is a communicating being but at a rudimentary level. He is still a long way from the verbal sophistication and confidence with which he will enter school when he is five years old.

The reasons why many hearing-impaired children do not acquire more than this rudimentary communication seem to be manifold. Absence of suitable hearing aids may be a factor, but it has already been pointed out that hearing aids alone cannot solve the problems of learning to speak. One factor seems to be that parents feel themselves to have made great efforts ever since their child was born. He has finally learned to speak a little and they can understand him. They feel this, understandably, to be such an achievement that they quite fail to see the gap between a child of, say, five and a half who speaks like a child of two and a half and the normal five-year-old who is capable of understanding complex stories, reciting poetry, following instructions from his teacher and holding complicated discussions about his pets and projects. The parents of the hearing-impaired child may feel that now their child has started to talk he will 'soon catch up' – they do not understand the enormous amount of development that would take place in a normal child between the ages of two and a half and five. Nor do they fully grasp that while a normal child covers this ground in approximately two and a half years, the hearing-impaired child may take twice or even three times as long to cover the same ground. He may indeed never cover it at all.

Parents also become very confused between their hearing-impaired child's speech and language development and his other assets. It is commonplace for them to feel anxiety on one hand and at the same time to look at their child's physical size, strength and skill at games and to tell themselves that he *must* be 'all right' – look how much stronger, braver and better at swimming he is than Garry-down-the-road! So accustomed are most of us to the idea that 'everyone can talk' that we find it difficult to believe that a well-developed boy who can play a competent game of football may be only two years old in his power to understand the spoken word.

When Andrew was brought, at nine and a half years old, for 'a little expert help with speech' his parents, though concerned about him, had no accurate idea of his low level of speech attainment. This intelligent boy could adjust the lawn-mower, paint the house, mend simple machinery and shop alone by pointing to objects and proffering money. His prowess at cycling, football and swimming made Andrew popular with other boys and he was much loved in the home. This boy's speech attainment was at the two years nine months level. Until his parents actually witnessed tests being carried out, they could not believe that their competent boy was unable to obey other than simple commands or to reply to any question beyond requests for his age, name and address. In general terms, the parents' natural admiration for their child, their hopes for him and their power to communicate with him through very simple words often cause them to greatly overestimate the level to which his speech has developed.

It appears that parents are also too ready to listen to the opinions of people who should be conversant with the speech skills appropriate to children of various ages but who, from years of working with numbers of hearing-impaired children who speak poorly, have no expectation that such a child will ever come anywhere near a normal child in speech attainment. These people are happy, when a hearing-impaired child says a few words, to assure parents that he is 'doing very well'. Kate, for instance (Audiogram Figure 11) was seven and a half when her mother received the opinion that she was 'doing very well indeed'. The same day, standardised speech and language tests showed that Kate understood as much as a child of two and three-quarter years and expressed herself at the same level. She showed many of the behaviour difficulties typical of hearing impairment and was becoming a great anxiety to her parents. Luckily for Kate, her mother preferred to be terrified by the second opinion rather than reassured by the first. The ultimate outcome, after some years of hard work, was a girl who was truly capable of understanding and communicating through spoken language.

It has already been said that there is a tendency for parents to feel that school, that magic institution, will solve the child's problems and that if only the child can go there, their job in teaching the child to speak will be over. Though many schools for the deaf and partially hearing do have specialised spoken language programmes and work hard at teaching children to talk, such schools usually encourage a great deal of parental involvement and expect as much effort from the parent in carrying out the programme as from the teacher. Again, parents are often too ready to believe, when told in the absence of such a programme, that the child is 'getting on all right'.*

Parental faith in the expert is great, partly because parents *want* to believe their child is doing well. Parents need the knowledge and courage to ask, 'Just *how* well is he doing? What is his present level of comprehension in years and months? What is his level of vocabulary? We know he can utter words, put words together, but what level of expressive language do these words represent? Just how far is he behind normal children of his age?'**

* It is distressing to see, in the course of clinical practice, young, hearing-impaired people in their late teens or early twenties who speak little or quite unintelligibly and to hear their worried parents say, 'But so-and-so always said he was doing so *well*!'

** The Reynell Developmental Language Scales devised by Dr Joan Reynell are constructed to test the level of attainment reached by a child in his comprehension of the spoken word and in his own power to express himself through words. The scales are used by psychologists, speech therapists and teachers of the deaf who have attended a special training course in their use. The level of attainment a child has reached is expressed in years and months. Together with other tests, the original Reynell Developmental Language Scales and the revised version have been much used by me in my clinical work with hearing-impaired children. I would like here to pay tribute to the benefits the scales have bestowed both as a tool of measurement and as a guide to the child's future spoken language needs.

If parents wish to be reassured about their hearing-impaired child's progress and not to increase their efforts on his behalf, this book is not for them. It is for the many parents who feel anxiety about their child, know that he does not speak like other children and want to help him to achieve more than the rudimentary stages of communication. These parents are already probably handling their child in as helpful a way as they can throughout the day, speaking clearly in short sentences and interpreting events as they arise in the home and the outside environment. Yet their child is still very far from a normal communicator. What else should these parents do? All of the following are true comments made by intelligent parents who understood something of hearing loss and who had a child whose level of communication was below the three-year level:

Mother of Nicola aged five and a half (comprehension of spoken language two years ten months): 'I want to help her but I don't know how.'

Mother of Michelle aged four and a quarter (comprehension of spoken language two years six months): 'They said to talk to her and we do, but she's still only just starting to say things.'

Father of Fred aged four (comprehension of spoken language two years): 'We've read all sorts of books, but they don't tell us what to teach him, or how.'

Parents of Peter aged five (comprehension of spoken language two years seven months): 'We've come to the end of knowing what to do next.'

Mother of Fiona aged eight years four months (comprehension of spoken language two years ten months): 'It isn't only that she doesn't talk properly. It's so dreadful that she understands hardly anything we say to her.'

The comments of Nicola's mother and Fred's father are particularly pertinent. Parents seem to find it easier to talk to a hearing-impaired baby or very small child, despite the lack of verbal response, than to a child who is older but retarded in his ability to understand spoken language. The language given to very small children is fairly standard, but there is something disconcerting about speaking to a bigger child whose range of interests has in all probability been limited by his handicaps and whose own verbal understanding and responses are far behind his years. Certainly some parents have a natural gift for finding things to talk about, but to provide a flow of conversation that is not only incessant but also interesting to the child is well beyond the reach of most people. The result is that most parents of hearing-impaired children talk to them much less than they believe and certainly too little for the child to make substantial progress. Many parents would provide more verbal input for their children if they knew how and the procedures described in the following chapters aim to fill this gap. They try to provide 'talking material' that is directed and structured towards solving particular difficulties in learning to talk from which I have over the years found hearing-impaired children to suffer. I have also found the material sparks off spontaneous ideas that parents might not otherwise have had, and increases the parents' awareness of many aspects of life and the environment, so giving opportunities for interesting their children and creating conversation between them.

While talking to a child can and should be enjoyable, to work through a definite talking programme with a hearing-impaired child demands self-discipline on the part of the parent and may not be welcomed, at first, by the child. It would be less than truthful to describe what follows other than as 'work' and it is therefore referred to as such.

9

How to Work with
a Hearing-Impaired Child

Before considering exactly *what* work to do, we must consider how to do it. The task is not an easy one and parents must be prepared to give up a great deal of time and energy, to have a great deal of patience, and always to remember how much slower progress will be than in the normally-hearing child. It must be remembered that the child looks at things in an entirely different way from the adult. Mostly, he *does not realise what is the matter with him*. He is often difficult and frustrated because he cannot communicate, but he does not know why he is difficult. Indeed, as far as he can see, it is everyone else in the world who is horrid and unreasonable. When his parents try to help him to learn, he is liable to feel more frustrated – partly because learning is difficult, partly because he is thinking of other things he might be doing, playing or watching television. To his parents, working with their child is a possible door to a better life for him. To the child, it is an imposition on his liberty. He sees no link between the efforts he is being asked to make and his frequent feelings of unhappiness arising from his handicap.

Having said this, parents must feel assured that it is a temporary stage only – how temporary depends upon many things. Usually, the more speech the child gains, the easier teaching and life in the home becomes because the child understands more and more that the parent is trying to help him. I have known few children who did not, in the end, come to enjoy the work entailed in learning to talk. Until he can enjoy the work for its own sake, the parent must make the work enjoyable enough to hold the child's attention.

Obviously the task varies with chronological age, and usually the older the child the more he is able to co-operate. In some older children and in most young children, concentration is poor at the outset and parents should not be surprised if their child works well for, perhaps, five minutes at a certain task and then tires. It is wise then to change the task. If the child has genuinely worked hard at, say, naming picture cards, then is the time to take out a jigsaw and play a listening game with the child – training him to put in the pieces as their names are said. When concentration span is again exhausted, then may be the time to play a game of acting out verbs so that the child works off surplus energy. Perhaps after this he may be ready for another session of sitting down and concentrating.

Sometimes it is difficult to decide whether a child is being tiresome or is genuinely bored. I have already dealt with the absolute necessity of giving hearing-impaired children firm discipline. If parents truly feel that their child is generally well-behaved yet finds his work on communication tedious, they should ask themselves whether they are doing their utmost to make the work as interesting as possible.

One way of maintaining attention is to work through the child's immediate interests. Mary, a profoundly deaf six-year-old, was restless and uncooperative even though apparently attractive teaching material was used. Without warning, she would get down from her chair and cross over to the doll's pram. No amount of coaxing, no amount of disapproval altered matters. The obvious solution was to structure Mary's learning round the doll. Accordingly, word-naming teaching consisted of the names of all the doll's clothes. The verbs taught – 'shaking', 'patting', 'wearing', 'rocking', 'dropping' – could all be acted out in connection with the doll. The doll could be placed *in* the pram, *in* the bath, *on* the table, *under* the cover. All this could be worked into an interesting and meaningful sequence. 'Baby's crying – lift her out of the pram and pat her. Rock-a-bye baby – let's rock the baby. Baby's not crying now – let's put her back in the pram,' etc. etc. Because she was interested in the doll and in the sequence of events, Mary learned all the relevant vocabulary very quickly.

The same child, in a fit of boredom, one day suddenly began to act out a lion, roaring and showing claws in a most life-like way! To tell her what a naughty girl she was would have been to throw away an opportunity. Mary knew none of the vocabulary involved, but was copying what she had seen other children do. The situation was quickly translated into pictures for her with a picture of a real lion. The words 'claws', 'roar', 'mane' were taught and also the vital word 'pretending'. 'Mary is *pretending* to be a lion.' She was then encouraged to act again and the vocabulary related to her performance.

Most children are interested in animals and will respond if the adult is lucky enough to find a live mouse, frog or even a ladybird. With a little thought the adult can abstract the relevant vocabulary, for example, a ladybird is 'tiny', 'red', 'black', it can 'fly', 'crawl', 'hide'. It is *on* the window, *in* the box, *under* the table.

Occasions such as Christmas or a birthday offer first-hand experience and genuine excitement. The relevant words and pictures should be produced in the week or two before the event so that they can be put into practice when the great day arrives.

Adults who are genuinely able to draw have an advantage. But those who cannot (and I am one) should not, and must not, give up with a despairing or self-satisfied 'I can't draw.' Anyone with fingers, paper and a good packet of felt tips can draw something. Children are perfectly satisfied with pin men or with simple line drawings. The important thing is to look for a salient feature in the child – red hair, a fringe or curls, and always draw him with this feature. Also to draw him as nearly as possible in a set of his own clothes and to draw Mummy and Daddy in their typical clothes. It is nearly impossible to find all the pictures required for teaching from magazines or educational suppliers, and a child's interest will be much better maintained if *he* is the star of the action or positional words being taught.

A diary is another way of maintaining interest. Once a child is about four years old a diary should be kept in a thick exercise book and written up by the mother each evening. 'I got up. I went to school. I came home. I watched television' should be avoided. The mother should get into the habit of noticing small, unimportant incidents that can be made interesting. 'I went out. I trod in a deep puddle. My shoes got wet. Mummy said "You must change your shoes." ' For younger children this may be quickly illustrated by a little picture.

Some work has to be done that cannot be done running about or in the form of an active game. It is good training for even a young child to accept the necessity for 'real work'. Children who have not learned to comprehend speech or to speak very much by seven or eight are usually more capable of understanding *why* they have to work and are able to sit down and concentrate though they often find it tedious. Young children find sedentary work very difficult to endure. Some parents dislike the idea of rewarding and consider that a child should not be bribed. If parents feel this, one must not argue – though it is noticeable that adults find it much easier to put in a hard day's work if they know it is the means of feeding their family or providing a summer holiday!

If the parent is in sympathy with rewards, a counter may be given for each correct response, i.e. a word said, or a picture pointed to, and ten counters gained exchanged for a smartie or a nut. Some children prefer a coloured sticker (to be stuck on a special card) as a reward; others will respond to 'I will tell Daddy what a good boy you have been.' One eleven-year-old rated a certain kind of biscuit very highly; a thirteen-year-old would prepare his work excellently for a small monetary reward. We should try to find out just what constitutes reward for any particular child and use this knowledge to help him. Failure should be greeted with a calm 'No, but let's try again,' genuine achievement always greeted with praise. Very tiny children, three-year-olds, are entitled to clapping for genuine achievement, but it is not wise to prolong this too far into the fourth year. I have found that as the child becomes more involved and interested in his work, rewards can gradually be dropped, the child becoming happy to complete tasks for the sense of achievement they give him.

I personally favour work being done as far as possible at the same time of day and in the same surroundings. It thus becomes part of the day's routine and is not questioned by the child. It is also part of the mother's routine and she allows time for it. At least an hour every day should be carried out, more if possible and certainly more at weekends. (Some parents are horrified by this, but many were even more horrified when they heard that the John Tracey Foundation requires parents to work twenty hours each week with a child!)

Though a table and chair of the appropriate height would seem essential for some work, long experience of mothers and their children suggests that each parent has an individual way of working. Several have told me that their child works best in bed just before going to sleep. One mother commented that the longer her son worked then, the more he felt he prolonged the day! Others simply report that the child is more relaxed when in bed. One young lady of six insisted that the only place in which she could listen to a story was in the bath! Since the results she produced by this method were excellent, who are we to argue?

Parental attitudes to time of day are similarly variable. Much work has, of necessity, to be carried out after school and most mothers give tea, a break and probably allow the watching of 'Play School' before bringing out the work. Several absolutely heroic mothers I have known started work with their children at 7.30 each morning. One mother did part of her daughter's work whilst waiting in the car for the older children to come out of school. Provided work is done regularly and done well, it does not matter where or how.

Something must be said of the people involved. As I have already stressed, the mother, who is at home all day and close to her child, is probably responsible for the main work. The father may be able to work with the child at weekends. For some activities (and these will be outlined later) two adults are an advantage and a helping hand from brothers and sisters can be invaluable. The attitude of siblings to the hearing-impaired child vary with age, sex and disposition, but as far as possible siblings should be trained to help their handicapped brother or sister, not to abandon it to the mother as 'her job'. However, an older sibling may have homework, and some have time but no patience or interest. A line must be drawn between exploiting the hearing child for the benefit of the handicapped, and letting the normal child get away without taking part in what should be a family endeavour. Only parents themselves should ultimately decide how much help to enlist from their normal children.

Some children are lucky enough to have supportive grandparents who truly share in the work. On the whole, since teaching a partially-hearing child is onerous work, the more helpers the better provided everyone is working on the same lines.

How much gesture should a hearing-impaired child be allowed to use? If the parents truly intend to put in all the hard work that teaching their child to talk implies, they should try not so much to inhibit gesture as to give the child words in which to convey his gestured message, however simple those words are. Mary, for instance, would pull an anguished face, rub her tummy and look appealing. Her mother would say to her, 'Talk, Mary! Say,

"Tummy sore." ' It is cruel to inhibit gesture if no alternative method of communication is available, but not wise to encourage it if oral communication is seriously intended.

Before leaving the subject of how to work, one last word on discipline. It is normal to all of us *not* to want to work and the less conscious control we have of ourselves, the harder it is for us to work. One senses in some children that the adults concerned are trying very hard to make work as interesting and as simple as possible, but that the child is not trying nearly as hard as he might. It is sometimes difficult to decide about this, but there are usually pointers. A child who says 'It's boring. I'm bored,' when presented with interesting material is to be suspected. Who taught him to use such words? My own feeling is that if he is capable of understanding that much, he can be told sharply that if he is bored, he had better interest himself in the project on hand. Some older children glance continually at their watches to see how long it will be before work-time is up. My own personal answer to this is to ask the child to entrust the watch to me unless he can promise to stop glancing at it. Some younger children are wild and defiant, get down a great deal from their seats for no reason and engage in other provocative and distracting behaviour. In such cases, it is up to the adult to maintain firm control of the situation, to promise that there will be no television or other recreation until the work is done or, in extreme cases, to ask the child to go outside the door or up to his bedroom until he feels he can do what is required of him.

The old-fashioned aphorism 'being cruel to be kind' is still applicable. Mothers who cannot bear to inconvenience their children or to see a momentary sadness are not considering the long-term incapacity their child may face if he cannot accept the discipline of work. Much better to have some unpleasantness and deprivation at four, five, six or seven years old than the bitter frustration of a lifelong handicap.

10

Learning More Words (1)
Naming Words

We have considered the framework of teaching the child and have mentioned listening techniques. How should more actual words be taught to him? Over and over again we find that in the absence of direct teaching what he has learned has been said to him loudly, often and very near the ear. David's mother had four children and repeatedly said to them loudly, whilst she was driving, 'Sit down!' 'Sit down!' was David's first utterance!

We must, therefore, teach words to a hearing-impaired child by saying them loudly, often and close to him. Parents will find it easier to keep track of what words their child is developing if vocabulary is taught in definite categories – naming words, doing words, positional words, descriptive words. Objection is sometimes made on the grounds that a normal child does not develop words in a categorical way. The answer is that of course he doesn't, but also that his mother doesn't have to keep her own ears open the whole time to try to keep track of his progress in language. Some professional people do teach language, very successfully, in a natural way, using their knowledge of language development to assess the child's progress. The parents with much less general experience will find that categorisation enables them to cover the ground in a systematic manner.

A naming word (or in old-fashioned grammatical terms, a noun) is the name of a person, place or object. These fairly stable things can be seen, heard, felt, smelled, and words representing them are as a class the easiest words to learn. The child will have learned the names of people and many objects in the home by the two-plus language level and the extent of this type of vocabulary very often reflects how much work his parents have attempted to carry out with him.

There is no better way to enlarge noun vocabulary than by the many picture-word games on the market – pairs, picture dominoes, lotto. The essence of word teaching is that it should be *fun*. One mother of a hearing-impaired child complained, 'You say "dog" every time you see a dog . . . "dog", "dog", "dog", and the child still says nothing.' Not surprising, since the child probably has no interest whatsoever in the dog and 'dog', 'dog', 'dog' gives him no inkling of the interesting properties (barking, biting, jumping) relating to dogs. Most children will learn, however, if an attractive game is spread on the table for them to play with their parents.

Supposing 'pairs' is selected. This is a game in which a pack of picture cards is turned face downwards on the table, and players try in turn to turn up two identical cards. Hearing-impaired children are good at remembering where things are, since their visual memory tends to be retentive and they quickly learn to localise cards. There must be a strict rule from the beginning that when a card is turned up, its name is loudly and firmly said by the adult until the child can say it, and after that by the child. Unless this rule is adhered to, the game loses its point as language instruction. A few cards at a time should be used to start with since hearing-impaired children are often impatient and cannot at first see the point of a game. To maintain interest, start with seven pairs (fourteen cards), where a whole pack would be used for a normal child of the same chronological age.

The same strict rules should be adhered to whatever game is chosen and parents should be firm about taking turns. The comments inherent in the games, 'Well done! You've got a pair,' 'It's my turn now,' 'Daddy's won,' are repeated so often that they are also valuable teaching. A list of games obtainable is given in Appendix 2.

The Invalid Children's Aid Association publish very cheaply black and white drawings of the first hundred words learned by a child. Not all these are naming words, but most are, and so good are they that it is tempting to stick each sheet in a scrap-book as a separate endeavour. The pictures are very easy to colour and look most attractive afterwards.

However, more pictures than this first hundred will be required and it may be better to incorporate them in a total scrap-book for the child. A large file with hard back, metal rings, loose leaves and reinforcers is a good investment and the aim is to fill it with pictures of objects familiar to the child. Apart from what the parents can draw themselves, pictures from magazines and catalogues can be used. It is a good idea for parents to go through the magazines when the child is not there, lest the operation lose its orderliness. The child can help when it comes to sticking the pictures in the book.

It is assumed by this stage that the child will know such familiar words as 'door', 'bed', 'table', 'chair' but it is amazing, once again, how many words a parent may *think* a child knows. Very often, he knows how to use the object, but he cannot locate it when the word is said, or name the object himself without prompting.

The child's own room should be a meaningful place to him and the mother should check just how many objects he can locate when she says a word and how many objects he can name without prompting. The parent then draws the objects in the book or finds pictures and labels them clearly in lower case letters. Suggested objects are: 'carpet', 'mat', 'picture', 'lamp', 'desk', 'shelf', 'mirror', 'duvet' (and other bedding), 'floor', 'ceiling', 'cupboard', 'bookcase'.

Once the child's pictures are in the book, parent and child play a pointing game with the book laid flat and the child laying a coloured counter on each picture he selects correctly on request. The advantage of a loose-leaf book is that sheets can be removed and also new sheets interpolated at any place in the book.

At this stage, the essentials in every room in the house should be learned, the objects the child sees and handles every day. Other groups of words relate to the meal table, the garden, clothes, parts of the body. Some children have a particular interest, for instance a pet or hobby, in which case the words appropriate to that subject should be added to the scrap-book.

Parents of little girls who do not have a doll's house may add interest by obtaining a large sheet of cardboard (30″ x 20″/76 cm x 55 cm) from an art shop and drawing a two-dimensional house with appropriate rooms, which are then filled with drawings of appropriate objects. Not all boys are averse to this, either! It is possible to buy two-dimensional cardboard houses with furniture but the somewhat unconventional nature of the furniture might be confusing to a hearing-impaired child.

The stress on orderliness will be noted – keeping bathroom pictures in a group, keeping garden pictures together. There are two reasons for this. One is that if pictures are pasted in higgledy-piggledy, the parent will soon become unsure just what the child knows. The other is that as I have said before, experience of hearing-impaired children has shown that they have much greater difficulty in categorising than do normal children. At later stages in language development, they find it difficult to tell one that 'Teddy', 'doll', 'ball', 'marble' are all *toys* or to give five examples of *vegetables*. Similarly, a hearing-impaired child with quite sophisticated language cannot select from a printed page the information relevant to a particular subject. 'Thinking in groups' is therefore an essential part of training from the beginning.

The reader may ask, 'If all the objects are in the house, why go to the trouble of making a scrap-book?' This is because the hearing-impaired child needs much reinforcement before he can actually master words. If he sees a mat on the floor, a mat in the doll's house and a mat in the scrap-book, his ideas of 'mat' are much stronger than if he has seen only one mat. All teaching needs reinforcement, using as many ways as the parent can think of to strengthen the child's auditory memory.

The parent will, for instance, make a special point of mentioning to the child during the daily routine the group of words currently being worked on: for example, 'Switch on your *lamp*,' 'I'm shaking your *duvet*,' 'Open the *cupboard door*.' The bathtime routine should always include mention of 'bath', 'hot tap', 'cold tap', 'soap', 'flannel', 'bath-mat', 'towel', 'heater', 'basin', 'tooth-brush', 'toothpaste', 'water'.

A further reinforcer may be a game played with small, identical coloured stickers. The mother says, 'Show me so-and-so' and if the child can locate the object, he is allowed to put a sticker on it.

Auditory memory may be further aided by the mother asking the child to point to two objects – either in the real room or in the scrap-book. 'Show me the *lamp* and the *carpet*.' Insist that the child points first to the object said first. Because his auditory memory is weak, the child is likely to remember the *last* object and point to it first. This encourages disordered thinking and it is unhelpful to correct word order at later stages.

Though some words have to be repeated many times to a hearing-impaired child before he can locate an object, let alone say the word himself, some words 'come' very quickly if they are attractive in themselves or have some emotive quality. One day, for instance, a live baby hedgehog suddenly appeared and actually ran into the room where a lesson was taking place. The profoundly deaf child present learned and retained 'hedgehog' because she was impressed by the experience. Yet this same child had the utmost difficulty in remembering words for objects she handled daily, apparently because their interest level was low. Another boy was terrified of the same hedgehog, turned his back and would not learn its name. Yet the same day he mastered 'marrow' after very little repetition, because, apparently, he was delighted by the size and weight of the object.

A word is comprehended when the child can respond correctly to 'Show me the —' It has been acquired when he can respond to 'What is this?' with the correct name. It is integrated when the child uses it spontaneously in conversation. There are still lapses of memory. A new word may 'go' under stress or excitement, or because an object is seen in different surroundings or is of a different size and colour from the familiar one.

Parents are often advised to use the simplest words possible in speaking to their hearing-impaired child, lest hearing too many words he becomes confused and fails to learn anything. While it is essential to use very simple *sentences* the simplicity can be overdone in naming words. Andrew, who came for help at nine and a half years of age with language levels of two and three-quarter years, epitomises this. Though he used soap, towel, bath, basin, plugs, taps, tooth-brush daily he knew only 'bath' and named all the other objects 'wash'. His mother, seeing Andrew's efficient use of objects and with the counsel of simplicity in her mind, had not grasped how impoverished was his actual store of words. At the age of nine and a half there was not only poor auditory memory but also years of bad habit to overcome and it took considerable time and patience to teach Andrew new naming words. It is easier, ultimately, to teach correct names for familiar things in the early years, and a great satisfaction to hear the various words taught uttered by the child.

Care should be paid, from the earliest stages, to the *way* in which a word is said. There is no point at all in a child acquiring a vocabulary of badly said words, for example, 'Di be the wee' (Give me the sweets). There is a special chapter on articulation (or saying words) and parents are advised to work towards clear speech from the earliest words before bad habits are formed.

It has already been pointed out how very important is the connection between saying and listening and it must once again be stressed that all the work on naming words should be done on the lines already described in the listening chapter, that is, with the parent's mouth covered once a word is known.

The following is a list of 400 plus nouns likely to be in the vocabulary of a normal child of three years old. Of course, there is a variation from child to child, depending upon the geographical location of the child's home and the interests and habits of the parents. 'Cicada', 'veranda' and 'yacht club' were for instance frequently used by Keith, an English child brought up in Trinidad. Children whose parents have particular hobbies pursued in the home will pick up words connected with these hobbies – 'saw', 'drill', 'vice', 'plane'. Some parents exclude all sweet things from the home, in which case 'chocolate', 'smartie', 'Coca-Cola', 'biscuit' will not be part of the child's vocabulary. Some words are very familiar to children without the child ever having seen an example of the real object. Good examples of this are some animals; children who have never seen elephants, mice or rabbits are quite familiar with the words from numerous pictures in children's books. Whilst it is, of course, vital to give hearing-impaired children first-hand experience of the object whose name is being taught, this is by no means always necessary in the case of objects that recur often in books, pictures and birthday cards. A word like 'postman' or 'milkman' on the other hand may well be a mystery to a child who is, perhaps, still asleep when the postman or milkman comes to the house, and pains should be taken to make sure that the child understands their identity.

Despite individual differences, this list of naming words should provide a basic guide, and in addition to being given in alphabetical order, the list has been re-grouped under subject headings in order to give the parent a framework within which to group words when putting together a file for the child. It can be copied out and placed at the beginning of the child's file. A word is ticked off the list when the parent has heard the child use it spontaneously in conversation several times.

Something should be said about *correct naming* of objects. Fortunately the current child-rearing trend is against any form of baby talk and children are no longer encouraged to say 'horsey' for 'horse', or 'quack-quack' for 'duck'. None the less, some infantile terms remain. Parents often describe 'cock', 'hen' and 'chick' as 'chicken', which can only lead to the child relearning words and ideas later. Similarly, sheep of all sizes are erroneously termed 'lamb'. 'Mug' and 'cup' are confused, 'saucer' and 'plate'. It will save time and energy at a later date if correct words are used from the beginning and differences in size and appearance clarified to the child.

Immature plural forms, such as 'mans', 'mens', 'mouses', 'sheeps', are, however, to be expected. They are frequent in the speech of the normally-hearing three-year-old and their appearance should cause no surprise or anxiety in the early communications of the hearing-impaired child.

A Basic Noun List

aeroplane	biscuit	butterfly	cigarette
ambulance	blackboard	button	clock
apple	blanket	cat	cloth
arm	blood	cake	clothes
baby	boat	camel	cloud
back	book	camera	clown
baddie	bookshelf	candle	coat
bag	bottle	cap	Coca-Cola
ball	bottom	car	cock
balloon	bow	card	coffee
banana	bowl	carpet	collar
basin	box	case	comb
basket	boy	cereal	cooker
bat	bread	chair	corner
bath	breakfast	chalk	cornflakes
bathroom	brick	cheese	cot
bear	bridge	chick	cover
bed	brother	chicken	cow
bedroom	brush	children	cowboy
bee	bubble	chimney	cradle
belt	bucket	chocolate	cream
bicycle	bulb	Christmas	crocodile
bike	bus	Christmas tree	cross
bird	butter	church	crown

cup	floor	hen	lighthouse
cupboard	flower	hill	lion
cushion	fly	hole	lip
daddy	foot	home	living-room
day	fork	honey	lock
desk	four	hood	lollipop
dinner	fox	hoop	loo
doctor	fridge	horse	lorry
dog	friend	hospital	lot
doll	frog	house	lunch
donkey	game	hungry	mac
door	garden	hurry	man
downstairs	gate	ice	marble
drawer	girl	ice cream	mark
dress	glass	I'm sorry	mat
dressing-gown	glasses	inside	match
drink	(spectacles)	iron	meat
drum	gloves	jam	men
duck	glue	jug	mess
duvet	goat	juice	milk
ear	goodbye	jumper	milkman
egg	goodnight	kettle	minute
elephant	grandma	key	mirror
end	grandpa	king	money
everybody	grass	kitchen	monkey
eye	guitar	kite	month
face	gun	kitten	moon
fairy	hair	knee	morning
father	hand	knife	mother
feather	handle	lady	motor-bike
feet	hanky	ladybird	mouse
fence	hat	lamp	mouth
field	head	leaf	mud
fight	hearing aid	leg	mug
finger	heart	lemon (drink)	mummy
fire	heater	letter	nail
fire engine	hedgehog	letterbox	name
fish	hello	lid	needle
flag	help	light	nest

net
night
nightie
nobody
noise
nose
number
nursery
   (school)
nut
orange
outside
owl
pain
paints
pants
paper
park
patch
path
pavement
pear
peas
pen
pencil
people
picture
pig
pillow
pin
pipe
plaster
plate
please
pocket
policeman
pond
postman
potty

powder
pram
present
puddle
puppet
purse
puzzle
pyjamas
queen
rabbit
rain
record
ring
road
roof
room
rope
round
roundabout
rug
salt
sand
sandwich
Santa Claus
saucepan
sausage
saw
school
scissors
sea
seal (sea-lion)
see-saw
sellotape
shampoo
sheep
sheet
shell
ship
shirt

shoe
shop
sink
sister
skateboard
sky
slide
slippers
smartie
smoke
snail
snake
snow
soap
sock
sofa
soldier
soup
spade
spider
sponge
spoon
square
stairs
stamp
star
stick
stone
story
sugar
sun
supper
sweater
sweets
swing
switch
sword
table
tail

tap
tea
teacher
teapot
teddy
teeth
telephone
television
tent
thumb
tie
tights
tissue
toe
toilet
tomato
tooth
tooth-brush
top
towel
toy
tractor
train
tray
tree
trousers
tummy
umbrella
upstairs
van
vest
wall
washing-
   machine
watch
water
watering-can
whale
wheel

wheelbarrow	window	work	yesterday
wind	woman	worm	zebra
windmill	wood	year	zoo

The House and its Contents

bag	cover	knife	sheet
basin	cradle	lamp	sink
basket	cup	lid	soap
bath	cupboard	light	sofa
bathroom	cushion	living-room	sponge
bed	desk	lock	spoon
bedroom	door	loo	stairs
blanket	downstairs	mat	switch
book	drawer	match	table
bookshelf	duvet	mirror	tap
bottle	fire	mug	teapot
bowl	floor	needle	telephone
box	fork	picture	television
brush	fridge	pillow	tissue
bucket	glass	pin	toilet
bulb	handle	plate	tooth-brush
candle	heater	potty	towel
carpet	home	purse	tray
case	house	record	upstairs
chair	inside	roof	wall
chimney	iron	room	washing-
clock	jug	rug	machine
comb	kettle	saucepan	water
cooker	key	scissors	window
cot	kitchen		

Food and Sweets

apple	chicken	lollipop	sandwich
banana	chocolate	meat	sausage
biscuit	cornflakes	nut	smartie
bread	cream	orange	soup
butter	egg	pear	sugar
cake	honey	peas	sweets
cereal	ice cream	salt	tomato
cheese	jam		

Drinks

Coca-Cola	drink	lemon (drink)	orange (drink)
coffee	juice	milk	

Living Things

bear	dog	hen	rabbit
bee	donkey	horse	sheep
bird	duck	kitten	seal (sea-lion)
butterfly	elephant	ladybird	snail
camel	fish	lion	snake
cat	fly	monkey	spider
chick	fox	mouse	whale
cock	frog	owl	worm
cow	goat	pig	zebra
crocodile	hedgehog		

People

baby	doctor	lady	people
baddie	everybody	man	policeman
boy	fairy	men	postman
brother	father	milkman	queen
children	girl	mother	Santa Claus
clown	grandma	mummy	sister
cowboy	grandpa	nobody	woman
daddy	king		

Toys and Playthings

aeroplane	doll	puppet	soldier
ball	drum	puzzle	spade
balloon	game	rope	swing
bat	gun	roundabout	sword
bicycle	hoop	sand	teddy
boat	kite	see-saw	tent
book	marble	ship	top
brick	net	skateboard	toy
card	paints	slide	

Meals

breakfast	lunch	supper	tea
dinner			

Shapes

cross	round	square	star
heart			

Vehicles

ambulance	car	motor-bike	train
bike	fire-engine	pram	van
bus	lorry	tractor	wheelbarrow

Body Parts

arm	feet	knee	teeth
back	finger	leg	thumb
bottom	foot	lip	toe
ear	hair	mouth	tooth
eye	hand	nail	tummy
face	head	nose	

School

blackboard	number	pen	teacher
chalk	nursery school	pencil	work
friend	paper	school	

Weather and Sky

cloud	night	sky	sun
ice	rain	snow	wind
moon			

Clothes

belt	dress	nightie	slippers
bow	dressing-gown	pants	sock
button	gloves	patch	sweater
cap	hanky	pocket	tie
clothes	hat	pyjamas	tights
coat	hood	ring	trousers
collar	jumper	shirt	umbrella
crown	mac	shoe	vest

Outside the House

bridge	hill	outside	roof
church	hole	park	sea
fence	hospital	path	shop
field	letter-box	pavement	smoke
flag	lighthouse	pond	stone
garden	mud	puddle	tree
gate	nest	road	wood
grass			

Others

blood	glue	money	shell
bubble	goodbye	morning	stamp
camera	goodnight	name	stick
Christmas	guitar	noise	story
Christmas tree	hearing aid	pain	tail
cigarette	hello	pipe	thank you
cloth	hole	plaster	tomorrow
corner	I'm sorry	please	watering-can
day	leaf	powder	wheel
end	letter	present	windmill
feather	lot	saw	year
fight	mark	sellotape	yesterday
flower	mess	shampoo	zoo
glasses	minute		

Learning More Words (2)
Action Words

An action word, or verb, is a doing word and is often felt by parents to be more difficult to teach than a naming word that can be seen and felt. Actually, once the technique of teaching action words has been grasped, they are not difficult to teach and are greatly enjoyed by the child. For one thing, they represent movement, a thing usually very meaningful to hearing-impaired children; for another, they represent a strongly emotive and oft-repeated action – cry, break, sleep, smack.

Many hearing-impaired children who come for help and who have some speech already say a healthy number of nouns. Catherine, at exactly four years of age had a noun vocabulary, on a standardised test, of a child of three years and eight months, but was using only half a dozen verbs that her parents could count. Catherine's general level of communication was two and a quarter years, twenty-one months behind her actual age, one reason for this being that she had never learned any doing words with which to join her naming words.

A three-year-old normal child should use approximately 200 verbs.* The 150 verbs on pages 110-11 form a suggested basic verb list, collected from experience of normal children and from teaching hearing-impaired children.

Some of these verbs are common to all children, but individual verb vocabulary, like noun vocabulary, varies greatly. A child with a mother who *crochets* and a father who *carves* wood will acquire these verbs early, whereas they will be absent in a child where no such vocabulary exists in the home.

* Whetnall, E. and Fry, D., *The Deaf Child*.

A Basic Verb List

ask	*drive	laugh	send
bath	drop	*lay	*sew
be	dry	like	shake
beg	*eat	listen	shine
bend	*fall	lock	shoot
blow	*feed	*look	shop
*break	*fight	make	show
bring	fill	melt	shut
*brush	find	*mend	*sit
*build	fish	mix	skate
bump	fly	move	*skip
burn	get	*open	*sleep
button	get up	pack	slide
*buy	give	*paint	smack
call	go	*pat	smile
carry	grow	*pick	smoke
*catch	guess	plant	splash
*chase	have	*play	stand
chop	hear	*point	stop
*clean	help	post	stretch
*climb	*hide	pour	stroke
colour	hit	pretend	suck
comb	*hold	*pull	*sweep
come	*hop	*push	*swim
*cook	*hug	*put	swing
crawl	hurry	*reach	*take
*cry	*iron	*read	talk
*cut	*jump	remember	tell
die	*kick	*ride	thank
*dig	kill	roll	think
do	kiss	*run	*throw
*draw	*kneel	sail	tie
dress	*knock	see	try
*drink	know	sell	turn

* Illustrated by LDA Photographic Action Cards, LDA Action Cards Sets 1 and 2, or Philip & Tacey Things-We-Do Pictorial gummed stamps. See Appendix 2.

Basic Verb List – continued

wait	want	wave	work
wake	*wash	wear	wrap
wake up	*wash up	wish	*write
*walk	*watch		

The more frequent and definite the action, the easier the action word. Suppose, for a start, the commonplace words 'jump', 'kick', 'run', 'push' and 'walk' are selected. The parent must be prepared to act these verbs in an interesting and exciting way. It is no use at all to sit down on a chair and tell a child about jumping. The parent must demonstrate jumping – jumping on the floor, jumping off the table, and she must make the child jump too, saying 'Mummy's jumping . . . Bobby's jumping . . . we're jumping.' This is exciting, and children whose attention span is shorter or who are lethargic, may need the physical activity before any interest can be aroused at all. Other children are easily stimulated and activity must be carefully controlled lest they become too excited or hyperactive.

As with naming words, an activity must be practised several times over before the child can be expected to learn the word. The parent should ask, 'What are you doing? You're jumping,' and may have to repeat this several times before the child can answer for himself.

For reinforcement it is possible to obtain wooden boy and girl dolls about seven inches (18 cm) high and make them do basic actions – kicking, jumping, falling, pushing, smacking, sitting, running and crying. Again the action should be clearly described: 'The boy is running. What is the boy doing? He is running.'

The child should also be requested to act out verbs on command, 'Run! Now jump! Now walk!' and also to make the dolls act, 'Make the girl run,' 'Make the boy lie down.' Picture cards of various verbs are obtainable – a list is given at the end of this book in Appendix 2, and about six of the cards that have been acted should be placed on the table and the child asked, 'Show me "The boy is jumping",' and 'Show me "The girl is sitting".' Children find it a great help to be given a goal – that is, if they can see the completion of an activity. When a card has been correctly selected therefore, the parent should say, 'That's right! Turn the card upside down.' The child then knows that when all the cards have been turned upside down that particular goal has been reached.

As well as teaching an actual word, it will be seen that in the total activity described several types of span are being lengthened. 'What is it?' contains three syllables. When he responds to 'What are you doing?', 'What is he doing?', 'What am I doing?' the child is comprehending a five-syllable question. On the expressive side (that is, in speaking himself) the child is lengthening his capacity to remember and to link words. Once again, when picture cards are used, the child should *listen* to the words, not only lip-read. When there has been an amount of repetition he will probably suddenly say quite naturally, 'Boy jumping', 'Girl walking', 'Baby crying'. At this stage with a child of three, four or five years of age, grammatical completion of the sentence (*The* baby *is* crying) should not be stressed. The achievement of joining two ideas together, 'Boy jumping', is a considerable feat. More can be expected from older children who may be able to read words and probably know that 'little words' should be included in a sentence. These children are more mentally mature and should have better auditory memory.

This is also an opportunity for teaching 'Who?' With six cards spread out, the child should be asked, 'Who is driving?' Some children, not understanding 'Who?', echo 'Who?' This should be inhibited by, 'No; listen: Who is driving? The boy,' until the child grasps the correct answer to the question.

Older children who concentrate well can learn many action words from pictures, but on the whole the parent must usually be prepared to demonstrate their meaning. With young children, almost everything must be demonstrated and verbs can be worked into a favourite and oft-repeated game, 'I'm *shaking* baby's cover – you *shake* it – baby's *crying*,' (life-like demonstration!) 'I'm *feeding* baby – you *feed* her,' 'We're *pushing* the pram.' If care is taken to keep the sentences very short and simple and the play routine enjoyable, the child will soon connect word with activity and begin to use the word himself.

Some very small children, or profoundly deaf children who have had no language until an advanced chronological age, may be unable to interest themselves at all in matters unconnected with themselves. In this case, the only pictorial form acceptable to the child

is a picture of the child himself engaging in the activity. A page
may be divided into four sections (as shown here) and simple line
drawings made. A double spread can be used for auditory training.
Usually once the action word has been personalised in this way,
the parent may locate it in an ordinary children's book or scrap-
book and will find that the child recognises it.

The natural progression from the step 'naming word-action
word' is to 'naming word-action word-naming word' or, in grammatical terms, from 'subject-verb' to 'subject-verb-object'. Some
verbs cannot take an object, e.g. 'The girl is crying,' 'The boy is
hopping,' but 'The boy is kicking' can be extended to 'The boy
is kicking the ball,' 'The boy is kicking the table,' or 'The boy is
kicking the box.' A normal child recognises this as logical and has

Mary is jumping

Mary is hopping

Mary is sitting

Mary is crying

(113)

no difficulty in making this progression. Hearing-impaired children, though they know that the ideas in 'Boy kick ball' are in some way related, are extremely confused about word relationship and order. Combinations like 'Boy kick kick,' 'Ball kick boy,' 'Ball boy kick' are then produced. These bizarre-sounding utterances worry parents a great deal, but we have to think of some of our efforts as adults to speak a foreign language to realise that the child's bewilderment and errors are natural enough. Some of the errors lie again in lack of sufficient listening to the rhythms of the sentence pattern and to the order of words involved.

It is also a great help if the parent taps firmly on the part of the picture that is being said: 'The *boy* (tap the picture) is *kicking* (demonstrate a kick) the *ball* (tap the picture).' Far from encouraging the child to gesture, he is by this time far too busy trying to conjure up the necessary words to join in the gesturing.

As many subject-verb-object combinations as possible should be taught to the child, for example:

> The boy is kicking the ball.
> The girl is kicking the ball.
> The man is kicking the door.
> The boy is cutting bread.
> The girl is cutting paper.
> Mummy is cutting the cotton.
> Daddy is climbing a ladder.
> The boy is climbing a tree.
> The girl is brushing her hair.
> Mummy is brushing her teeth.
> The boy is brushing the dog.

Ability to draw such combinations is an advantage and as the following page shows, such drawings make excellent auditory training material. Once again, with young children, the achievement of a three-word combination is considerable, and correct grammar should not be insisted upon. The child is making good progress if he can, when given any of the cards listed at the end of this book, describe them in terms of subject-verb, or subject-verb-object.

As with naming words, verbs need to be reinforced all through the day by the parent drawing particular attention to actions that are being currently learned. It is advocated most strongly that the

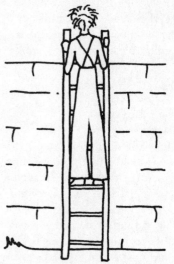

The boy is climbing
the ladder

The boy is climbing
the tree

The cat is climbing
the wall

The girl is climbing
the ladder

doing words being learned are definitely highlighted and also that the mother try deliberately to work them into the child's daily diary. One confusing feature of 'doing words' is, of course, the way in which some of them change according to the time being spoken of:

(Today)	I *buy* sweets.
(Yesterday)	I *bought* sweets.
(Today)	I *find* a ladybird.
(Yesterday)	I *found* a ladybird.

Little deaf children have not enough language to tell us if this confuses them, but one normal three-year-old announced on coming out of nursery school, 'I *drawed* a picture.' 'You *drew*,' corrected her mother. 'No, I never *drew* in nursery; I told you, I *drawed*,' persisted the child, thus showing clearly that she regarded the words as referring to two different activities. Older hearing-impaired children have also been able to indicate, when helped with their diaries, that the present and past forms of verbs seem to them to refer to different activities. Time and use clarifies the problem; once again small illustrations in the diary are a great help and also linking with a time word: '*Yesterday* I found a ladybird.'

Another aspect of 'doing words' may be described as 'What things do what?' or 'What do we do with what?' A three-year-old is able to reply to many such questions as:

'What flies?'
'What burns?'
'What boils?'
'What stings?'

In order to train the hearing-impaired child in this sort of response, collect a number of objects that have a well-known function. Suggested objects are:

a toy broom	a toy car	a little shoe
child's scissors	a pencil	a doll's spoon
a small gun	a toy chair	a toy boat
a key	a toy cup	a little ladder

Present the child with four of these and ask him appropriate questions (always remembering what a useful auditory training exercise this is):

'Which one do we shoot with?'
'Which one do we cut with?'
'Which one do we throw?'
'Which one do we sit on?'

If the child's answers are wide of the mark, he is often kept working at the task if the adult makes a joke of the mistake and pretends to use the object in the way the child has suggested, e.g. the adult pretends to shoot with the chair. It must of course be made clear that amusing though the child finds this, amusement is not enough and he must learn to select the object appropriate to the question. Once the uses of twelve objects have been mastered it is not usually necessary to use further real objects.

Jigsaw puzzles are a useful interim step between real objects and pictures. These puzzles need to be of a particular type, in which one whole puzzle piece depicts a single object such as a house, a shoe, a dog, a jug and is fitted into a plain background. Appropriate puzzles are listed in Appendix 2. In puzzles with about ten pieces, all the pieces are removed when working with the child; in puzzles with over twenty objects pieces should be removed a line at a time, so that the child is coping with six or seven pieces at most. As with the three-dimensional objects, he is asked:

'Which one do you live in?'
'Which one do you put milk in?'

It will be a long time, probably, before the hearing-impaired child can answer questions such as 'What cuts?' without a visual clue, but when he has mastered this exercise he has taken a valuable step forward. He has learned to associate the uses of an object with an object without the name of the object being said. 'Which one do we cook with?' is more sophisticated and abstract than 'Show me the pan.'

At this stage the child needs almost endless experience of 'doing' words. If the child enjoys looking at books, many of the verbs he has acted out, or seen on picture cards, can be reinforced by his parents looking at books with him. Books with plenty of familiar action in them should be selected. It is worth while looking carefully at all sorts of books in a children's bookshop, since books suitable for what parents are trying to teach a hearing-impaired child are sometimes written with a quite other purpose in mind. *Silly Billy* in the 'Books for Me to Read' series is a good example.

Really a reading book, it is full of verb action which a hearing-impaired child will enjoy. In order to help the child to *listen* the relevant picture and the print should be covered while the parent describes the action *in his own words*, slowly and clearly, 'Billy is asleep.' The picture is then shown and after the child has examined it, the page turned and the picture on the next pages covered. The parent says, 'Billy is walking to the bathroom.' The story is continued in this way, showing the picture after a sentence (the parent's own words, not the text) has been said:

'Billy is washing – he is putting on his shirt – he is combing his hair – he is eating an egg – he is cleaning his teeth – he is putting on his shoes – he is waving to Mummy – Mummy says "Don't play. Go straight to school." '

(Luckily, Billy gets into all sorts of mischief and is late, which enlivens the story.) This is such a very useful book that it is one to return to later, when the whole text may be used.

Meanwhile, the parent should try to remember as nearly as possible what he has said to describe each picture so that the same language is repeated each time and becomes impressed upon the child's mind. Other clear and simple books with an emphasis on action words can be used in the same way and a list of appropriate books is given in Appendix 2.

It can happen, particularly with profoundly deaf children, that existing reading material is exhausted long before the child is able to use an adequate number of verbs. Once again, a persevering parent can make up little stories about simple but outstanding happenings in their child's life. One severely deaf three-year-old boy much preferred such stories to anything that could be bought in a shop and used to demand re-reading of a current story a dozen times a day. Just as a normal child does, this intelligent little boy finally knew his 'stories' by heart. One such story, actually about another child, is given on page 119. This is somewhat similar to a diary, but has the advantage that it can be done in the present tense and, because each action is illustrated, the child has more motivation to demand repetition. When presented to the child, the story is not, of course, drawn in the chart-like form shown on page 119, but presented page by page.

It is not at all hard to find books for children up to about seven years old, but it can be difficult to select appropriate books for

Mary
and baby are playing

Baby pulls Mary's hair

Mary is cross

Mary puts
baby in the cupboard

Mary shuts the door

Mummy opens the door

Mummy
is picking baby up

Baby is smiling

older children who are still at an immature level of language. These children are not able to speak much but they can and do feel very hurt and insulted if 'babyish' books are produced. The best solution is Longman's 'Breakthrough to Literacy' series, intended to interest older children in reading whilst at the same time maintaining their dignity. The series is long, interesting, well illustrated and full of action. Once again the picture should be covered (and also the print since the aim is listening not reading) and the parent should describe the action in his own words, working in as many chosen verbs as possible.

Despite what has been said about the perils of 'babyish' material it can happen, because of his lack of experience, that a hearing-impaired child enjoys books that his hearing peers would find beneath them. Roger was a severely partially-hearing boy of ten and a half whose large size and lack of language seemed to pose problems in story material. These Roger solved himself by taking from the shelves the Ladybird 'Easy Reading Books' – traditional fairy stories such as *Goldilocks and the Three Bears* and *Red Riding Hood*. He would ask that they be told to him and, as he gained more language, his therapist read aloud to him the simpler ones. 'A beautiful story,' he would sigh, 'I love stories.'

It is too easy to dismiss Roger as a hopelessly immature and perhaps not very bright boy. He was actually an average child who, as a little boy, had missed all the normal fairy-tale experience because of his hearing loss. It was completely understandable that he should feel the necessity to make up his lack.

12

Learning More Words (3)
Positional Words

Positional words or prepositions denote the spatial relationship between person and object or between object and object. 'Mummy is *in* the car,' 'The ball is *on* the table.' 'In' here denotes the spatial relationship between Mummy and the car. 'On' denotes the spatial relationship between the ball and the table.

It has already been said that normal children begin to develop understanding of prepositions round about two years of age. The normal child will also utter the prepositions he has heard. The prepositions 'for' and 'with', for instance, tend to develop in relationship to people because adults have said to the child, 'Here is a cake *for* Bobby,' 'Go *with* Daddy,' 'We're going *to* Grandma's.' 'In' and 'on' may also be used shortly after the second birthday or even before, because the child has heard 'Put your ball *in* the pram,' 'Sit *on* the bed.'

The hearing-impaired child finds some prepositions difficult for several reasons. Prepositions are short, unstressed words. We do not say, 'Put the ball *in* the basket.' We say, 'Put the *ball* in the *basket*.' The hearing-impaired child, with his short auditory memory, has difficulty in remembering the two stressed naming words, 'ball' and 'basket'. The small unstressed word denoting the relationship between the ball and the basket is difficult both to hear and to lip-read. Its function is far more obscure than that of a naming or action word and he comprehends it only after much practice.

Some hearing-impaired children have a great deal of difficulty with spatial concepts in themselves. We are partly conscious of *where* we are because sound comes to us from someone or something *overhead*, *beside* us, *behind* us. This information is severely curtailed in the case of a hearing-impaired child who has difficulty in locating the direction from which sound comes. When this confusion is added to the apparent unimportance of the word in the sentence, it will be seen that the hearing-impaired child does not receive prepositional messages in the manner that a normal child does.

The prepositions to be expected in the third year of normal speech development are:

up	down	for	in	from
into	off	on	at	beside
out	to	onto	over	
round	under	with		

Of these, 'up' and 'down' are usually fairly easy because of the marked and continuous movement of going up and down stairs and the regularity of this occurrence. 'Up' is often therefore an early word in the vocabulary of hearing-impaired children.

The hardest words on the list are undoubtedly 'in', 'into', 'on' and 'onto' which lack dramatic movement, audibility and visibility. It may take long and patient teaching before a hearing-impaired child can differentiate between 'in-ness' and 'on-ness' but both words are essential to language development and little progress can be made without them.

1. *Teaching with large objects*

A strong cardboard box of the type groceries are packed in and large enough for the child to climb into is needed and also a strong basket. A round, open cat- or dog-basket is ideal, because it has no handles and can be reversed – for the converse reason a plastic laundry basket with handles is not so good. A strong wicker waste-paper basket may be used instead of a dog-basket.

Ask the child to climb into the basket. Lift him in if he does not grasp the idea, and then comment, 'You're *in* the basket,' stressing the 'in'. 'Now, climb *into* the box – you're *in* the box.' (The child's name may be used instead of 'you'.)

How quickly he masters the idea depends upon the individual child and his particular problems. If he is enjoying the game, continue to ask him to climb into the box and basket.

If he seems to understand 'in', then 'on' may be added and a variety of commands given:

'Climb onto the box.'

'Climb into the basket.'
'Climb onto the box.'
'Climb into the box.'
'Climb onto the basket.'

It is always interesting to see how readily a child masters the concept of reversing a hollow object such as a basket in order to convert 'in-ness' to 'on-ness'. Once a child is reversing objects with facility, he has almost certainly grasped the central principle of the exercise.

If things are going well, further objects should be added – a sturdy table, a chair, a bucket (this looks and sounds very like 'basket' and should be added with care). 'Off' may be added:

'Jump off the table.'
'Jump off the basket.'
'Jump off the box.'

The child should always be told when he has performed an instruction correctly, 'Good! You jumped *off* the table,' or 'Good! You are *in* the box.' The fact that the child himself is performing the actions powerfully reinforces his awareness of position. Occasionally the child, even at this early stage, will want to tell the parent what to do, which is an excellent exercise.

2. *Teaching with small objects*

Use a large, plastic cup, a small, strong empty box and a basket without a handle – a fruit punnet or one of a set of plastic building baskets is ideal. These objects are chosen because they are flexible to manipulate and because they ought, by this stage, to be very familiar to the child as words. Use also a variety of attractive small objects whose names are very familiar to the child – a car, a little wooden house, a key, a dog, a bird, an aeroplane.

Train the child to respond to a variety of commands:

'Put the key *in* the cup.'
'Put the dog *on* the box.'
'Put the house *on* the box.'
'Take the key *out of* the cup.'
'Push the dog *off* the box.'

If the child is making good progress, the word 'under' may be added. 'Under' appears at about three years of age in normal speech development. It is recognised as more difficult than 'in' or 'on' because of the 'disappearing' element, i.e. the key *under* the inverted cup is invisible. However, it has been found that hearing-impaired children, learning the word at a later chronological age when they are more mentally mature, do not find the 'invisibility' feature a problem. They find 'under' easier than 'in' or 'on' because it has two syllables and the audible and fairly noticeable 'd' consonant.

A child who can manipulate its six small objects 'in', 'on', 'under', 'off' and 'out of' the three large objects is making good progress and should certainly be introduced to 'over' and 'round'. 'Over' brings great satisfaction, partly because 'over' is a two-syllable word that is easy to see, partly because jumping 'over' something has a marked sensation. 'Round', though not so easy to see as 'over', is an easy and enjoyable action.

It could be asked, 'If "in", "into", "on" and "onto" are so difficult, why introduce them first?' The answer is because they *are* so difficult and at the same time so essential. The number of times we use these words in conversation is extremely high and the earlier they are started, the sooner the child will learn. The introduction later of the easier prepositions will probably, worked into games, enable the child to continue working on the harder ones.

3. *A further exercise with objects*

Many hearing-impaired children will have mastered the short list of prepositions given and will not need further practice with objects. Unfortunately, there are those who find prepositions difficult and are bored by them without having grasped their meaning. Great care must be taken, for instance, that the child really understands what is said to him and is not just making, to one set of objects, responses that he cannot transfer to another situation.

Peter, partially-hearing with language levels between two and three years, started at a chronological age of just five years to be very good with his box, basket, cup and various small objects. When he was placed in a different situation, however, he became confused and could not carry out prepositional commands reliably. This was so even if the commands were given in a room familiar to him such as his bedroom – he could not put his hair brush *on* the bed, nor his book *under* it. The prepositions were related only to an already learned situation.

This, unfortunately, is a very familiar predicament of hearing-impaired children and prepositions must be practised in as many different situations as possible. Peter's mother set up what she described as an 'obstacle course' in the garden – she directed Peter to climb *into* the laundry basket, stand *on* the table, jump *off*, crawl *under* the net, jump *over* the plant pot and run *round* the chair. She varied the instructions as far as she could, requiring different things of him on the next round.

A series of small empty packets and boxes and a doll provide similar reinforcement. This time the doll is made to go through the 'obstacle course', directed by the parent and manipulated by the child. It is very easy to cut a convincing bridge to go under from a tissue box – and also interesting to see what happens when the doll is directed to go *round* the bridge after one or two trips *under*. This activity, of course, provides a much better opportunity for quiet listening than the games involving the child himself in physical activity.

'To', 'for' and 'with' can be acted out in the ways already described. The child may be asked, 'Give the cup *to* Daddy,' 'Give the cake *to* Grandma,' and games may be played involving giving milk, tea, sugar, biscuits, etc. at a doll's tea party. 'To' is another small unstressed word. Probably the child learns to respond to the nouns involved rather than to 'to' itself, but 'to' does not seem to be as troublesome as 'in' or 'on'. This may be because 'to' is also used in connection with places and 'going *to* school', 'going *to* the shops', 'going *to* the park' are all part of daily routine. One severely deaf girl of eight had, however, great difficulty with 'to' which she always omitted. She became clearer when the four corners of the table were marked 'school', 'shops', 'park', 'swimming pool' and she was asked to make her fingers 'walk' *to* one of the places, saying meanwhile, for instance, 'I am going *to* the swimming pool.'

'With' is a visible word with its marked lip and tongue movements. It too may be acted out: 'Go the kitchen *with* Daddy,' 'Go to the bathroom *with* Grandma.' (The 'with' of the agent, 'I cut bread *with* my knife', is a more advanced stage.)

A hiding game is very attractive to young children who have to rehearse 'in', 'on', 'under' many times. Two adults make the game easier to play, but if the mother is on her own with the child, she hides a familiar object (a toy mouse is popular) in the room whilst the child waits outside. She then goes to the door and says, 'Ready. Where is the mouse?' Mother and child search together, the mother verbalising:

> 'Is it *under* the rug? . . . No!'
> 'Is it *under* the table? . . . No!'
> 'Is it *on* the table? . . . No!'
> 'Is it *on* the basket? . . . No!'
> 'Is it *in* the box? . . . Yes! Here's the mouse!'

It is advisable to use as a hiding place only large, familiar objects whose names are known to the child. The power of a child to see the object and pounce on it before the verbal routine is completed varies very much. Though traditionally sharp-eyed, some young hearing-impaired children will pass by a table with the mouse underneath it and never notice. The mother must, therefore, gear the hiding of the mouse to the searching capabilities of the child.

Logically, the child himself should then hide the mouse but this is often a failure because, knowing where the mouse is, the child cannot resist sharing the secret with the adult the moment the latter enters the room! (This lack of secrecy is not confined to hearing-impaired children!)

Considering its obvious simplicity, or perhaps because of it, 'Hide the Mouse' is amazingly popular. It also has the virtue of teaching that very important word 'where?' and reference will be made to this again later.

It will be noticed that although a great deal has been said about prepositions, no mention has yet been made of pictures. This is because prepositional words are essentially three-dimensional and lose some of their characteristics when viewed two-dimensionally. Objects 'in' another object are difficult to see, and though objects can be portrayed *under* a bed or table, they cannot be satisfactorily drawn under a mat or a cushion. Learning Development Aids none the less publish preposition cards which may be used by children who are very sure of the meaning of the words. Philip & Tacey publish two boxes of preposition cards and four strip books containing other pictures. Of these, some are at a more advanced level than that being discussed here, but the appropriate cards may be abstracted and used for auditory training.

If a profoundly deaf child still has great difficulty with prepositions when all the games already described have been exhausted, a chart may be made similar to the one drawn on page 128 and used as a vehicle for auditory training. The obvious difficulty is that of drawing clearly enough and the adult must make the child and the objects as near reality as possible. The child is asked, using his own name, 'Show me Mary is on the table,' 'Show me Mary is under the mat.' A counter is placed on each square as it is correctly selected. The number of squares included depends upon the progress and maturity of the child. Such a chart has the advantage that the child can concentrate on listening without any moving about and it certainly has worked on occasions for me when all else has failed.

Because of the necessity of keeping comprehension ahead of utterance, no mention has yet been made of the child uttering prepositions himself. Sometimes, particularly with partially-hearing children, the work carried out on comprehension does result in use by the child. Often, however, the child has also to be encouraged to use prepositions in his own speech and his using them reinforces understanding.

Box, basket and cup can be used again and the six small articles placed 'in', 'on' and 'under' whilst the child watches. The parent then asks, 'What is in the cup?' The child replies and the parent reinforces his reply, with 'Yes, that's right, the mouse is in the cup. What is in the box?' etc., until all the objects have been retrieved. A game can be played whereby the child retains objects he has dealt with correctly, whilst the parent keeps those over which the child has made an error.

The child may also be asked, 'Where is the mouse?' and when the child responds, 'Yes, that's right, the mouse is in the cup. Now where is the key? Good, the key is under the box.'

'Where is the –?' and 'What is in the –?' can also be played round the room for variety. The preposition cards of LDA and of Philip & Tacey also have a great advantage in that the child can be encouraged to describe what is happening on each card: 'The dog is in the kennel,' 'The girl is under the bed,' etc.

Despite the difficulties presented by two-dimensional material, some books are excellent in helping to transfer the child's experi-

ence of prepositions to ordinary books. Stan and Jan Berenstain's *Bears in the Night* is a simple, delightful and dramatic story composed almost entirely of prepositions. Some of these, such as 'between' and 'through' would not have been dealt with at the stage here described but most of the other prepositions will be now familiar and the bears, proceeding 'Out of the window, down the tree, over the wall, under the bridge, around the lake . . . up Spook Hill,' are quite irresistible. The story can be acted round a room or in the garden or on a miniature scale with bricks, small trees, bears and other basic props. Many are the hearing-impaired children who can ultimately recite the entire story from pictures.

Rosie's Walk by Pat Hutchins is similarly composed of prepositions. *Buster is Lost* in Macmillan Educational's Language in Action Series has prepositions as its special feature and very simple basic language. Stan and Jan Berenstain's *Inside, Outside, Upside Down* is also helpful at this stage. Properly, 'inside' and 'outside' are naming words and 'upside down' a descriptive word. However, the book contains 'in', 'on', and 'off' and gives a very good sense of movement and position that seems to belong to this stage of teaching. Its simplicity of language makes *Inside, Outside, Upside Down* very useful.

From here the child can be asked questions about ordinary picture books provided the pictures show positions of objects clearly. Jean and Gareth Adamson's Topsy and Tim books are helpful, with cats *in* baskets, babies *in* cots, objects *on* tables and Topsy and Tim going *to* this or that place *with* Mummy or Daddy. The child can again be asked, 'What is on the chair?' 'Where is the rabbit?' 'Where are Topsy and Tim going?'

Other books containing suitable prepositional material are listed in Appendix 2 at the end of this book. Obviously, parents must use prepositional words worked upon whenever possible during the child's daily routine. 'Get *into* the bath,' 'Put your mug *on* the table,' 'You jumped *over* the puddle,' 'Put your feet *under* the table properly, please.' Once a child can understand and use basic prepositions, his comprehension and speech really do seem to take on another dimension. Many mothers have said that life in the home becomes much easier because the child can be asked to fetch articles of clothing, toys, etc. for himself and to perform simple tasks for his mother.

13

Learning More Words (4)
Descriptive Words

Descriptive words tell us about quality or quantity – colour, shape, size, texture, weight, amount and other attributes. An elephant is *big*, a mouse is *small* or *tiny*, a man is *tall*, a pillow is *soft*, there are *lots* of smarties, the basket is *heavy*. Hearing-impaired children often use essentially emotive descriptive words very early, e.g. 'broken', 'naughty', 'more', 'another', 'sore', 'good', because they are, once again, related to something happening – punishment, reward, medication, a second helping of food. They utter these words in the early years of learning to talk and continue to prefer them for a very long time to other words taught to them. (Mark, though he knew a considerable number of descriptive words, once said 'broken' twelve times in a one-hour session.)

Size

'Big' and 'little' may also be acquired spontaneously but if not, are easy ideas to acquire. Two sets of objects of markedly different sizes are required:

a big doll (7″/18 cm high)	the littlest doll that can be found
a big plate (4″/10 cm diameter)	a doll's plate ($\frac{1}{2}$″/13 mm diameter)
a big car (4″/10 cm long)	the littlest car that can be found
an ordinary household pudding spoon	a doll's spoon
an outgrown child's shoe	a doll's shoe
a tennis ball	a tiny ball (the high-bounce variety)

It should be possible to keep all these objects in a shoe box. The adult draws two circles on a piece of paper or on a formica-topped table, one circle 10″ (25·5 cm) in diameter, the other 4″ (10 cm) in diameter. She sorts the objects, big into the big circle and little into the little, saying 'Big doll . . . little doll . . . big spoon . . . little spoon . . .' and so on until all the objects are placed. She then asks the child to sort the objects into the circles again, speaking herself. The child is then asked: 'Show me the little car,' 'Show me the big spoon' etc. An object can be taken out of a circle when it is selected, though this has the disadvantage that when the other is asked for, it must be an obvious choice. The game may be played the other way round. That is, the pile of objects is sorted, on instruction, into the two circles. Children do not usually have difficulty with the concept of big and little, but if there is a problem, this is a place where gesture is helpful – holding the arms wide when 'big' is said and contracting the hands for 'little'. To transfer the idea of big and little to two dimensions, pictures on cards approximately 4″ x 4″ (10 cm x 10 cm) may be used:

a big house	a little house
a big girl	a little girl
a big boy	a little boy
a big ball	a little ball
a big cup	a little cup
a big table	a little table

These cards can be placed in two lines and make a useful auditory training exercise: 'Show me the big boy' etc.

The 'Read It Yourself' series contains two excellent and inexpensive books to reinforce the idea of 'big' and 'little', entitled *What is Big?* and *What is Little?* See Appendix 2.

Colour

The parents of hearing-impaired children have often taught them colours because they are an obvious thing to teach. Any child, hearing or not, has to have a certain level of mental maturity to be able to perceive differences in colour at all and this readiness to 'see' colour usually comes at three or four years of age. Coloured round counters are an indispensable part of working with a hearing-impaired child and can be difficult to obtain in shops. Those obtained from the Educational Supply Association have the advantage of including orange, brown, black and white as well as the usual red, green, blue and yellow. Mother and child should begin by sorting the red, blue, green and yellow counters into piles of various colours, the mother naming the colours clearly. The child can then be asked, 'Give me a blue counter,' 'Give me a yellow counter' etc. This is another good auditory training game and an element of activity is added if counters are spread round the room and the mother says, 'Fetch a red counter' and so on, making piles of each colour as the child fetches counters to instruction. The child should then be asked to name the colours when the mother holds up a counter and says, 'What colour is this?' Once a child is ready to learn colour, the idea comes quickly, but there is often a period of perhaps a week when the child really knows the colour yet sometimes says the wrong name. This seldom lasts long and, once past, the mother can turn to a book in which colours are bright and definite ('Topsy and Tim' books are once again excellent) and ask, pointing to an object, 'What colour is this?' If the child is confident in his replies, the mother can safely pass to the next stage, where she does not point at all but asks, 'What colour is the coat? What colour is the sky? What colour is the ball?' There is a definite step up in comprehension between 'What colour is it?' when the mother is pointing to the object and 'What colour is the coat?' when no gesture is used. Similarly, 'What colour is Tim's coat?' or 'What colour is Mummy's coat?' is even more difficult because coats and hats of several colours may be depicted. Both levels of comprehension make good exercises in auditory training.

The child should be encouraged, from this point onwards, to use objects and colour together – red bus, blue sky, green coat, etc. To some children, the French way of tackling this seems more logical and they say the object first, 'bus red'. This is lack of listening experience and will pass with practice. Once red, blue, yellow and green have been mastered, white, black, brown, orange, pink and purple are usually learned very quickly and the child should be taught to respond to 'What colour is so-and-so?' using not only the full colour range, but also two-colour objects, e.g.'The coat is red and blue!'

A popular colour game to extend comprehension is 'I am thinking of something red.' The mother says this choosing an easy object in the room and the child must guess the object, responding each time with a full sentence: 'You are thinking of the door!' The child himself then says, 'I am thinking of something –' This is excellent practice for the extension of auditory memory and word linking.

Small books to reinforce teaching of colour are given in Appendix 2.

Shape

The first shapes learned are round and square. When dealing with very small children who have little idea of the difference between the two, it is helpful to fill a square box with round and square objects – small square packets, square bricks, round lids, doll's plates. Put all the objects on the table and sort them out with the child putting round objects into a round container and square objects into the square box, at the same time naming the shapes. Then ask the child to sort for himself whilst the adult names, and finally, as with the colours, ask him, 'Give me something round. Give me something square,' until he has learned to comprehend the shape names. Then, picking up an object, ask, 'What shape is this?'

Other shape-descriptive words are 'oblong' and 'oval'; one would not expect a child of this language age to say 'triangular', 'half-moon-shaped' or 'diamond-shaped'. 'Triangle', 'star', 'half-moon', 'diamond' are naming words, but often used by young children and it is convenient to teach shape words together. Any shape puzzles already in the home will be useful, but although names of puzzles are included in the back of this book, they are comparatively expensive to buy for a short period of teaching. Educational Supply Association make an excellent geometric tracer giving ten basic shapes. The child can trace round these—each should be marked clearly in lower case letters 'round', 'triangle', 'half-moon' etc.—and the words can be taught in the same manner as other words.

Familiarity with and ability to name shapes is very important for reading, writing, mathematics and also for the ability to describe an object accurately.

Colour and Shape

An excellent exercise in listening is to ask a child at random, 'What colour is it?' or 'What shape is it?' Unless he is listening hard, when asked 'What shape is it?' he will reply with a colour. Special geometric shapes can be bought, but shapes can be made at home out of two sheets of cardboard, 20″ x 30″, bought from an art shop. The following should be made:

12   squares, each 3″ x 3″ (7·6 cm x 7·6 cm)
12   circles, each 3″ (7·6 cm) in diameter
12   triangles, 3½″ (9 cm) each side
12   squares, 1½″ x 1½″ (4 cm x 4 cm)
12   circles, each 2″ (5 cm) in diameter
12   triangles, 2¼″ (5·8 cm) each side

The shapes should be coloured red, blue, yellow and green in equal numbers, i.e.,

3   big red squares
3   big red circles
3   big red triangles
3   little red squares
3   little red circles
3   little red triangles

and so on for each of the other colours. The shapes are spread on a big table and the child is asked, 'Find me a big red triangle,' 'Find me a little red square,' etc. This again is an excellent vehicle for auditory training, demanding that the child listen carefully and also retain the instruction in his head while he finds the object of the right size, shape and colour.

Again, the cards can be spread round the room and the child asked to fetch them. In this way he has, of course, to retain the instruction even longer. The child should then be asked to sort the shapes, colours and sizes into groups and should be encouraged to describe them: 'A big red square,' 'A little green triangle.' Also circles, squares and triangles of one colour can be grouped together and termed '*all* yellow,' 'The yellow shapes are *all together*' – both useful words.

Adventurous parents may wish to make more than basic shapes and also to use other colours.

Other Descriptive Words

A hearing-impaired child requires to learn first of all descriptive words that are highly meaningful in terms of colour, texture or emotion. As with round and square, very young children need to *feel* a variety of objects.

The following objects can usually be found in the home and put into various boxes for the child to sort out:

A box of Hard and Soft object – nut, pencil, stone, egg-cup, marble, cotton wool, fur, foam rubber, wool, small soft toy.

A box of Long and Short objects – ribbon, tape, shoe-laces, string, candles, pencils of definitely long and short lengths.

Tall and Short objects – containers of various sizes, e.g. some shampoo bottles are tall, whereas a vanilla bottle or spice container is short.

Straight and Curved objects – pencils, felt pens, pieces of wood, a short ruler, ornamental combs, hair clips, a fork, an old spectacle frame, crescent-shaped pastry cutter.

Same and Different objects – the coloured shapes previously mentioned can be used. Any two taken out of a box simultaneously are bound to be either 'the same' or 'different'.

Empty and Full objects – a number of little boxes, some full to the top, some empty (spice boxes and pepper tubs are handy). Contents may be anything harmless – shells, rice, dried peas, but need changing to maintain interest.

Heavy and Light objects – various stones, a piece of lead, a piece of brick, a piece of iron, cotton wool, a ping-pong ball, latex foam, a feather.

Open and Shut objects – boxes open and shut. A paper house with windows cut out that will open and shut.

Pretty and Ugly objects – plastic monsters, plastic snakes and frogs, artificial flowers, lace, toy rings, necklaces. (This is a difficult box. What children consider pretty and what an adult considers pretty varies a great deal.)

Shiny objects – mirror, toy jewellery, a spoon, pastry cutters, foil. A number of dull objects need to be included to show the meaning of 'shiny', but the word 'dull' is not usually acquired at this stage.

Rough and Smooth objects – rough stones and bricks, a rough piece of old towelling, a kitchen scrubber, sandpaper, cellophane paper, velvet, silk, a doll's china saucer.

Sharp objects – objects need to appear sharper than they are and still to be handled with care – a pin, a needle, scissors, skewer, knife. The polarity 'blunt' would not be taught at this stage, but blunt objects, a wooden spoon, a pencil, a felt pen with its top on, need to be included.

There is considerable language teaching in these boxes, which need to be tackled slowly – one a week would be sufficient. To take the Full and Empty boxes as an example, the adult may say, 'Let's open the *big* box, shall we? Take off the lid. What's *inside*? *Little* boxes. What's *inside* the *little* boxes today? I'm trying to open one – I can't open it – it's *stiff* – that's right, you try. Oh! You're *strong* – you've opened the box! It's *full*; there are *lots of* shells inside. Don't spill the shells. Shut the box. Now let's look at the *next* box. It's *empty*; there's nothing in it,' etc.

The child may sort the objects in a box, e.g. the Rough and Smooth box, into two piles, whilst the adult names the qualities. The contents of a box are then muddled up and he is asked to select 'something smooth' or 'something rough' and to name qualities and objects for himself. The contents of all the boxes can finally be muddled up for selection and naming. It then becomes apparent that an object may, of course, have more than one quality. A *tall* pot may be *smooth*, a *heavy* stone may be *rough* and *shiny*.

Not all descriptive words can be presented as polarities or illustrated by the above method, but many can be taught very easily if a little ingenuity is used.

Five-year-old Michelle was lifted on to a five-foot high wall (carefully held) and sat there, looking somewhat appalled. 'It's a high wall,' said her therapist. 'You're sitting on a high wall. You're high up.' Michelle was lifted down, ran straight indoors to her mother and announced, 'Michelle high wall. Mama – look!' She had not previously known the word 'high'.

'Next' is often learned because the mother says, 'Now, let's look at the next picture.' 'Hot' and 'cold' can be learned by taking the child round the house and showing him objects. Mark, three years old, seated firmly on his therapist's hip, put his hand into the deep freeze, under the cold tap, held a piece of ice and stepped briskly into the December cold outside the door. He then felt the radiator, and hot water, the hot tank and inspected the gas and boiling kettle. The fact that he gave the latter a wide berth showed that he was well aware of the concept of heat and only lacked the word.

Mary learned 'wrong' because, a left-hander, she wrote her name

too big

too small

too big

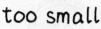

too small

too big

too small

from back to front. A none the less agile child, she learned 'upside down' from standing on her head and 'right way up' by assuming her natural position. Both 'inside out' and 'back to front' were frequently related to her clothes, as was 'new'. 'Strong' was learned immediately she received a new ring file for her work. 'Come on, pull, open it,' said her therapist. 'You're *strong*,' and thereafter Mary never forgot the word, flexing her arms to demonstrate strength!

One of the first words many hearing-impaired children use is 'later' because they are frequently told they may have so-and-so 'later' or 'after'. 'Better' frequently refers to a tummy-ache or cut. If the adult is on the alert, words that seem difficult and abstract can frequently be interpolated. Thus, if Mark is inattentive, his therapist says to him, 'I'm waiting, Mark,' and if this brings no response, 'I'm *still* waiting!' Good effort is greeted with 'That's good, *very* good,' and poor effort with '*Quite* good, but let's try again.'

'Too' may be learned by a series of simple drawings (see page 137) but much success with descriptive words lies in the adult watching carefully for opportunities when they may be used.

If a young child has difficulties in joining a descriptive word to another word, it is possible to make drawings as on this page. Not only can the drawing be used for auditory training, but the child

hot kettle   hot sun

hot tap   hot coffee

can be asked to name each picture. With a little ingenuity, this can be done with a number of descriptive words.

It is also possible to draw a sort of composite picture showing many qualities several times over, as in the example on page 140. Say to the child, 'Find me something long. Very good. Now find me something else long' (thus using the valuable word 'else'). 'Now find me something short. Now something straight.' This is good listening practice and children enjoy looking, particularly if the adult privately adds some new items from time to time. The picture done for the child should be brightly coloured and on a larger scale than shown here – about 18″ x 12″ (45 cm x 30 cm). (The descriptive words 'big', 'little', 'cold', 'curved', 'same', 'different', 'happy', 'hot', 'long', 'short', 'open', 'sad', 'sharp', 'sore', 'straight', 'tall', 'ugly', 'wet', 'upside down', 'round', 'square', 'oblong', 'oval', 'right way up' and 'thin' appear in the picture.)

Some children as young as four years old, particularly if they are only partially deaf, do not require the detailed approach outlined so far. Older children probably need a more straightforward approach whatever their hearing loss is, partial or severe. It is possible to obtain from LDA a set of sixty cards depicting descriptive words (see Appendix 2). The descriptive words illustrated in that set are marked with an asterisk in the list of words given on pages 143-4. Two packs can be used in order to play a pairs game. The cards as they are supplied are divided into five sets of twelve cards but it is as well to use only about six words (i.e. twelve cards) to begin with. The twelve cards are turned face downwards, muddled up on the table, the aim of each player being to pick up two similar cards. A firm rule must be made, as when playing the same game with naming words, that the picture must be described each time it is turned up – 'a fat man', 'a thin woman', etc. The adult speaks until the child has listened enough to say the words for himself. Some children love this game. Others prefer simply to learn in the usual way to select and describe the cards. The game must be reinforced by general activity round the room and house. 'I want you to find me something long. Good! Now find something thin. Now find something heavy.' A goal of, say, twelve objects can be set so that the child knows how much work he has to do.

The 'This is my Shape' series by Derek and Lucy Thackray (see Appendix 2) covers 'big', 'little', 'thin', 'fat', 'tall' and 'round' and

is suitable, because of vocabulary, for older children. *This and That* in the Macmillan Educational 'Language in Action Series', with its delightful and expressive drawings, is suitable for all ages and includes thirty-two descriptive words.

Number words such as:

| a few | all | another | both | least | each |
| lots of | more | most | no | some | none |

are, of course, descriptive words and some like 'more' and 'another' are easily acquired. Others can be difficult to understand. A game can be played with counters:

> 'Give me *all* the counters.'
> 'Give me *some* of the counters.'
> 'Give me *both* yellow counters.'
> 'Give Daddy *lots* of counters.'
> 'Give Daddy *another* counter.'

The child may also be asked when everyone has counters in front of him:

> 'Who has *both* yellow counters?'
> 'Who has *most* red counters?'
> 'Who has *least* red counters?'
> 'Who has *more* blue counters, Mummy or Daddy?'
> 'Who has *a few* counters?'
> 'Who has *no* counters?'
> 'Who has *all* the counters?'

This sort of training, like colours, requires that a basic number sense has developed. The understanding of these words is quite essential for the learning of mathematics. Ladybird Books' *More Words for Numbers* illustrates many of these words and will be useful as reinforcement, but number words, like positional words, are most easily comprehended in relation to actual objects.

Actual numbers are often taught to the child by the mother. This teaching can be varied and reinforced by a variation of the number game just described:

> 'Give Daddy two red counters.'
> 'Give Bobby one blue counter.'
> 'How many counters has Daddy got?'
> 'How many counters have you got?'

At this stage, superlative adjectives should also be taught. Even normal children find it difficult to grasp the difference between comparative and superlative, and often announce about one of two objects, 'This is the biggest.' At this stage no attempt is made to teach the comparative of regular adjectives.

Three of a stack of coloured, graded play baskets are placed on the table and the child is asked, 'Which is the biggest?' If he does not know, he is shown; then three more baskets are placed on the table and he is asked again. If a stack of graded rings or beakers is available, these can also be used three at a time. Once the child is reliably pointing to the biggest object, several sets of graded objects are placed on the table at once, for example:

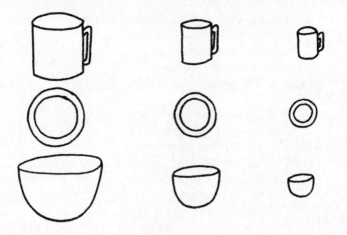

and the child is asked at random, 'Show me the biggest ring. Good. Now show me the biggest mug,' etc. When this is well established 'Show me the smallest' is introduced. From here it becomes a simple matter to teach 'longest', 'tallest', 'strongest', etc.

Despite the desire of the hearing-impaired child to adhere to his 'old' descriptive words, his new words can mean a great deal to both him and his parents. Many hearing-impaired children have had a very sharp appreciation of the quality of an object and no words in which to voice this. Two weeks after being introduced to descriptive words, one child was heard murmuring to herself 'Smooth . . . smooth . . .' as she fingered the case of her radio machine. On dropping a box of eggs and breaking one, Kate announced firmly, 'It was a *weak* egg.' Mark was taught 'ugly' and this word was thereafter used to him with effect when he was saying consonants poorly. Even when the child does not use the words immediately himself, they give much greater meaning to the speech of the people speaking to him.

Descriptive Words

after	*empty	naughty	*shiny
again	far	near	*short
asleep	*fat	new	shut
back to front	*frightened	next	silly
bad	*full	nice	small
*bare	*funny	*noisy	smooth
better	good	*old	*soft
big	*happy	*open	*sore
*brave	hard	poor	sorry
*bright	*heavy	*pretty	still
broken	*high	quick	*straight
*clean	*hot	*quiet	*strong
*cold	hungry	*quite	*tall
*crooked	*ill	ready	*tired
*cross	inside out	real	too
*curly	late	*right	*ugly
*curved	later	right side out	upside down
*dark	left	right way up	very
*dead	light	*rough	warm
*deep	little	*sad	wet
*different	*long	*same	wicked
*dirty	lost	*sharp	*wrong
else	magic		

Amount Words

all	both	*lots of	no
*a few	each	more	other
another	least	most	

* Illustrated by LDA Description Cards. See Appendix 2.

Number Words*

one	four	seven	nine
two	five	eight	ten
three	six		

Shape Words

circle	heart	round	star
diamond	oblong	square	triangle
half-moon	oval		

---

* Children vary greatly in their ability to appreciate numbers.

14
Learning More Words (5)
Other Factors

Binding Speech Together

It may seem, because speech has been discussed in relation to naming words, doing words, positional words and various types of descriptive words, that a fragmented approach is being described. It must be realised that in teaching the child to use these words, he will steadily put the various pieces together. It is only by considering the various categories of words that not only the child but also his parents will have attention attracted to areas which could otherwise remain extremely weak and never blend together to form the meaningful pattern that is speech. In speaking to their child continually in a meaningful way, his parents are presenting him with a whole pattern and by bringing in words they have been specifically teaching, they are blending these 'highlighted' words into the pattern.

Telling Stories

Stories should be a vital and enjoyable part of any child's life and the hearing-impaired child has even more need of them than the normal child since a story binds together ideas, vocabulary and previous experience. Stories for a hearing-impaired child must be much more carefully chosen and told than those for a normal child. The advice in the John Tracey Clinic Correspondence Course for Parents of Pre-School Deaf Children cannot be improved upon:

1. Stories must be true to life. They must be about real people or about animals which behave in a real way. Fairy stories which contain matter outside the child's experience should be excluded.
2. Illustrations should be very clear and simple, with firm colouring within definite lines.
3. The story line should be clear and simple. A good pay-off line improves the story.

4. The adult should *tell* the story from the pictures, not attempt to read it.

5. The adult should choose, beforehand, which pictures to talk about and what to say. Extraneous parts of the book should be clipped firmly with a bull-dog type clip. The adult should keep the book in his own hands and inhibit any desire by the child to grab at or pull the book.

6. Simple 'props' may be used to make the story more real, but not so many that attention is distracted.

The John Tracey programme assumes that the child will lip-read. The adult sits opposite the child and holds the book picture-side-down against his chest. He catches the child's eye, says a short sentence and reveals the picture. If a child is extremely deaf, and predominantly a lip-reader, this method is excellent. However, I have found that children with well-trained considerable residual hearing do not wish to watch the face when a story is told. For these children, it is better still to sit opposite them, place the book flat on the table and cover the picture. With the child looking down and waiting for the picture to be revealed, the first sentence is uttered. After the picture has been shown, the sentence may be repeated.

Thus the 'Breakthrough' reading book *I Fell Over* would be told as follows:

1st page:	The boy and girl are running to school.
2nd page:	The boy falls over.
3rd page:	The girl falls on top of the boy.
4th page:	Oh dear! They have both fallen over!
5th page:	The girl is standing up. She's not hurt!
6th page:	The boy gets up. He's hurt his knee.
7th page:	His knee is bleeding.
8th page:	The boy is crying. The girl says, 'Don't cry!'
9th page:	Mummy is coming.
10th page:	Poor boy! He's hurt – but Mummy is wiping his knee.
11th page:	Mummy is taking the boy home.
12th page:	She is washing his knee.
13th page:	She is putting a plaster on it. (Here produce 'prop' – a piece of plaster)

14th page: The next day the boy and his friend go to school again.

15th page: The boy shows everyone his knee. His teacher says, 'You are brave!'

A list is given in Appendix 2 of stories that can be used in this way. The 'Breakthrough' series are some of the shortest stories, and shorter stories should be told first until the child's auditory (or visual) attention span has lengthened enough for him to enjoy a longer story. Once a story has been told, the child may handle the book himself. To ask for a story a second time is an excellent sign. It is as well to put books that are being used for teaching away out of the child's reach, lest he tire of the pictures and so cease to learn further words. Some books of repetitive type can be read as they stand, e.g. *I Can Smell* by Ronald Ridout. 'Props' should certainly be used for this book – if even half a dozen of the strongly scented objects described can be brought out as a surprise, reading will be greatly enhanced.

The sense of rhythm of hearing-impaired children is normal, and many listen with pleasure to Ainsworth and Ridout's *What Can you Hear?* with its very strongly marked repetitive rhythms.

A child may ask questions about the pictures related to a story which should, of course, be answered, but in many cases a story is enjoyed without comment and the child himself should not be questioned. Too much questioning about a story at this early stage can destroy story sequence and so diminish the pleasure in the story that the child does not want it retold. It should always be obvious to the adult whether or not the child understands what is being said to him. His steady gaze if he is a lip-reader, or his rapt, listening posture show attention and understanding. Fidgeting, fiddling with objects or inappropriate comments show the reverse. The stories listed in Appendix 2 are only suggestions – the parent will find others in bookshops and libraries and should keep the salient features required in mind. Stories should be told to the child from the very beginning of the work outlined in Chapters 10–14.

Children who can read a little may wish to read a story for themselves. Again, understanding or lack of it is obvious and if the child clearly does not understand what he is reading, because the actual text of the book is difficult, he should be discouraged.

Questions

Questions are an extremely important feature of speech. A child questions to find out about his environment and unless he goes through a period of intensive questioning, speech cannot develop fully. Hearing-impaired children are delayed in their questioning, the marked questioning of the hearing three- and four-year-old sometimes being absent in hearing-impaired children until six or seven years old, even when a child has received a great deal of help with speech. I have seen hearing-impaired children who have not had massive help with speech until seven, eight or even nine years old start the intensive questioning typical of the three- and four-year-old as late as ten years old. The hearing-impaired child must therefore be stimulated to ask questions both so that he learns how to phrase a question and so that he gains information. The best way to train a child to ask questions is to question *him*.* In this way the adult finds out how much the child has comprehended of what has been taught to him as well as teaching the word patterns that the questions take.

Every feature of speech teaching described so far has included questions to be put to the child. These must, as each is mastered, be asked of the child in relation to a picture. Once again, the picture should be clear, colourful, with enough detail to stimulate the child but not too much to confuse him. Questions about a picture should be a regular part of each day's routine.

What is it?

Who is it?

Where is so-and-so?

What is the boy (girl, etc.) doing?

What is the boy (girl, etc.) riding (climbing, etc.)?

Who is riding (feeding the baby, painting, sweeping, etc.)?

Which one do we sweep (shoot, wash, etc.) with?

What do we do with a spade (spoon, etc.)?

What is on (in, under, up) the table (box, chair, tree, etc.)?

Who is on (in, under, up, etc.)?

Who is sitting on the chair (as opposed to the floor)?

What colour is the boy's coat (girl's dress, mummy's hat, etc.)?

What shape is the box (sun, mirror, etc.)?

* Berry, M. F., *Language Disorders in Children*.

(148)

How many boys (girls, men, etc.) can you see?

Who has the brush (spade, spoon, etc.)?

Who is wearing a blue (red, yellow, etc.) coat (shoes, dress)?

Which one is fat (thin, long, short, etc.)?

These questions may seem simple but when all the questions are put together, it is a considerable feat for the child to answer them, and ability to do so shows some mastery of speech comprehension. A child should *always* be required to answer a question in sentence form, for example:

> Adult: 'What colour is the little girl's dress?'
> Child: 'The little girl's dress is green.'

This comes hard at first when auditory memory is short and some professional people object to it on the grounds that it is 'not natural' since normally-hearing children do not answer questions in this way. However, normal children do not have the vast difficulties of auditory memory of deaf children. Answering in whole sentences is one way to exercise auditory memory and to practise getting word order right.

It is quite difficult to find appropriate material about which to answer questions. Books such as Macmillan's 'Language in Action' *Cat and Mouse* with its action-full, bold yet uncluttered pages is ideal and the Ladybird 'Talkabout' series is also suitable. Since suitable story material is also often suitable questioning material, books already used as stories and finished with should be put away and then brought out again to be used for questioning. 'Topsy and Tim' books, for instance, have opportunities for questions on every page. Some books, however, like *The Story of Miss Moppet*, are excellent stories but do not have pictures that lend themselves to questioning.

It has already been said that older children may be offended by young children's books, but most find the 'Breakthrough' series acceptable and luckily the series is extensive!

Sequence Cards

As already stated, hearing-impaired children find putting things in order difficult. This applies to sounds in words, words in sentences and also to incidents in a simple story. The Invalid Children's Aid Association produce, very cheaply, a set of ten picture stories simply drawn in black and white. Each story can be cut up and, if wished, the pictures outlined in colour and mounted on card. The aim is for the child to tell the story from the pictures. The sequences range from four to seven pictures and it is wise to start with a four-picture sequence. The adult showing four cards says, for instance, 'Here is a story about a naughty dog taking some meat. Let's talk about the pictures.' By questioning the child and by the adult adding some information, the child becomes familiar with the pictures. Then the adult says, 'Which picture comes first? Yes, tell me about it. Now, which comes second? Tell me about it. Which comes third? Which is the last picture?' (This is good teaching of ordinal numbers.) The child then tells the whole story again, giving as much information as he can remember. There will obviously be mistakes in sentence formation and words omitted, but provided the child is doing his best, these should be overlooked. A child's rendering of a story might be: 'The lady going home with basket. The lady putting meat on table. Dog watching. Lady gone away. The dog taking meat. Lady say "Naughty dog. Come back."'

The adult has, in most cases, to judge whether further prompting will improve performance or merely make the child tired of the activity. At a later session, probably the next day, the cards should be shuffled and the child should be asked to order them unaided and tell what he remembers of the story.

Sequence work of this type can only be carried out with a child who is thoroughly familiar with the preliminary word lists. It is practice of words already mastered and should not be attempted until the child is familiar with the earlier work. The child may, therefore, have been working for six months or even a year before sequence work is attempted.

Encouraging Connected Speech in Daily Living

Certain situations occur over and over again in a child's life – greeting people, thanking people, saying goodbye, asking for objects. Parents would not allow a hearing child to come into a strange house without saying, 'Good morning' or 'Hello' and it is even more important to train a hearing-impaired child to perform these courtesies. He should *always* say 'Thank you' and should always ask for an object in a full sentence:

'Please may I have a drink?'
'Please may I go to the bathroom?'

In the early stages this is hard work and means a word-for-word repetition after the mother, but after a time auditory memory and word sequencing become habitual.

> Good morning
> Good night
> Yes, please
> No, thank you
> Hello
> Goodbye
> I'm sorry

should be established as early as possible.

One of the most natural displays of good manners came from Mary who, though she had little speech, had always been trained in courtesy at home. Bringing a friend to see her therapist, she smilingly performed, without any prompting, a rudimentary introduction: 'Davies – that Cathy!'

Widening Comprehension by Question Games

This series of small games is designed to widen comprehension and to encourage correct sentence structure. None is intended to last longer than five or ten minutes at the outside, though each can be returned to later.

1. *I am thinking of –*

   This has already been suggested in relation to colour, but 'I am thinking of something in the room' or 'I am thinking of a shape' can also be played. The child must answer '*Is* it so-and-so?' When the child has guessed correctly the roles are reversed and he asks the questions.

2. *Who has the mouse?*

   This requires several people, one of whom conceals a toy mouse in his fist whilst the child goes out of the room. All fists are placed on the table and the child returns to ask, 'Who has the mouse?' 'You must guess,' replies an adult and the child then asks, 'Is it Mummy?' etc. Any adult asked replies, 'No, I have not got the mouse.' When the child finds the mouse it is someone else's turn to go out.

3. *Which hand will you have?*

   The child covers his eyes while one adult hides a tiny object in his fist and calls, 'You can look now!' The child replies, 'I will have this hand.' Only when he guesses correctly first time can he be the one to conceal the object.

4. *Marbles into a bottle*
Small children can be given a marble at a time to drop into a large, long-necked bottle. The child may not release the marble without saying, 'I am dropping the marble into the bottle.'

5. *The 'Don't' game*
This requires that the child is completely familiar with action words. It is most popular, but must be played in a restrained and humorous way, lest it become rough. The adult tweaks the child's hair gently and the child says, 'Don't pull my hair.' Other 'don'ts' are:

> 'Don't push me.'
> 'Don't pull me.'
> 'Don't kick me.'
> 'Don't smack me.'
> 'Don't bite me.'

It should be remembered, before disapproving of this admittedly primitive game, how very often normal children do, and say, this sort of thing to one another. (The Ridout book listed in Appendix 2 *What Can You Hear?* which reiterates 'Don't move a hand, don't move a foot' links up well with this game.)

6. *The 'Do You Like' game*
This should follow the 'Don't' game because of the sentence structure involved. Three or four real foods known to be liked or disliked by the child are produced and the child is asked, 'Do you like so-and-so?' If he does not know the meaning of 'like' this can be made clear by adults showing obvious enjoyment or dislike for a food. The child is taught to answer, 'I like . . .' or 'I don't like . . .' so-and-so.

Once the concept is established, real food is abandoned and pictures are produced both of liked and disliked foods, the parent continuing to ask, 'Do you like so-and-so?' and eliciting a full reply. Then the pictures are given to the child and he is encouraged to ask the question.

7. *The 'Where Are You Going?' game*
Two adults are helpful in establishing this game. One adult leaves the room and the other asks, 'Where are you going?' while

the other adult replies, 'I am going to the kitchen' (bathroom, bedroom, garage, etc.). Once the idea is established one adult can play with the child and they take it in turn to be the person to leave the room.

This game can also be played with boy and girl dolls. The four corners of the table can be marked 'kitchen', 'bedroom', 'garden', 'park' (or other locations) and the child asks, 'Where is the boy going?' or 'Where is the girl going?' A further variation is for the adult to ask the child, 'Guess where I am going.'

8. *Guess What I am Making*

Variations of the last game are 'Guess What I am Making' with a doll's pan and spoon as props, and 'Guess What I am Going to Do' (cook the lunch, find Daddy, feed the baby, wash the car, etc.).

9. *The 'Can You?' game*

The child must be helped to understand 'I can' by the adult demonstrating:

I can hop   I can jump   I can walk   I can run

The child is then asked 'Can you run?' etc. and invited to demonstrate his skill. Once the idea of 'I can' is established, the child is asked the questions and must reply in speech. Other questions are added, 'Can you drive?', 'Can you fly?' and the child is taught to answer, 'I can't drive,' 'I can't fly,' etc. The child's comprehension is extended by pictures of other objects being produced and 'can' questions being asked about them, e.g.

'Can an aeroplane hop?'
'Can an aeroplane jump?'
'Can an aeroplane eat?'
'Can an aeroplane sleep?'
'Can an aeroplane fly?'

Alternatively:

'Can a dog run?'
'Can a cat run?'
'Can a boy run?'
'Can a table run?'
'Can a mouse run?'

This is very good comprehension practice. The 'Read It Yourself' book *What can jump?* mentioned in Appendix 2, is useful as reinforcement.

10. *The 'Who Gave You?' game*

More than one adult is needed for this game. The adults present each pass the child a small object and he is then asked 'Who gave you the –?' He replies and then becomes one of the donors and the person to ask the question.

11. *The 'Who Did That?' game*

The child leaves the room while an adult misplaces an object: say, puts a vase of flowers on the floor. The child returns and asks 'Who did that?' The adult replies and it is then the child's turn to do something.

12. *The 'What Am I Doing?' game*

The adult mimes one action – swimming, flying, cooking, eating, sleeping, walking, running, pushing a pram, etc. – and says 'Guess what I am doing.' The child replies, 'You are kicking a ball' or whatever the action is. When the child mimes the adult may pretend to make a mistake in guessing and the child taught to say, 'No, I am *not* kicking a ball.'

These games should be introduced slowly and in small quantities, but played by the adult with liveliness and enthusiasm. One new game every two weeks is sufficient and it is better to stop a game well *before* a child tires of it so that he may wish to resume it the next day. Though the 'games' are extremely simple and would not interest a normal child, one must remember that hearing-impaired children enjoy simple things that they can understand and are much less sophisticated in their games than normally-hearing children. The fact that action and movement are linked with words is sufficient to make the game interesting; once again, the word becomes magical when *it causes something to happen.* All the games are quite useless unless the child uses the sentences involved correctly. Children who read or who are learning to read, are at an advantage, but whether or not the child can read, each sentence should be written in large lower case letters on a piece of card, thus:

> Where are you going?
> I am going to the

When the child has read, or tried to read the replies two or three times, the card should be removed and he should try to remember the sentence. Even non-readers or poor readers should be given a card. Not only will this encourage reading, but even when reading skills are inadequate the card seems to be a definite aid.

Acting out Sequences with Simple Props

This can only benefit a child who, again, has firm mastery of basic vocabulary and has begun to make sentences in response to questions.

Sequence cards have the limitation that the sentences used are 'subject-verb-object' – 'The girl is holding so-and-so,' 'She is looking at so-and-so.' Acting out a simple scene with a small amount of doll's furniture once again makes a situation three-dimensional and allows for more variety of speech.

Props should be kept to a minimum, lest the child be distracted. For instance, the adult may put on the table a doll's bath, a girl doll and a mother doll. The adult then enacts a small sequence: 'Mummy says to the girl, "It's time for your bath." The girl takes off her clothes. She gets into the bath. Mummy starts to wash the girl. The girl splashes. Mummy says, "Don't splash; I'm all wet." The girl splashes again. Mummy says, "You are naughty. I will be cross." The girl says, "I'm sorry." Mummy says, "Get out of the bath." The girl says, "I want to play." Mummy says, "Get out of the bath at once." The girl gets out.'

The sequence is then acted again but this time, while the adult tells the story, she asks the child to fill in pieces as the story unfolds by asking questions:

'What is the girl doing?'
'Where is the girl?'
'What does Mummy say?'
'Is Mummy cross?'
'Who is the girl splashing?'
'What does Mummy say now?'
'What will the girl do now?'
'Where is the girl going now?'

Sequence stories should be fairly short and need to contain some dramatic incident – a birthday, Father Christmas coming, looking for a lost object (he is looking *under* the bed, she is looking *on* the chair, she is looking *in* the box, etc.) Naughtiness of a doll is always acceptable as a topic!

The procedures and material so far described should be regarded as things a hearing-impaired child should be taught in an endeavour to raise his level of verbal communication. It is NOT *a programme to be carried through simply as it is written down here. It is up to parents to select items from procedures and materials so that a balanced work schedule is created for a child.*

Thus one week's work might consist of the following items:

1. Learning to listen to, comprehend and name articles on the meal table (not food). Responding to the question, 'What is it?'
2. Learning to listen to and comprehend eight to ten action verbs. Responding to the questions, 'What am I doing?' 'What are you doing?' 'What is he/she doing?'
3. Learning to comprehend and name some descriptive words. Finding in the environment articles that could be described by these words.
4. Practice for positional words.
5. Keeping the daily diary.
6. Hearing stories.
7. Responding to as many questions as the child has mastered about a picture and generally discussing the picture with the adult.

The parents probably have additional ideas about helping the child that they wish to work into the daily programme. It cannot be stressed enough that the set things taught – definite naming words, action words, positional words and descriptive words – are intended to act as a framework. The natural language that the parent gives to the child during the daily routine fills out this framework and makes it living language. The framework is given because many parents of hearing-impaired children told simply 'Talk to your child' have an increasing feeling as the months go by of 'getting lost', of 'not getting anywhere' and of 'not knowing what the child knows'. None the less, the framework is useless unless regular work is carried out and unless that work is related to everyday life by spontaneous conversation between parent and child.

15

The Outcome of Effort

I have spoken of the hearing-impaired child who, though he may be four, five, six or seven years old or even older physically, is still at the two or two plus level in speech and language. A parent, faced with the considerable amount of work I have outlined, is entitled to enquire what may be the probable results if he undertakes it; whether his child will gain in speech and language development and how much he will gain. I can safely say that I have never known a case where, if the child was placed on a routine based on the ideas and materials described, there was no improvement. This is so whether the work was carried out by myself or by parents. How much improvement depends upon how conscientiously and imaginatively the parents work and on the level of cooperation, degree of hearing loss, previous experience, efficiency of hearing aids and intelligence of the child. The length of time needed to cover the work is also dependent upon these factors and has extended, in my experience, from six months to between two and three years. On the whole, parents report after one year a considerable improvement in the child's understanding of speech, and to a lesser degree improvement in his own speech. Marked improvement in speech does not develop until listening and looking patterns are well established; this takes a considerable time and it is most unlikely that, after one year's work, the hearing-impaired child's speech will resemble that of a normal three-year-old. In younger hearing-impaired children, it is more immature in every respect; in older children it may be more sophisticated in content but inferior in grammar. Articulation is likely to be poorer in both age groups.

Let us look at some achievements of real children.

David (Audiogram Figure 13)
David's failure to understand speech or to speak himself was a mystery until hearing loss was diagnosed just before his third

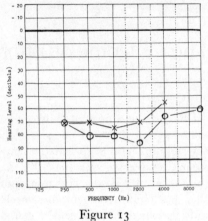

Figure 13

O – Right ear   X – Left ear

birthday. He was then fitted with two body-worn hearing aids and received some excellent early training in a school for deaf children. At four years old David transferred to a partially-hearing unit and also came for speech therapy, his mother commenting, 'He's come on very well but we want him to say sentences.' David's comprehension was at the two years six months level. He said many single words and joined two words ('big bus') but did not make sentences except those specifically taught in relation to his daily routine ('Please may I have a drink?'). He had already been taught, at school, to read a little. David was shy and afraid of separation from his mother. He was also a very active child, investigating his surroundings and climbing fearlessly to obtain objects he required. His physical activity would subside once he was mentally interested. Though no intelligence tests were ever carried out, his later academic career and attainments suggest that David is a bright boy with high motivation to learn. David was placed on a work plan based on the word lists and material described. The work was carried out at two hourly speech therapy sessions each week and supported by daily practice with a most well-disciplined and conscientious mother. David was the youngest of four children and the whole family united to help David at the weekend. At four years and three months, different body-worn hearing aids were tried and David's response to sound improved.

By four and a half, David had covered the work described in

Chapters 10–14 and had a verbal comprehension age of three years eleven months. Such questions and requests as: 'Where has Eleanor gone?' 'What did you have for lunch?' 'Do you want chocolate or sugar biscuits?' 'Pass me your plate and then pick up your napkin,' were readily intelligible to him. His expressive speech level was three years two months and the following is a sample of his own speech taken down verbatim during the testing period:

'Shopping look – big car – I got big car – ball in the car – car is in the house – looks too big – there's little car – the broom is in the car – broom broom – there's a cake – what is it? – dog? – rabbit? – the dog won't run – this is a fast boat – some pencils to colour with – colour the balloons – the money go round – peoples finished – where's the baby? – put it down on the floor – this is a daddy – it's a muddle bed – that's better.'

We see that words in all categories are developing and sentences forming. Articulation (even 's') was accurate apart from 'ch' which David replaced by 'sh'. This little boy, who has been mentioned in earlier chapters, had much in his favour. One year and three months after this speech sample was taken, when he was five years nine months old, speech was entirely normal and just before six years old, David entered a school in which there was no partially-hearing unit, and ceased specialised treatment. He did very well in school work and read extensively to himself for his own pleasure, showing excellent understanding of all types of reading material.

David was, first and foremost, a listener who frequently played or drew at the same time as conversing with an adult. Probably lip-reading is an aid to him, but it is certainly not his prime means of comprehending spoken language.

Mary (Audiogram Figure 14)

Mary, the third of four children, was found to be profoundly deaf when she was two years old and was fitted with body-worn aids. At three and a half years, since there was no day school for deaf children within reach of her home, Mary was placed in a partially-hearing unit, but made progress neither in learning to understand speech nor in saying more than a few words. Her parents brought her for speech therapy at four and a half as a last resort. They were extremely worried about her and though they tried to help her had no clear idea how to do so. The child was totally out of touch with the speech of other people and had no realisation that it was a channel of communication between herself and them. So low were her language levels that language tests had to be abandoned. She showed she understood 'Where's Mummy?' by reliably turning her head towards her mother but no other understanding of words could be detected. She could say about eight words spontaneously, including 'please' and 'thank you', 'fish', 'bag', 'horse' and 'flower', but could not locate the pictures for these words when the names were said to her. She was unresponsive even to loud sound and it was found that, unknown to her parents, one aid was broken internally. Even in good repair, the aids supplied to Mary would not have provided enough amplification to help her. Neither ear mould fitted well.

Mary engaged in excessive physical activity to compensate for normal outlets and while running and jumping she occasionally broke into babble – 'bah-gah bah-gah'. She gestured when she required something and had acquired some unconventional deaf signs (e.g. thumbs up for 'all's well') but had never been taught any conventionalised sign system. She was very clinging with her mother, since this was her only firm line of communication, and would not allow her mother to leave the room. Her nights were poor and her inability to explain her needs or to appreciate why she could not have certain objects led to frequent fits of screaming and crying during the day. Concentration was very poor, Mary

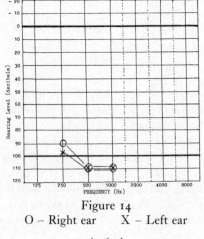

Figure 14

O – Right ear   X – Left ear

either going into a dream or wriggling incessantly when asked to sit down to a definite task. Intelligence had been tested by a psychologist who specialised in assessing deaf children, and was found to be average.

Mary was fitted with two powerful body-worn aids and given two hourly speech therapy sessions a week, her mother and other staunch helpers doing a considerable amount of work with her between visits. Work was initiated to make her aware of sound and of the face as a source of information. For a considerable period, even into her sixth year, the type of very early experience described in Chapter 7 had to be filled in. Mary responded to this by developing not only more babble but also a great deal of jargon and the names of familiar objects in her environment. Because of her extreme deafness, late aiding and untutored state, progress was very slow and after two and a half years the work outlined in Chapters 10–14 was still being carried out again and again in as many different ways as possible to enable Mary to gain understanding. Outside circumstances made the task of Mary's parents even harder than that of parents of other hearing-impaired children and the extreme nature of Mary's handicap made progress slow. The parents none the less toiled on without complaint and were rewarded by Mary's slowly becoming able to understand speech in a way that made life in the home much easier:

'Go upstairs and fetch my handbag, please.'
'We can't go out because it's raining.'
'Do you want me to read you another story?'
'Your birthday is a long time yet.'
'The boys are coming home soon.'
'Go and look at the tree in the garden.'

When Mary was six years and ten months old it was possible to carry out language tests with her with the following results:

Verbal Comprehension: three years.
Verbal Expression: two years four months.
Word Naming Test: four years four months.

The child could now enjoy all sorts of stories aided by pictures, particularly appreciating Ladybird 'Easy Reading Books'. Situations could be explained to her and she was accessible to reason. Her own speech showed a preponderance of single words, but also the joining of many words:

> 'Mary going school.'
> 'Daddy milking cows.'
> 'Sophie eye better.'
> 'Where –?'

Well-structured sentences were on the increase:

> 'I am going to bed.'
> 'I am going on holiday.'

She possessed some basic general knowledge, understanding for instance the functions of the milkman, the postman and dustman etc., the imaginary nature of fairy-tale characters and the structure of her own day and week. She had even learned that a person has only one birthday, one celebration of Christmas and one summer holiday in a year! She had started to read and though she found this difficult she could read the first two Ladybird 'Key Words Easy Readers' books and could recognise the words she had learned there in other contexts. She showed imagination in her ideas for play which she could partly verbalise to other children; her general hyperactivity was much reduced and concentration was better. Mary was far more integrated with other people and could enjoy outings and parties without her mother. Situations could be explained to her and she was far more accessible to reason. Though she still cried and screamed a great deal, she was often able to give a reason for her tears even if only 'So-and-so hit me.'

When Mary was six and a half years old, her body aids were replaced by specific power post-aural aids for a trial period. It was obvious, both from aided audiometry and from Mary's reaction, that she received increased sound messages through these aids. She was now much more accurate in selecting one word to command from such groups as 'cock', 'clock', 'cross', 'cot', and she was very responsive to sound about her. When, owing to an oversight, she was separated from her post-aural aids during a speech therapy session she showed anxiety and asked for them repeatedly until they could be brought to her.

Obviously there is still a vast amount of work to be done, but Mary is no longer an isolated little girl. It need hardly be stressed that early appropriate aiding and suitable training would have helped her to a much better start. There was, however, an advantage in her being presented for speech therapy knowing almost no words – correct articulation was taught from the start and is today remarkably accurate.

Mary is predominantly a lip-reader, fixing her eyes on the speaker's face with unwavering attention while a story is told to her and obviously deriving high meaning therefrom. There is no doubt that the sound derived from her aids is also of great value to her since, when they are removed, she loses control of the pitch of her voice, of the rate and rhythm of speech and of her articulation.

The examples of David and Mary have been selected as being extreme ends of the spectrum of progress I have known. Most of the children treated by the methods I have described fall somewhere between the two.

16

Increasing Understanding (1)
Vocabulary and Speech

Parents who have worked systematically with their child to teach him the things described in the last chapters will have no difficulty in extending their teaching to include the material about to be discussed. The earlier stage often involves a struggle; the child does not quite know what is required of him, he is unaccustomed to working, language is a new sphere to him and concentration is probably poor. The parent is likely to be as unused as the child to the sort of organisation and effort required. From now onwards, progress should be faster, both comprehension and spoken language taking shape much more rapidly, and the child becoming not only willing, but even eager to work and expressing his curiosity of the world about him by constant enquiry.

Parents who come to this book at this point, feeling that their child has covered the earlier ground but is still retarded in speech, are advised to consider certain points carefully. Vocabulary given in the early chapters will be included in this second half, but a child will be deemed to have mastered all the stages in comprehension already described. The best measure of language comprehension and speech skills is professional assessment by a psychologist, speech therapist, or teacher of the deaf, trained to administer language tests that will determine the exact level of language development that the child has reached.* If it is genuinely impossible to obtain professional testing, the parents should run through the earlier comprehension and listening work *without using gesture*. If the child can do the work, the experiment will soon be completed; if he is unable to do it, it is useless to proceed with more complex work.

* The Reynell Developmental Language Scales, devised by Dr Joan K. Reynell, can be given only by qualified psychologists, speech therapists and teachers of the deaf who have attended a course specifically designed to teach the administration of the test.

Secondly, parents whose child is really able to do the earlier work and converses quite freely, often still overestimate performance. A boy of seven years old who had never had formal structured teaching, had none the less made fair progress and was deemed by his parents to be 'doing well'. Formal testing showed that though the boy certainly talked a great deal, he was a full three years retarded in comprehension, and even more in his ability to express himself. The amount of speech present was of immature type, but its presence had deceived the parents into believing that their son was doing much better than was actually the case. They were considerably shaken by the amount of work that still remained to be done and by the extent of the boy's speech retardation.

Thirdly, a child who has mastered earlier speech skills informally may present problems in teaching (poor concentration, lack of motivation) that a child taught in a structured way has overcome.

Lastly, parents intending to start work on material contained in the current section should familiarise themselves with the actual teaching techniques described in Chapters 9–14 since these will not be repeated in detail.

Reading

So far, only casual mention has been made of reading. Hearing-impaired children are often taught to read very early in life in the belief that, since they can't hear or talk, if they can only use their eyes and hands to read and write, they will be able to communicate through these channels. Unfortunately, this is far from completely true. Reading is only partly a visual activity. To have meaning, the print seen by the eye must, like the sounds heard by the ear, be interpreted by the brain. For this interpretation, a fund of vocabulary of all classes is necessary, but, even more complex, an ability to understand the relationships between words that give a sentence its meaning.

Kate, who at seven and a half years old had scant speech and language, had been taught to 'read' and demonstrated this skill by picking up a Ladybird Easy Reading Book and reading aloud. The first few words were read clearly, but deteriorated progressively into gabble. When asked, 'Show me the words "Grandmother's house" ' and 'Show me "wolf" ' Kate was at a loss. What was even more serious, when the sentence 'Put your book on Mummy's chair' was written on a card, though Kate could read the words she had no idea what they meant or how to act upon them. 'Reading' had developed without any reference to comprehension of language and was almost useless to the child.

In many ways, reading of this type is much worse than no reading at all. The child who does not read at all can be taught to do so, but the child who thinks he has already learned is most reluctant to be taken, as he sees it, back to the beginning and made to think what he is reading about. Ideally, reading skills should grow gradually out of the speech and language work carried out with the child and no effort should be made to teach the hearing-impaired child reading at an earlier age than he would have learned had he been a hearing child. It has already been said that naming words should be clearly labelled and question forms read aloud. Practice should also be given in matching sentence and picture. Action cards, for instance, should be accompanied by a sentence to be matched to the appropriate picture.

> # The boy is kicking the ball

Work on positional words should be accompanied by making sure that the child can read 'in', 'on', 'under', 'off', 'up', 'down', 'around', 'to', 'out of'. *Bears in the Night* (see page 129) is an easy book to read and so are many of the other books recommended in Appendix 2. Flash cards should be made of each word a child is asked to read, e.g.

> # bed

All the flash cards should be kept in a box and reviewed as part of daily speech practice.

Many parents are very anxious to place their child on a reading scheme, but reading schemes that are excellent for normal chil-

dren contain vocabulary that speedily becomes beyond the understanding of a hearing-impaired child, and consequently there is a
danger of the 'reading without understanding' syndrome developing. The most practical type of scheme is one that demands that the
child reads words that require him to *do* something, e.g. 'Colour
the roof red.' In this way, reading and comprehension are firmly
linked from the beginning. It is also most important that, in the
early stages, only short sentences are read and the meaning checked,
if not by the child performing an action then by his relating the
words to a picture. I have found the Ladybird 'Key Words' Reading Scheme good because of the high ratio of pictures to words.
At approximately Book 6a and 6b level vocabulary and sentence
construction become too complex for most hearing-impaired children but the words in the first six books form a useful nucleus of
reading vocabulary.

The daily diary is another vehicle for meaningful reading, and
its entries should, by this stage, be a little longer and more complex
– but still very clearly and carefully written by the adult. The
child should attempt to read each entry back to the parent.

Daddy came home. He said, 'How pretty your new dress is! Did Mummy buy it today?' Daddy, Mummy and I all went to have supper at Grandma's house.

A further way of making reading meaningful is to encourage
reading of well-known material. Since the child will already be
familiar with basic fairy tales from the stories told to him, Ladybird
'Read it Yourself' books are excellent reading material. The first
four books, *Goldilocks and the Three Bears*, *The Three Billy Goats
Gruff*, *Sly Fox and the Little Red Hen* and *The Elves and the Shoe-
maker*, contain basic vocabulary and sentence structure and have
high interest and meaning. Two slightly more difficult levels (two

sets of four books each) are also available. The 'Laugh and Learn' series by Terry Hall contains useful vocabulary, often repeated. It is full of activity and has a strong comic element that appeals to young children.

For hearing-impaired children, reading is a good servant but a bad master. When reading can be kept firmly linked with known language, it is a wonderful aid in that it reinforces auditory memory of words, and shows in visual form the order of words in a sentence. It can also clarify meaning when both auditory and visual comprehension through lip-reading break down. James, for instance, was asked, 'Fetch me the smarties, please,' and fetched the basket since 'smarties' and 'basket' are both auditorally and visually similar. Two repetitions failed to help him, but a swift writing down of 'smarties' showed James his error.

Developing Further Language Skills

So far, the vocabulary dealt with has been related to the child's immediate surroundings. The next step is to increase the child's vocabulary so that it covers not only all aspects of the wider environment the child moves in, but also some of the vocabulary we know at second hand. Thus we all of us know what a 'whale' is though few of us have actually seen a real whale in the sea.

Before further naming words are taught, however, positional words should be extended. (The reason for this will become obvious presently.)

> behind
> in front of
> above
> beside
> between

should be added in that order, to the original list given on page 122. By this stage, with his previous training firmly established, the child should find the integration of new positional words much easier than when they were first introduced. Each word should none the less be made known carefully to the child, one at a time, and games played round the room as before. It should be ensured that some furniture is placed so that the child can really get *behind* it. The concept of 'behindness' is difficult and often confused with 'under'. The following type of instruction should be given:

> 'Stand *behind* the blue armchair.'
> 'Sit *in front of* Mummy's chair.'
> 'Hold your hand *above* the television.'
> 'Kneel *beside* the radiator.'
> 'Stand *between* the television and the red chair.'

Once the child is confident in placing himself, the routine with the large and small objects on the table should be carried out, first asking the child to place objects, then, when they are placed, to say where they are. 'Beside' and 'behind' are sometimes confused by very deaf children because there is similarity, both visually and auditorally.

Learning More Words

Parents looking at the word lists given on pages 199-223 and feeling overcome with horror, should consider firstly that these lists include the 900-plus words that their child already knows from the earlier lists and, secondly, that their child's auditory memory will have been extended by the work already carried out. The word lists given are not an attempt to assess the vocabulary of a normal child, and any child, normal or hearing-impaired, will have words personal to himself that are not on the list. Most parents will be able to find examples of what they consider to be omissions from the list. These lists simply represent words that I have taught to numbers of hearing-impaired children over the years in an attempt to bring them to a level where they can begin to understand varied conversation, read meaningfully and benefit from what is taught to them in school. Parents should not attempt to teach all the words in any one category at once. Some will already be known to the child, and parents should now introduce only such new words from any list as seem meaningful to the child and within his scope. Guidance will be given later for further enlargement of vocabulary.

An alphabetical list of words has been given at the end of this book, but the same words have also been grouped into lists at the end of Chapter 17 to help parents to keep track of what their child knows, and what he doesn't know, in relation to any one subject. Some of the lists, for example, body parts, are an entity and easily taught as such. Other lists can be grouped together to form a project; the farm, the countryside, and many birds and animals belong together. It is suggested that a certain number of such projects should form an important part of teaching so that the child learns not only naming words but positional and descriptive words. Suggested projects are:

> The street, with its typical objects,
> people and vehicles.
> The shops and their contents.
> The countryside, farm, birds and animals.
> The garden, garden tools, birds and plants.

There is a variety of material available related to these topics and each allows for a considerable amount of activity. At least one, possibly more, are major features of the lives of many children. The home with its many sub-divisions has not been selected, since it was dealt with in Chapters 10–14.

In considering which project to work upon with a child, his own interests should be considered. If a child has been born on or near a farm, he will be familiar with farm animals and the countryside, and a project about these things will come easily to him. Many children have rarely visited the country, and it therefore means little to them.

The Street, People and Vehicles

Most children, town- or country-dwellers, are familiar with a street, its objects, vehicles and people, and accordingly a street has been chosen to illustrate how this type of project work is carried out. The basic aim is to present a street in as many different ways and through as many different materials as possible.

Using a sheet of drawing paper 33″ x 23″ (84 cm x 57 cm) draw a street with roads, pavements, kerbs, corners and crossroads and a zebra crossing. Objects should be clearly marked in lower case letters. Shops should be added, with shop names written clearly to encourage reading, and shop contents drawn with felt tip pens. A church, a garage, public house, post office, flats, bank, bus shelter, cinema – anything found in the child's own shopping area should be included. While the adult will find it easier to prepare some of the work beforehand, the child should also be encouraged to help since drawing the street will necessitate his observing the real environment more closely and feeling involved in the project. Small objects should be drawn on white card: bus stop, flag, grating, 'keep left' sign, lamp-post, letter-box, litter bin, post, puddle, statue, telephone box. The child should be taught to select to instruction and to name them by the same method used on page 98, always remembering to include auditory training. He is then asked to place them in the street to instruction:

'Put the litter bin *beside* the butcher's shop.'

'Put the flag *on top of* the church.'

'Put the letter-box *between* the butcher's shop and the greengrocer's shop.'

'Put the puddle *on* the pavement *beside* the baker's shop.'

'Put a white cloud *above* the church.'

Figures of people – butcher, dustman, lady, man, boy, girl, toddler, policeman, postman, sailor, workman and traffic warden – should then be added. Once the child is able to name them, he can be asked to manipulate them in the street scene:

'Make the window cleaner *cross* the road.'

'Make the lady *walk through* the gate *to* the church.'

'Make the girl *run up* the street *to* the supermarket.'

'Make the policeman *stand in front of* the butcher's shop.'

'Make the traffic warden *stand at* the corner.'

Various vehicles may then be added to the scene. As the child becomes familiar with the various objects and people, he may want to be the person to give the instructions while the adult carries them out.

Parents may ask why they should trouble to make a street scene when there is probably a perfectly good street near their house and also when books show pictures of streets. One answer is that children love objects on a miniature scale and that they feel much more involved in anything they have helped to make. Secondly, a child's attention is more easily held if he can manipulate something in response to what is said to him. As Andrew's mother said, 'I notice Andrew's eyes light up when you bring out something he can actually handle.' A model gives wide opportunities for auditory training, and lengthening of auditory memory span, and the constant reiteration of naming words involved in giving instructions is almost bound to result in the child learning them. Positional words have definite limits. On a flat, two-dimensional scene, 'behind' and 'under' really are the same thing, and should be omitted. 'In front of' and 'beside' can be confusing.

Once a child has mastered one simple instruction well, two should be attempted, for example, 'Put the lorry in the garage. Give me the postman.' *The child should not be allowed to touch the pieces until the complete instruction has been spoken.* If he carries out one instruction and *then* listens for the second, the exercise is a waste of time in terms of lengthening auditory memory.

To begin with, instructions should be simple but, as the child becomes more practised and confident, greater complexity may be introduced. Descriptive words can be used; shape and colour words, 'full', 'empty', 'dirty', 'clean', 'zig-zag', 'fat', 'high', 'long', 'quickly', 'upside down', 'right side up', 'curved', 'forwards', 'backwards', 'sideways', 'biggest', 'smallest', 'same', 'different', 'straight':

'Put the van on the zig-zag line, turn the lorry upside down.'

'Give me the smallest person, show me the empty bin.'

'Put the girl on the high wall, put the lorry by the corner.'

'Make the policeman walk backwards towards the supermarket.'

'Show me the longest pavement, show me something round.'

'Put the tallest person between the baker's shop and the greengrocer's shop.'

Number words may be included:

'Touch each person and one of the cars.'

'Show me all the buildings.'

'Show me two of the shops and three of the people.'

'Are there more people, or more buildings?'

For a child to be able to operate on those instructions, he must be able to understand every word in a sentence or he will make a mistake. There can be no guessing, all gaps in comprehension soon become obvious. It is impossible to enumerate all the instructions that can be given, and it is up to the parent to utilise the lists provided and to use flexibility and ingenuity to improvise instructions. If the adult will treat the project as a lively and amusing game, the child will join in and see it as fun. Any feeling by the adult that it is a dreary, childish activity will also percolate to the child just as quickly. The adult should be able to judge when a child is following instructions well and when he is floundering. Persistent failure is bad for a child and in the event of several failures in a row, easier instructions should be given. It should be remembered that the concentration and interpretation required is very difficult for the child, and that about ten instructions at a sitting are ample. A normally-hearing five-year-old should be able to carry out an instruction containing three parts, e.g. 'Put the book on the table, shut the door, then bring me the book that is on the chair near the door,'* but this is not to be expected from a considerably older hearing-impaired child without months of training. An advance from one to two parts in an instruction is a marked achievement. When one parent, probably the mother, has worked daily with the child for a week, the other parent should take a turn to check the child's progress. A child becomes accustomed to one adult's choice and mode of giving instructions, and a change of adult will often reveal inadequacies in basic comprehension.

The home-made project should be backed up by collecting pictures related to buildings, people and vehicles and also by observing them in the street. Half an hour standing on the pavement beside a busy junction enabled therapist and child to spot and name all the vehicles learned apart from the fire engine. Driving along a street discussing the sights with a child is a hazardous business; walking is preferable if people and buildings are to be observed to the full.

A list of helpful books is included in Appendix 3. Especially recommended is Richard Hefter's delightfully simple *Word Book* since this provides pictures with captions relating not only to street, people and vehicles but also to many of the other groups of words listed in this book. It is laid out in such a way that auditory training is easy to do from each scene depicted. At this stage, not all the material in the excellent 'Words Your Children Use' series by Edwards and Gibbon is necessary. The books relevant to the street project, *Travelling by Land*, *People We Meet* and *Buildings* contain more words than are needed at this level, and in some places the text is too difficult. It is recommended that the suitable pictures be used and the books put away and brought out later when the filling in of more difficult words is attempted.

Not to be missed is *In the Town* in the 'Create a Story' series by Kiddicraft, a strip book of many combinations. This is an

* Valentine, C. W., *Intelligence Tests for Children*.

excellent vehicle for questions and the earlier questions given on page 148 should be amplified by those based on the games on pages 151–6.

> 'I am thinking of something in the
> picture that is red – can you guess what it is?'
> 'Who has red shoes?'
> 'Which house do you like best?'
> 'Where is the little boy going?'
> 'The aeroplane can fly – can you fly?'
> 'Who gave the ice cream to the little boy?'

Additional questions might be:

> 'What do we do with a letter-box?'
> 'What is in the little boy's satchel?'
> 'Where is the mummy taking the little girl?'
> 'Who put the car in the garage?'
> 'What is the lady waiting for?'
> 'Who is taking the little girl across the road?'
> 'Who is down the hole?'
> 'What is in the lady's basket?'
> 'Which building is the tallest?'

If the child cannot reply to a question, the adult should show him how to do so, but return to the question at a later stage to see whether the child has mastered it.

A project of this type involving the learning of many words and skills is not intended to be rushed through quickly. It is intended to last about a month, perhaps longer, but to be interspersed with other work so that it does not become tedious. Some children who work on a project of this type will learn naming words but will be unable to master more than a single, simple command. These are often fairly young, very deaf children and they should not (indeed cannot) be pressurised into trying to achieve more, but should be allowed to gain what they can from the project and pass on to another. At the other end of the scale, there are children who become very excited by the venture and not only reel off the names of buildings, people and vehicles at every opportunity, but also begin to link more words together and to talk far more.

The Shops

This again is suitable for most children. Though many things are

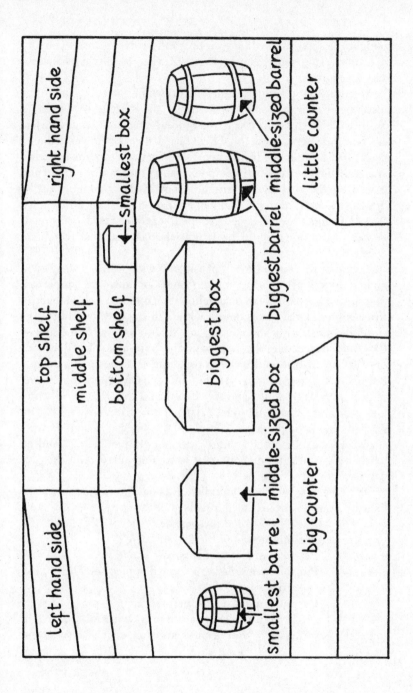

bought in a supermarket, toys, clothes and hardware are still bought in ordinary shops and many mothers still visit the butcher's, baker's and greengrocer's.

An empty shop similar to the one drawn on page 175 should be made but preferably on a larger scale – about 16″ x 10″ (40 cm x 25 cm). This can be used as a background in teaching many different kinds of shops, a suitable fascia board always being added on a flash card. A catalogue from a good seed firm will provide beautiful and realistic pictures of fruit and vegetables that can be cut out and placed on the shelves and anything not in the catalogue can be drawn (bananas, oranges, melons, etc.). A child should be shown that fruit and vegetables are grouped separately in a real greengrocer's shop and should be taught the class words 'fruit' and 'vegetables'.

A shop of this sort makes it possible to widen the words used in giving directions. 'Top', 'middle' and 'bottom' are important descriptive words and can be taught with a miniature chest made of three empty match boxes bound with 'Tuf' tape. Show this to the child, demonstrating and naming top, middle and bottom drawers. Carefully concealing the box whilst a button is placed in one drawer, say to the child after producing the chest, 'There is a button in the top drawer.' If the child pushes open the correct drawer, say, 'Well done!' and give him the button. If not, show him his error and remove the box, saying, 'No, that's not right. You opened the wrong drawer!' Explain the names of the drawers again and make another attempt with the button. Some children 'click' very quickly; with others it is trial and error and the idea dawns gradually.

Once the idea of 'top', 'middle' and 'bottom 'is firmly established, it can be applied to the shelves of the shop:

'Put *all* the *red* apples *on* the *top* shelf.'
'Put the carrots *in* the *biggest* barrel.'
'Put the oranges *on* the *middle* shelf.'
'Put the melon *between* the red apples and the green apples.'
'Put the lemons *above* the oranges.'

As will be seen from the picture, there is scope for practice of 'biggest', 'middle-sized' and 'small'; also for 'edge', 'corner' and 'middle'.

'Put the plums *in* the *corner* of the *big* counter.'
'Put the grapes *at the edge* of the *little* counter.'
'Put the bananas *in the middle* of the *top* shelf.'
Once the articles are placed, the adult can ask:
'What is on the middle shelf?'
'What is in the biggest barrel?'
'What is on the top shelf above so-and-so?'
or alternatively
'Where are the oranges?'
'Where are the grapes?'
The child should always answer in a whole sentence as before. 'Gap' is a useful word that may be introduced here. A child may be shown the gap between the two counters, two boxes or between the box and the barrel and taught to name it.

Normal children do not know in any detail what is contained in a fish shop, baker's shop or butcher's shop until they are quite mature, but a chemist's shop, while difficult to draw, is easy to make from objects contained in the home. The parent should look at the list of words related to 'Inside the House' and 'Illness', collect relevant items such as shampoo, nail-brush, soap, plaster, tooth-brush, powder, lipstick, pills, medicine and cream and set up a simple chemist's shop on the table. If the child possesses a toy till and plastic money, the game is doubly popular. The child will gain a great deal of natural language from this shop game, as opposed to the more formal training offered by the two-dimensional shop.

'Good morning. What can I do for you?'
'Good morning. I want some shampoo.'
'What kind of shampoo do you like? This
kind? Or that kind?'

Finding the items a 'customer' requires (cotton wool, a nail-brush and plaster) is also a good exercise in auditory memory. A grocer's shop stocked with tins and packets from the store cupboard is also popular.

Ladybird *Shopping with Mother* is always useful. It is so simple that it can be read as it stands, but it is also useful to show the child a picture of a shop and ask him to name a few of the items bought there.

Obviously, going to the real shops with the mother whenever

possible is excellent reinforcement. Children are often at school when shopping is done, but if it is holiday time I am always sad to hear a parent say, 'He's such a nuisance, I always leave him at home when I go shopping.'

The Farm, Countryside, Birds and Animals

This can be a very important project, containing as it does many ideas and objects that occur in later stories and education. Country children have no difficulty in learning even words like 'cowshed' but to many town children the country remains a mystery. Andrew, a confirmed town-dweller, remained resistant to country ideas and learned few country words. Both he and his therapist realised that he could not really do without them when, at eleven years old, he was listening to her telling a story without pictures, and suddenly asked her, 'What is a stream?' A strong effort should be made to teach what is, after all, basic vocabulary, even if it is not in tune with the child's immediate interests.

Two sheets of drawing paper can be sellotaped together to make an area 66″ x 46″ (167 cm x 116 cm). On this can be drawn and painted fields, roads, lanes, rivers, streams and ponds. A hill can be made by padding beneath the paper with small pieces of crumpled up newspaper. Any fences the child possesses can be used to enclose fields, but fences and hedges can also be cut from card and stuck on. Woods can be made with cut-out trees and a farmhouse, stables, cowshed, pigsty and henhouse made of small cardboard boxes. Most children own some farm animals and people that can be placed in the scene. There is scope here for people to move about, e.g.

'Make the farmer come out of the farmyard, walk
down the lane and cross the bridge.'
'Make the cows walk through the gate, down the
road and into the next field'

Because hearing-impaired children know so little they are inclined to accept with joy what a hearing child the same age would reject as babyish. A severely deaf child of eight years old I knew was enchanted by just such a project as this. For those who are less ambitious, Uniflex make a two-dimensional farm, a card background upon which plastic pieces can be placed. There are many delightful books related to the country, farm and animals, some of which are listed in Appendix 3. Another 'Create a Story' book, *In the Country*, provides valuable reinforcement, and young children appreciate *Who Lives Here?* by Eileen Ryder. This is a repetitive book, and children often learn to recite parts of it, or at least to provide the last word of a sentence: 'Who lives here? The bird lives here. This is a –' The Ladybird *The Farm* with its emphasis on both baby animals and counting is also indispensable. Apart from *Topsy and Tim on the Farm* many of the earlier 'Topsy and Tim' books have strongly rural illustrations that reinforce country vocabulary. If a hearing-impaired child rarely goes to the country, a strong effort should be made to take him and to show him farms, hedges, streams, fields and woods. Some children who have been quite often know the appearance of country objects, but never quite place them due to the lack of a verbal label.

Gardens

Some children have parents who are keen gardeners, in which case it may again be worth making a small two-dimensional plan of a garden with small movable pictures of garden tools, flowers, insects and birds. As with shops, a garden gives good scope for various shapes, sizes and colours; round and square lawns, big, middle-sized and small flower beds, long and short fences, high and low walls. 'Corner', 'middle' and 'edge' can be used again. A suggested plan of a garden is given on page 180. A garden project would serve the same purpose as that of the street or the shops, to repeat vocabulary and to lengthen auditory memory by asking the child to carry out varied instructions.

The Zoo

A certain amount of formal work is essential to help the child to acquire vocabulary and comprehension. The following suggestions are given with less formal teaching in mind, but it is still essential that the child actually makes solid gains in vocabulary from each topic introduced. Children gain most from being exposed to toys and pictures when they have recently experienced or are about to experience the real thing. Mary, for instance, was promised a visit to the zoo. The visit was discussed, the days were crossed off on her calendar and a pretend zoo was made on the floor, using bricks and

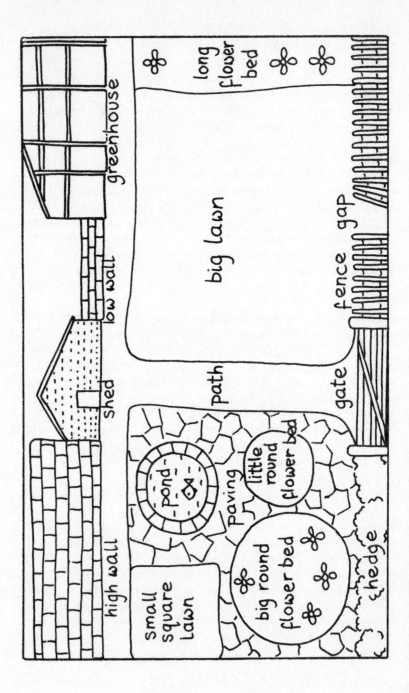

greenhouse

long flower bed

big lawn

low wall

shed

high wall

small square lawn

pond

paving

little round flower bed

big round flower bed

path

gate

fence gap

hedge

cardboard boxes for animal enclosures, each of which was care-fully labelled. Mary had never seen a zoo or a wild animal but, stimulated by excited anticipation of the promised treat, she learned all the animals' names and was actually able to recognise each animal when it was shown to her at the real zoo.

The Seaside

The seaside has no reality for a child if he has never been there, but most children nowadays have either an annual holiday or at least a day's outing to the seaside and this is the time to work on all the seaside material. The seaside is a particularly meaningful experi-ence for a hearing-impaired child with its taste of salt and candy floss, and the feelings of the waves, the rough sand and the warm sun. One child enjoyed a freezing holiday on the English coast so much that it stimulated some of the first words she ever put together: 'Everybody cold, wet sea!'

Railways and Stations

Railways and stations are not, in this jet age, as popular as they once were, none the less boys love this topic if a small toy railway is used, and not all girls are averse to it. Any railway set, even the variety with plastic rails and a push-along engine, will suffice provided it is arranged in an interesting way. Tunnels and bridges can be made with bricks and a simple railway station with the main features labelled. There is good scope for positional words: *over* the bridge, *through* the tunnel, *round* the corner, the engine is in *front*, the carriages are *behind*, the train is climbing *up* and running *down*. There seem to be few books about trains nowadays but, though a little difficult, *The Little Red Engine Goes to Market* is popular. Once again, a visit to a real station scores highly as does a ride on a train.

Since teaching should follow, as far as possible, what is hap-pening in the child's life, *Christmas* is the time for learning Christmas words and for hearing the Christmas story. *Seasonal* projects can be made up at the right time of year from words on the lists and a child can be encouraged to note, say, spring signs and to draw a picture of them. If a child starts *swimming* lessons and enjoys them, then is the time to learn the appropriate words.

Four-year-old Michelle clamoured, 'I want fun fair' and mimed licking candy floss. Her parents had not warned the therapist of the visit to the fair planned for after her lesson, but previous plans were immediately abandoned in favour of her being taught 'candy floss', 'coconut', 'big wheel', 'bumper car', etc., all of which were strongly reinforced by the real thing. Adults often miss golden opportunities such as this one from sheer thoughtlessness.

Books and pictures relevant to topics are included in Appendix 3. One or two other ideas may be helpful.

The *outside of the house* can be made with detachable parts – chimney, slates, knocker, number, letter-box, steps – that the child can remove and assemble.

Body parts can be taught by giving the child a packet of small round adhesive labels ($\frac{1}{4}''$/ 6 mm diameter) to stick on a doll as each part is said, and to peel off the second time round. While no one wishes a child to dwell unduly upon *illness*, an ill doll who is put to bed, dosed, nursed and visited by the doctor can generate a great deal of language in a small girl. *Fairy-tale people* should be gradually introduced once the child has a good store of 'real world' knowledge. It is only when he has this that the child can appreciate witches, giants and trolls and it is then quite easy to make him realise the meaning of 'pretend'! The *weather* can, as the child progresses, be added to the daily diary: 'Today it rained hard and I wore my raincoat.'

The materials that things are made of are included in the vocabulary list as being important, but a hearing child will not understand about materials and their origins until he is about seven years old. When the time comes for a hearing-impaired child to learn this, a shoe box of materials – cotton, wool, rubber, stone, clay, plastic, lead, etc. – should be collected so that the child can see and feel what is meant by them. Edwards and Gibbon's *What Things Are Made Of* is excellent supportive teaching. A child can be asked both to go round the house and say what he thinks objects are made of and also to tell five objects in the room made of certain commonplace materials.

17

Increasing Understanding (2)
Vocabulary and Speech

Action Words Again

The basic action words previously learned now need to be increased. *The Hop, Skip and Jump Book* by Jack Kent is full of useful action words and should be worked through slowly and systematically since it is difficult to find another collection of such vivid action pictures. The book contains some Americanisms, like 'mail' for 'post', and the words are written in capital letters which, unless a child is reading very easily, should be altered to lower case letters. A bulldog-type clip should be clipped on the pages not being worked upon to prevent the child looking ahead and tiring visually of the contents before he has learned sufficient words. Several of the action scenes depicted can be used for auditory training and word recognition; a page should not be abandoned until most of the action words it contains have been learned. The book contains several attractive stories without words that can be told by the child. Not all actions are marked and the adult needs to be on the alert – for instance, the boy on the first page is obviously 'shouting' though this is not stated. Some of the scenes contain excellent opportunities for discussion, for instance the school scene, which shows numerous children engaged in multifarious activities whilst the teacher has her back turned at the blackboard. Children are always amused if asked, 'What will the teacher say to *him* when she turns round? And what will she say to *her?*'

The action words on pages 219-23 have deliberately been kept simple. Some verbs in the language change radically in meaning if a preposition is added, for example, 'move up', 'move in'; 'take in', 'take up', 'take on', 'take over'. Such complexities are deemed to be beyond the scope of this book. 'Wash' and 'wash up' are however listed separately since a child learns quite early that the former may relate to any object while the latter always relates to dishes.

On the Action Word list on pages 219-23 many of the words are marked *. Such words are depicted in the following:

Things-We-Do Pictorial gummed stamps –
Philip & Tacey
Gonville Associational Picture and Vocabulary sheets –
Philip & Tacey
Action Cards, Set 2 – Learning Development Aids
Photographic Action Cards – Learning Development
Aids
The Hop, Skip and Jump Book by Jack Kent

It may take a little ingenuity for the parent to see all these words because they are by no means always captioned.

Of those words that remain many which cannot be illustrated can be worked into the child's daily routine if the adult will only think about it. For instance when Mary, at five years old, was making careless mistakes, her therapist always said, 'Think!' tapping her forehead. When Mary tried to recall a word she was asked, 'Can you remember?' and the top of her head was tapped. Despite their abstract nature, 'think' and 'remember' were some of the first words that Mary used – and she used them correctly. At three and a half Mark had quite enough speech to make his view-point known in opposition to that of an adult and was told, 'Don't *argue* with me, please!' If hearing-impaired children do not learn these types of word it is due to a lack of imagination and seeing the right moment by the adults around them.

Many of the words on the list are either very familiar or easy to act out and demonstrate to the child with or without simple props, for example:

> *bursting* a blown-up paper bag
> *calling* for someone to come
> *dialling* a telephone number
> *boiling* water
> *staring* at something
> *folding* a piece of paper
> *pricking* one's finger
> *peeling* an apple
> *whispering*

No one suggests that a hearing-impaired child should try to learn all these words quickly. They are intended to be absorbed over a long span of time. None the less, his parents should try to ensure that the child *is* gradually learning by introducing a few new action words each week and reinforcing them throughout the week by working them into a conversation and into the daily diary. Some children find it very difficult to learn unless words are illustrated and personalised and rehearsed again and again by, say, the child putting a counter on a picture when either the sentence or a single word is said. The drawing requires some artistic skill.

Descriptive and Less Tangible or Discrete Words

Like action words, descriptive and non-concrete words can be worked into a conversation or story if the adult will keep an eye on the word lists and consider what the child does not know. Stories often give an opening – either the adult realises that a word is unknown or, when a child has developed to a certain stage, he will ask a meaning. Much lack of learning comes from lack of alertness on the part of the adult who goes on using the same old words because he feels a child will not understand new words, or because using old words is easier. Descriptive words are harder to demonstrate and act than are action words, but some can easily be shown: for example, tight clothing, loose clothing, a sour lemon, tangled hair, a tidy table, an untidy table, a blank page, a crack, a crash, footprints, footsteps, a fright. All children love acting, but because movement and facial expression are so important, a hearing-impaired child enjoys dramatics even more than a normal child. Some words can only be acted with two people, but this is easily done with a word or two of prior consultation. It is always a delight to see the look on the face of a child when one adult pushes through a door in front of another or snatches something from the table. 'What bad *manners*!' comments the second adult. Very often the child will then demand to join in, actually saying, 'Now me! I act bad manners, please!' Many adults are much too inhibited with hearing-impaired children or perhaps feel that dignity and discipline would be impaired by their demonstrating 'bad manners', 'a scream' or 'a thud'. In fact, the child's respect for the adult is in no way lessened, provided it is made clear that pretending has limits and must end when its purpose has been achieved.

Positional Words

Once a hearing-impaired child has mastered basic positional words – 'in', 'on', 'under', 'off', 'out of', 'to', 'up', 'down', 'over', 'round' and 'with' – he probably uses them himself and does not forget them. Positional words can still, however, confuse him when they occur in a sentence containing other words and he may easily forget words like 'above', 'towards', 'between', 'behind' unless they are rehearsed frequently. Practising the positional words known and gradually acquiring new ones should be a continuous process and a child should be asked to carry out ten instructions each day, such as:

'Walk *along* the straight crack in the lino.'
'Lean *against* the wall *near* the door.'
'Put the button *among* the pencils.'
'Put a sticker *above* the door.'
'Stand *in front of* the cupboard.'
'Sit down *near* the television.'
'Walk *towards* the door.'
'Put your hand *through* the handle of the basket.'
'Make your fingers walk *across* the table.'
'Put two red pencils *together*.'

Instructions should be varied so that the child does not become accustomed to a set pattern and, for the same reason, adults should take turns at giving instructions. Tedium may be avoided by providing a box of mixed objects (some doll's tea things in coloured plastic, some coloured bricks and buttons of various shapes and sizes, a large and some smaller boxes, a few toy dolls and animals). The child may be asked:

'Make the girl walk *along* the box.'
'Put all the cups *together*.'
'Make the horse jump *over* the orange cup.'
'Put a big button *through* the handle of the jug.'
'Make the girl lean *against* a small box.'
'Put the horse *among* the bricks.'

Younger children cannot be expected to do more than this or to handle simple double instructions like:

'Put the horses *together*; put a cup *in* the box.'
'Put the *little* boxes *in* the big box; give me a brick.'

When older children of seven, eight, nine and ten years who have poor comprehension are being taught, considerably more may be expected and positional words, number, shape, size and amount words should gradually be included:

'Put a *brown* horse *in the middle* of the table and take the *biggest* button *out* of the box.'

'Give me the horse that is *nearest* the girl.'

'Turn *two* of the cups *upside down* and put the *smallest* button *on* the big box.'

'Make the *biggest* boy walk *towards* the *other end* of the table, then give him *to me*.'

'Pick up *one* of the cups and put your *little* finger *through* the handle.'

'Show me *all* the *round* things on the table and put something *square on* your chair.'

'Put *some* red things *in* the box – show me the *red* things that are *not* in the box.'

'Put *all* the blue things together and put something *green among* them.'

A child will often understand enough of a story to both satisfy and benefit him without necessarily understanding all of it. To carry out instructions, the value of every word must be understood and there are few more searching tests of verbal comprehension. Even an older child will have to practise over many months to become efficient at carrying out the sort of instructions outlined above.

Why? – Because

Normal children ask 'Why?' so incessantly at four years old that some mothers respond with the old saying, 'Why? Why? Apple Pie!' with some logic, since when the child first asks 'Why?' he doesn't wish to know the answer, only to practise asking the question. A desire to know the answer develops at about five years old. Hearing-impaired children are usually late in asking 'Why?' questions and it is most important that they should be stimulated to do so. Sometimes, despite all the stimulus provided and the verbal material fed into the child, 'Why?' still does not develop.

As soon as the child is responding to the earlier questions 'What is it? Where? Who? Which?' he should be asked 'Why?' when he is looking at pictures.

'Why is Topsy wearing a raincoat?'

'Why is Mummy happy?'

'Why is Daddy cross?'

'Why is Tim crying?'

'Why is Daddy wearing a warm scarf?'

Once again, Topsy and Tim presented in familiar situations with their expressive faces are ideal material. If the child does not know the answer, he should be told and once again, when he answers himself, he should use a whole sentence. An ability to answer 'Why?' questions usually develops quite quickly, but a hearing-impaired child may have to be asked 'Why?' many, many times over a long period before he asks 'Why?' himself. Once he does begin to ask, his questions proliferate and a most important milestone in the development of language has been reached. The parent must be prepared, as with a normal child, for an 'asking but not wanting to know' stage, which may last a considerable time but is most valuable as language practice.

Though the logical answer to 'Why?' seems to be 'Because', another answer may be 'to so-and-so', e.g.

'Why is the man running?'

'He is running to catch the bus.'

Unless both forms of answer are encouraged, the child is inclined to believe there is some magic in 'because' and will use it slavishly, so inhibiting the learning of the 'to' form.

LDA make 'Why – Because' cards, but these require a more mature understanding of situations than is displayed by hearing-impaired children when they are first introduced to 'Why?' The cards are, however, very useful once the child has gained more experience.

When? – Time

The question 'When?' develops even later than 'Why?', because until they acquire language, hearing-impaired children can have little sense of time. They often use 'later', 'after' or 'morrow' early in learning to talk, but this is because they have often been assured that something they are not going to acquire immediately will be given then. Thus, to Mary everything was 'morrow' – even her birthday (actually a good eight months distant) and even by her sixth birthday she knew nothing of days, weeks or seasons.

To begin to give a child some sense of time structure, the days of the week should be written in upper and lower case letters about 2″ (5 cm) high, thus:

Monday
Tuesday
Wednesday
Thursday
Friday
Saturday
Sunday

This chart should be pinned up in the child's room. An arrow made of postcard should be fixed with a large paper-clip or bull-dog type clip beside the days and moved first thing each morning to the correct day. The mother should stress, at getting up time, 'Today is Monday' and outline whatever detail is particular to that day. 'Today is a school day. After school you are going swimming. We go swimming every Monday.'

The full date 'Monday, 17th April' should of course head the daily entry in the diary, but time may none the less remain a vacuum to many children. The most satisfactory solution is to make a chart for the entire year out of drawing paper and sellotape. A full chart measures about 9″ (23 cm) deep by about twelve feet (three and a half metres) long, and a small section is given on page 190. The tiny drawings, personal to the child, should be made before the event (as opposed to afterwards in the diary) thus giving some sense of future just as the diary gives a feeling of past (as Mary said, 'Finished-over'). The learning of verb tense, at a later stage, is dependent upon these concepts. If the chart is conscientiously kept then 'yesterday', 'today', 'tomorrow', 'this week', 'last week', 'a long time', 'a very long time', will come to have meaning and also the important time words – 'now', 'every day', 'soon'. Seasons can be marked on the chart and important events such as birthdays, Christmas and Easter.

The obvious place for the chart would seem to be running round the wall of the child's room, but this makes it difficult to add little drawings and write notes. There is something to be said for rolling it up and keeping it in a long narrow box. The unpacking may seem a nuisance but it involves language. 'Let's unpack your *calendar*. Unroll it. Fetch some bricks and put them on that end. Now put some bricks on the other end. Good. Cross off *yesterday*. Show me *today* – that's right, *today* is Tuesday. Granny is coming. Show me *tomorrow* – that will be Wednesday. Granny and Mummy

MONDAY	TUESDAY	WEDNESDAY	THURSDAY	FRIDAY	SATURDAY	SUNDAY
MONDAY 20 swimming	TUESDAY 21	WEDNESDAY 22	THURSDAY 23 dancing class	FRIDAY 24 Jane's holiday begins	SATURDAY 25	SUNDAY 26 easter eggs
MONDAY 27 no swimming	TUESDAY 28 Granny is coming to stay	WEDNESDAY 29	THURSDAY 30 dancing class	FRIDAY 31	APRIL SATURDAY Granny goes	SUNDAY 2
MONDAY 3 swimming	TUESDAY 4	WEDNESDAY 5	THURSDAY 6 dancing class	FRIDAY 7 Jane is having new shoes	SATURDAY 8	SUNDAY 9
MONDAY 10 Swimming	TUESDAY 11 school begins again	WEDNESDAY 12 Put tortoise in garden	THURSDAY 13 dancing class	FRIDAY 14 Charlotte's birthday	SATURDAY 15 Melissa is coming to tea	SUNDAY 16
MONDAY 17 Swimming	TUESDAY 18	WEDNESDAY 19	THURSDAY 20 dancing class	FRIDAY 21 Daddy going in aeroplane	SATURDAY 22	SUNDAY 23

are going shopping. Let's draw them. Now let's roll up the calendar carefully and put it away.'

Parents should also be aware that because they themselves realise when it is morning, afternoon and evening, this is by no means so clear to a hearing-impaired child. They should make it clear to the child what time of day it is and what activities are appropriate to that time of day even if, once again, they have to make a simple chart.* The child should be asked 'When?' questions:

> 'When do you go to school?' (In the morning . . .)
> 'When do you come home from school?'
> 'When does Daddy come home?'
> 'When are you fast asleep in bed?'
> 'When do you have breakfast?'
> 'When do you have supper?'

The big calendar may be used to ask more difficult questions:
> 'When does school start again?'
> 'When is your birthday?'

Even if the child can only point to the day and the mother has to provide the words, this is still a valuable activity.

Some parents attach a good deal of importance to telling the time by the clock. Although this must be learned at some point it can, like reading, be a quite meaningless activity unless it is firmly related to the real happenings appropriate to each hour. The same thing is true of a mechanical recitation of the months or seasons. 'Christmas is in December. December is a long time yet,' has meaning, while a gabbled 'January, February, March, April, May, June . . .' may have no meaning whatsoever.

Once again, many 'When?' questions will have to be asked of the child before he himself asks 'When?' The child who asks 'When?' has progressed a considerable distance in language.

---

* A normal child should be able to reply to the question, 'Is it morning or afternoon?' at five years old. The midday meal is taken as the dividing line (C. W. Valentine, *Intelligence Tests for Children*).

How? Questions

The easiest type of 'How?' question is:

'How do you sharpen a pencil?'
'How do you cut bread?'
'How do you dig a hole?'
'How do you boil water?'

since such questions involve knowing only the agent through which an action is carried out. Young children can learn this. More difficult is:

'How tall is Mary?'
'How long is the road?'
'How much money have you got?'
'How long will you be?'
'How often do you have a swimming lesson?'

These questions involve either knowing a specific length, weight, amount of time or a comparison, like, 'Mary is as tall as I am.' At the level we are discussing, it is not suggested that these questions should be attempted, apart from, of course, 'How old are you?' which should certainly be taught, along with the full name and address of the child.

Hearing Stories

Whatever specific teaching is carried out, the hearing-impaired child should continue to hear stories as part of his daily routine. Some delightful stories such as *Wide-awake Jake* and *Sylvester and the Magic Pebble* (see Appendix 3) contain difficult vocabulary and language, but their basic idea is so enjoyable that they should be told to the child by the method described on page 145. By this time, however, the child's vocabulary and comprehension should be much improved and it should be possible to read him selected stories in the words of the book. Stories should have good illustrations and a simple text. One of the best is again a 'Breakthrough' book in the 'Joke Series': *Shirley Sharpeyes* is dramatic, repetitive and original, and never fails to give infinite pleasure. The book should again be placed on the table with the illustrations covered until the text has been read – the adult becomes amazingly adroit at reading upside down! By this stage many children are able to read and wish to read the book themselves after it has been read to them. It must be ascertained, if necessary by questioning, that he really understands the book before he is allowed to do this. From now onwards, reading and being read to become a valuable source of new vocabulary. *Shirley Sharpeyes*, for instance, simple though it is, contains the descriptive words 'hairy', 'furry' and 'lumpy' and the book should not be put aside before the child observes and feels real objects with these qualities. A list of books that can be read as they stand is given in Appendix 3.

Encouraging Expressive Speech

Much stress has been placed upon the child *understanding* words and ideas since without understanding there can be no progress. It is likely that as a result of the work done with him, the child will now be able to understand far more than he can express and this is a desirable thing since expression grows out of understanding and it is likely that the child is already speaking far more, joining words together and using the words that he has learned. None the less, the child is likely to have difficulty with word sequencing, to leave out words, to make mistakes such as 'I did bought' and to be unable to recall words that he would recognise if they were said by someone else. So great, often, is the hearing-impaired child's difficulty in expressing himself that it is hard to understand what he means to say. There are many ways in which a hearing-impaired child can be helped to express himself more clearly.

1. Pairs of cards and constructing sentences round pictures.

   The child is given a series of about ten names, 'Mummy', 'Daddy' etc., on slips of card and an equal number of familiar pictures. He must select a name and a picture and make up a sentence, like:

   > 'Baby sleeps in a cot.'
   > 'Daddy pushes the lawn-mower.'

   The whole point of this exercise is to make the child think for himself. If he seems stuck he should be asked, 'What do you *do* with a lawn-mower?' (if that is the picture) – 'Yes, you push it. Well, *who* pushes it? Yes, Daddy. Now tell me the whole sentence.' The purpose is defeated if the child simply repeats the adult's thought.

   'What Goes With What?' puzzle dominoes (Abbatt Toys) provide opportunities for this sort of linking though a child cannot be expected, when for him linking requires such hard thought, to get through the whole game at a sitting. DLM make two sets of Motor Expressive cards, the purpose of which is to pair two related objects by constructing a sentence.

It is even harder for a child to look at one picture of a single object and make a sentence about it. When children build these sentences they should be discouraged from repeating the same sentence again and again. One repetition may reinforce the original sentence but when, for instance, 'Daddy pushes the lawn-mower' is said for the third time, the parent should try to question the child to elicit other thoughts, e.g. 'Daddy took the lawn-mower to the shop.'

2. Talking about a picture.

This sounds simple, but is in reality a most difficult task for a child and he may merely enumerate the objects that he sees. The adult should give some help by asking a few questions, and should encourage the child to make sentences about the action, colour, shape, size and number of things seen in the picture.

3. Sequence cards.

Lists of sequence cards in addition to those listed in Appendix 2 are given in Appendix 3. Once again, the child must put these in order and tell the story. By this stage, the adult should ask for more elaboration. For instance, a popular sequence by LDA depicts the story of a cat who, seeing a goldfish in a glass bowl, climbs on to the table, catches the fish, breaks the bowl and disappears. The child should be asked questions about things actually shown in the picture:

> 'Who does the cat belong to?'
> 'Where is the lady?'
> 'Who left the door open?'
> 'What will the lady say when she sees the mess?'
> 'Will the lady know the cat broke the bowl?'
> 'Where has the cat gone?'
> 'When will the cat come home?'
> 'What will the lady say to the cat?'

An activity like this encourages thought, mental agility, imagination and correct sentence construction. Once the pictures have been thoroughly discussed, the child may be helped to assemble his expression if the story is written down for him to first read and then retell.

Look, Think and Write contains numerous stories to tell from pictures. It is intended to stimulate a child to do written work, but it can be done orally. The stories can be cut up to make sequence cards, though this involves sacrificing the story on the back of the page.

Ladybird Easy Reading Books provide further excellent sequencing material. Make sure the child knows the story well, cover the print and ask him to tell the story from the pictures. By this level, the more advanced stories, i.e. Grades II and III may be used.

4. Detection of absurdities.

Children very much enjoy seeing what is wrong with a picture, and verbal adroitness is necessary to explain, for instance, that 'The river is flowing over the bridge instead of under it.' The term 'instead of' is a useful one and indispensable when dealing with the excellent 'What's Wrong?' cards made by LDA. Also useful are the Macdonald 'Zero' series which each contain a page of absurdities, but also other pages to talk about. Some of these pages are a good exercise in future and past tenses. Of the first picture the child is asked, 'What do you think *will* happen to this boy?' On turning over a sequel is given and the child may be asked, 'What *happened* to the boy?'

5. Problem solving.

Because of their inexperience and difficulty with thinking, hearing-impaired children frequently find it hard to see any solution to a simple problem if it is presented in words. Though they are quick to act when they *see* a problem, like bringing a plaster if someone cuts himself, the same problem couched in words defeats them. This is not so much lack of understanding of the words used by the questioner, but a real difficulty in thought. A problem such as 'This little girl is going to be sick. What should we do?' would be easily solved by most normal four-year-old children, but I have seen it defeat hearing-impaired children of six, seven, eight, nine and even ten years old. The simplest way to present such a problem is by persuading a normal child to act it out with high drama. This puts the problem on a slightly symbolic level and seems to get the deaf child's mind moving more quickly than by using a doll.

Situations acted out with simple props and a co-operative child assistant may be as follows:

Charlotte has cut her knee.

Charlotte is going to be sick.

Charlotte's nose is running.

Charlotte's hands are dirty.

Charlotte is very hungry.

Charlotte is tired.

Charlotte is crying.

Charlotte has spilt her tea.

Charlotte has forgotten her school case.

Charlotte feels very cold.

The hearing-impaired child should be encouraged to see that there may be more than one solution to a problem: for example, a cut knee may be washed, it may be bandaged, TCP may be applied or a plaster may be put on.

The next stage is to dispense with the real person and to use dolls but no other props. This takes the problem further from the concrete to the abstract.

The lady has missed the bus.

The boy has a headache.

The little girl has a cold.

There is no food in the house.

The girl's dress has a big hole in it.

The car is running out of petrol.

The girl has no handkerchief.

It is raining hard and Mummy has to go
    to the shops.

The dog has hurt his paw.

The little girl is lost.

The boy's shoe has a hole in it.

The boy hits his sister.

The boy's hair is too long.

The boy's shoes and socks are wet.

The girl has toothache.

The lady has lost her front door key.

The child should be encouraged to make the dolls act, provided he also verbalises the solution, and once again as many solutions as possible should be found. A child who can solve these problems has considerable language and has come some way in overcoming the problems in thinking that beset the hearing-impaired child.

It will be found that, as a result of being exposed to so much verbal material, so many questions and so many discussions, a deaf child has become talkative – sometimes extremely so. He is most unlikely to know all the vocabulary given on the lists, because these are intended to extend further than the work carried out so far. However, he understands much of what is said to him and he wants to reply, and to keep the conversation going by asking questions. This is more than half the battle and the parents should not be too concerned if word order is poor and mistakes are made, like, 'Where you bought it?' or 'Him arm broken.'

The following illustrates the sort of progress that may be made after carrying out a programme based on the procedures described in Chapters 10–17.

Polly (*Audiogram Figure* 15)

Polly's hearing loss – no hearing whatsoever in the right ear and an appreciable loss in the left ear – was diagnosed when she was two years and three months. Polly was fitted first with a body-aid and then, at three years three months, with a powerful post-aural aid. Her audiogram is shown in Figure 15.

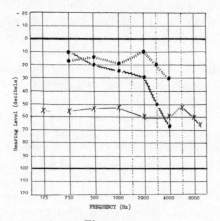

Figure 15

×—× – Left ear with headphone.
•ᴡᴡᴡ• – Free field test using body aid.
•ııı• – Free field test using post-aural aid habitually worn.
    Electrocochleagram revealed no response in right ear.

Because her problem was not diagnosed, Polly received no handling appropriate to a hearing-impaired child as an infant toddler and no special help until she was over three. When first seen in the speech therapy clinic she was four years and four months old and had reached a level of two years and six months in comprehension of speech. Her own speech was sparse, consisting of names of objects and a few phrases, 'Daddy gone to work', 'Mummy orange present'. Polly had no general emotional problems and was an extremely well-behaved girl. She gave the impression, however, that she somehow realised that she was cut off from other people and that she was bewildered and very distressed by this.

Normally, Polly would have received weekly or even twice-weekly speech therapy sessions but before this could be arranged, a change in her father's job resulted in the whole family moving two hundred miles away. Polly and her mother were therefore seen by the speech therapist at roughly three-monthly intervals, usually for a two-hour session. Polly's mother was given a list of ideas for work and loaned material to work with until another visit could be arranged. This schedule was followed for the next three years, the type of programme outlined in Chapters 10–17 being roughly adhered to, but the parents essentially doing the work themselves and also, because of distance, having to supplement the information given to them by using their own initiative. During these years, her parents were successful in teaching Polly to speak and she also became a fluent reader. She received a little professional help with pronunciation, but the basic language work was carried out by her mother.

At seven years and four months it was obvious that Polly was an entirely normal child. On being shown a picture of a wigwam, she remarked, 'That's a tepee. When I was six years old, I would have said "tent" but now I am seven I say "tepee".' Her understanding of speech was appropriate to her age and her own conversation showed a knowledge of all aspects of time, of simple geography, of the books she had read and of the natural wild life existing round her home.

At seven and a quarter years Polly entered a school for normal children. She was one year older than the average age for her class, but needed no supplementary help in learning what was taught.

She mixed well with other children and had become a happy and confident child.

The interesting feature of Polly's story is that, because distance made more regular help impossible, Polly's parents had themselves to develop her speech with only periodic guidance and assistance. That they did so with such success and were rewarded with a normal daughter who spoke so well is a great tribute to their hard work, devotion and resourcefulness. Her parents and speech therapist agreed that had Polly had the benefit of regular sessions with the speech therapist, she might have acquired normal speech a little earlier than she did, but that the difference in time would have been marginal. This is one more indication that while the knowledge and ideas professional people offer are certainly helpful, it is the parent of the hearing-impaired child who is the key factor in his success or failure.

Word Lists

Air

aerodrome	control tower	helicopter	parachute
aeroplane	engine	hovercraft	pilot
aircraft	glider	jet	runway
airport	hanger	journey	

Animals

badger	foal	kid	ram
bat	fox	kitten	rat
calf	fur	lamb	sheep
cat	goldfish	mare	snout
claw	guinea-pig	mice	sow
cow	hamster	mouse	squirrel
cub	hare	otter	tail
deer	hedgehog	paw	tusk
dog	hide	pig	vixen
donkey	hoof	pony	whisker
fawn	horn	puppy	wolf
fin	horse	rabbit	

Bicycle

bell	fork	pump	spokes
brake	handlebar	rear light	tyre
chain	lamp	saddle	wheel
crossbar	pedal	saddle bag	

Birds

beak	claw	goose	robin
bill	cock	gull	sparrow
blackbird	cuckoo	hen	swallow
blue tit	dove	owl	swan
budgerigar	duck	parrot	thrush
canary	duckling	peacock	turkey
chick	feather	pigeon	wing

Body Parts

ankle	finger	lip	skull
arm	flesh	little toe	sole
back	foot (feet)	moustache	spine
beard	forehead	mouth	stomach
big toe	gums	muscle	(tummy)
blood	hair	nail	teeth
bottom	hand	neck	thigh
brain	head	nose	throat
cheek	heart	palm	thumb
chest	heel	pore	toe
chin	hip	rib	tongue
ear	jaw	scalp	tonsil
elbow	joint	shoulder	vein
eye	knee	skeleton	waist
eyebrow	knuckle	skin	wrist
face	leg		

The Car

bonnet	bumper	hand-brake	key
boot	engine	handle	number
brake	gear	headlamp	number plate

The Car – *continued*

pedal	steering wheel	tyre	winking light
roof	switch	wheel	wipers
safety belt	tail light	windscreen	

Christmas

bells	Christmas	decorations	paper chains
carol	pudding	Father	present
carol singers	Christmas	Christmas	reindeer
Christmas card	stocking	holly	sledge
Christmas	Christmas tree	mince pies	turkey
present	cracker	mistletoe	

Clothes, Cosmetics, Personal Possessions and Appearance

anorak	cream	hood	patch
apron	crown	jacket	pattern
belt	cuff	jeans	petticoat
bib	curl	jersey	pinafore
blouse	diary	jumper	pinafore dress
boot	dimple	kilt	pipe
bootees	dot	knot	pleat
bow	dress	lace	plimsolls
bow tie	dressing-gown	ladder	pocket
bracelet	dungarees	lighter	pom-pom
buckle	fan	lipstick	pony tail
button	freckles	locket	pouch
cap	fringe	loop	powder
cape	frock	mac	pullover
cardigan	glasses	medal	purse
check	glove	mittens	pyjamas
cheque book	gown	money	raincoat
cigar	handbag	muff	ribbon
cigarette	handkerchief	nappy	ring
cloak	hat	nightdress	sandals
clog	hearing aid	overall	sash
coat	hem	pants	scarf
collar	high heels	parting	scent

Clothes – continued

shawl	stitches	swim suit	T-shirt
shirt	stocking	tab	tunic
shoe	strap	tag	umbrella
shorts	stripe	tartan	veil
skirt	stud	tassel	vest
sleeve	suit	tie	waistcoat
slipper	suitcase	tights	wallet
sock	sunsuit	trousers	wig
sole	sweater	trunks	wrinkle
spot			

Country and Farm

acorn	farmer	lake	saddle
badger	farmhouse	lane	scarecrow
bank	fence	log	sheep
barley	field	marsh	sheepdog
barn	fleece	meadow	shepherd
barrel	flock	moss	signpost
bee	fold	mountain	snail
beehive	forest	mushroom	spring
blossom	forge	nest	stable
bog	frog	nettle	stall
brook	gate	oats	stile
bull	goat	orchard	stirrup
camp	goose	pasture	straw
chart	hay	peak	stream
chick	haystack	pigsty	stump
churn	hedge	pine	swarm
cock	hedgehog	plough	thatch
coop	hen	pond	toadstool
corn	hen-house	pool	track
cottage	herd	pump	tractor
cowshed	hill	reed	tree
crossroads	hive	rick	trench
crow	horse	ridge	trough
ditch	horseshoe	river	valley
farm	kennel	road	view

Country – continued

village	web	wheat	wood
waterfall	well	windmill	yard

Drinks

beer	coffee	lime juice	ribena
chocolate	coke	milk	water
Coca-Cola	lemonade	orange juice	wine
cocoa	lemon juice		

Fairs and Circuses

acrobat	coconut	lion	swings
band	conjuror	lion tamer	tent
big wheel	elephant	prize	tightrope
box office	fortune teller	ring	tightrope
bugle	gipsy	ringmaster	walker
bumper car	ghost house	roundabout	toffee apple
cage	helter skelter	safety net	trainer
candy floss	hoopla	sawdust	trapeze
caravan	hot dog	stilts	trumpet
clown	juggler	strong man	waxworks

Fairyland

angel	fairy	knight	troll
devil	godmother	magician	unicorn
dragon	ghost	mermaid	wand
dwarf	giant	monster	witch
elf	gnome	ogre	witch's broom
fairy	goblin	sorcerer	wizard

Family

aunt	daughter	husband	sister
baby	father	mother	son
brother	grandma	Mummy	uncle
cousin	grandpa	parents	wife
Daddy			

Food

apple pie	crust	marmalade	sandwiches
bacon	custard	meat	sardines
baked beans	dough	meringue	sausages
batter	doughnut	mince	shepherd's pie
beef	dumpling	muffin	shortbread
beefburgers	egg	mushroom	shrimps
biscuit	fat	mutton	soup
bone	fish	noodles	spaghetti
bread	fish fingers	nut	steak
bun	flour	omelette	stew
butter	gravy	pancakes	sugar
cake	ham	pastry	swiss roll
casserole	hamburger	pepper	syrup
cereal	honey	pie	tart
cheese	hot dogs	plum pudding	tea
cheese spread	ice cream	pork	toast
chicken	icing	porridge	toffee
chip	jam	potatoes	treacle
chocolate	jam tarts	prunes	trifle
pudding	jelly	pudding	tuna fish
chop	ketchup	ravioli	turkey
Christmas cake	kipper	rice	veal
cornflakes	lamb	rice pudding	vinegar
cream	lard	rusk	wedding cake
crisps	liver	salad	yogurt
crumb	loaf	salmon	Yorkshire
crumpet	margarine	salt	pudding

Fruit

apple	fig	orange	raspberry
apricot	gooseberry	peach	rhubarb
banana	grapefruit	pear	strawberry
blackberry	grapes	pineapple	tangerine
cherry	lemon	plum	tomato
dates	melon	prune	

Garden Tools

axe	hose	roller	watering can
broom	lawn-mower	spade	wheelbarrow
fork	rake	trowel	

The Garden

ash	fountain	path	soil
birdbath	grass	paving	spray
bonfire	greenhouse	pebble	sprinkler
border	ground	post	stick
bud	hammock	pot	stone
bush	hosepipe	rockery	terrace
can	ivy	roller	tub
earth	lawn	sandpit	wall
fence	leaf	seed	water lily
flower	manure	shed	weed
flowerbed	mud	shrub	worm

Inside the House, the Home

attic	cellar	loft	sitting-room
basement	cloakroom	loo	(or living-
bathroom	dining-room	(or toilet)	room)
bedroom	kitchen	playroom	

Hall and staircase

banister	hook	latch	stairs
bolt	landing	passage	telephone
chain			

Features of most rooms

bulb	electricity	light	socket
carpet	floor	lino	switch
ceiling	handle (of	mantelpiece	wall
curtains	anything)	plug	window
door	heater	radiator	window-sill
door knob			

Sitting-room

armchair	cushion	picture	stool
ashtray	film	plant	switch
bellows	fire	poker	table
bookcase	fireplace	radio	telephone
carpet	frame	record player	television
chair	lamp	rug	vase
clock	mat	shelf	wallpaper
curtain	photograph	sofa	

Cleaning materials

carpet sweeper	mop	scrubbing	tea towel
cloth	polish	brush	vacuum
duster			

Kitchen

basin	dustpan	mixer	spin dryer
bin	electric cooker	mould	stove
bottle	frying pan	oven	tin
bowl	gas	refrigerator	tin opener
box	iron	rolling pin	toaster
bucket	ironing board	saucepan	tray
cooker	jar	scale	washing-
cupboard	kettle	sink	machine
draining board	lid		

Meal table

china	fork	napkin	saucer
coffee pot	glass	pepper	spoon
cup	jug	place mat	teapot
dish	knife	salt	teaspoon
egg cup	mug		

Bedroom

alarm	blanket	comb	cupboard
bed	brush	cot	drawer
bedcover	chest	cradle	dressing-table

Bedroom – continued

duvet	hot water	mirror	sheet
hanger	bottle	pillow	wardrobe
	mattress		

Dining-room

candlestick	table	tablecloth	trolley
chairs			

Bathroom

bath	pottie	tiles	towel rail
bath mat	shampoo	toilet (loo)	tube of
nail-brush	shower	tooth-brush	toothpaste
pipes	soap	tooth mug	washbasin
plug	sponge	towel	water

Tools

chisel	nail	screw	tack
hammer	saw	screwdriver	vice

Useful objects in the house

basket	envelope	plaster	stamp
battery	glue	postcard	straws
camera	ladder	pram	string
candle	letter	rag	tape recorder
cardboard	matches	rope	tissues
carrycot	newspaper	sellotape	tobacco
comic	oil	sewing	torch
drawing pin	peg	machine	

Sewing box

cotton	pin	tape	thimble
elastic	scissors	tape measure	thread
needle			

Found in the house

bills	dirt	indoors	steam
cobweb	downstairs	rubbish	upstairs
corners	dust	smoke	

Illness and Misfortune

accident	gargle	mumps	sick
aspirin	germ	operation	sling
blister	headache	pain	splint
blood	hiccoughs	patient	splinter
bruise	ill	phlegm	spot
chickenpox	infection	pill	sprain
cough	injection	poison	stethoscope
crutch	jab	pulse	sting
cut	limp	pus	surgery
doctor	lump	rash	swelling
dose	measles	scab	tonsils
faint	medicine	scar	tummy ache

Insects

ant	caterpillar	grasshopper	moth
bee	dragonfly	ladybird	slug
beetle	flea	maggot	spider
bluebottle	fly	midge	wasp
butterfly			

Meals

breakfast	elevenses	picnic	supper
barbecue	lunch	snack	tea
dinner			

Outside the House

bell	drainpipe	gutter	outside
brick	dustbin	knocker	padlock
chimney	garage	moon	paint
cloud	gate	number	path

Outside – continued

porch	sky	spout	sun
putty	slate	star	tile
roof	smoke	steps	wall
scaffolding			

The Park

bench	drinking	notice	see-saw
bowling green	fountain	paddle boat	shelter
branch	duck	park keeper	slide
bridge	flower bed	peacock	swan
cafe	grass	pond	swing
conker	lake	railings	tennis court
deer	litter	roundabout	turf
dog dirt	litter basket	seat	waterfall
drake	maze		

People

actor	cashier	lollipop man	sailor
actress	chauffeur	man	Santa Claus
archer	child	men	soldier
bachelor	children	milkman	sweeper
baddie	cook	nun	tailor
baker	dentist	nurse	teacher
beggar	doctor	page	thief
blindman	driver	painter	toddler
boy	dustman	paper boy	traffic warden
bricklayer	garageman	parson	tramp
bride	gipsy	pilot	twin
bridegroom	girl	pirate	waiter
bridesmaid	greengrocer	plumber	widow
builder	grown up	policeman	window
burglar	hairdresser	postman	cleaner
butcher	jockey	prince	woman
captain	king	princess	workman
carpenter	lady	queen	

Plants and Flowers

blossom	daffodil	lavender	snowdrop
bluebell	daisy	poppy	thistle
buttercup	dandelion	rose	tulip
crocus	holly		

Railway and Station

barrier	footbridge	newspaper	sleeper
bridge	goods train	stall	slot machine
buffers	green flag	oil	station
carriage	guard	overhead	station clock
cloak room	guard's van	wires	station master
coach	left luggage	passenger	subway
compartment	office	points	suitcase
corridor	level	porter	ticket
diesel engine	crossing	rack	ticket
electric engine	luggage	railway line	collector
embankment	luggage rack	red flag	train
engine	luggage van	seat	truck
engine driver	mail	siding	trunk
express	mail bag	signal	tunnel
fare	mail van	signal box	turntable

Reptiles

adder	crocodile	tortoise	viper
alligator	snake	turtle	

Seaside and Boats

anchor	buoy	crab	fishing rod
bandstand	cabin	crane	foam
barge	canal	deck	funnel
bay	canoe	deckchair	harbour
beach	captain	dock	island
boat	cargo	dolphin	jelly fish
breakers	cave	fish	jetty
breakwater	channel	fisherman	keel
bucket	cliff	fishing line	lifeboat

Seaside – *continued*

lighthouse	quay	seaweed	submarine
limpet	raft	shark	tide
lobster	rigging	shell	trawler
mast	rock	shingle	vessel
navy	rowing boat	ship	voyage
net	sail	shoal	wave
oars	sailors	shore	whale
ocean	sand	shrimp	wharf
octopus	sandcastle	spade	wreck
pier	sand pie	starfish	yacht
port	sea	steamer	

School

absent	desk	mark	piano
address	dictation	master	playground
answer	division	maths	playtime
arithmetic	dot	message	plus
art	exercise	minus	poem
atlas	figure	miss	point
attention	form	mistake	prize
badge	friend	model	pupil
ballpoint	girl guide	music	reading book
blackboard	globe	nature	recite
board	grace	nib	recorder
book	handwork	nonsense	register
boy scout	headmaster	nought	report
chalk	headmistress	number	rhyme
champion	hockey	order	rubber
chart	holiday	pad	ruler
charter	hymn	page	question
class	ink	pageant	satchel
clay	length	paint	sir
cloakroom	lessons	paper	space
concert	letters	paste	spelling
crayon	line	peg	stage
cross	list	pen	story
dance	map	pencil	studio

School – continued

sum	term	time-table	violin
surname	test	total	width
tambourine	tick	tune	word
teacher	time	verse	world
team			

Shape Words

circle	half-moon	oval	star
cross	heart	round	triangle
diamond	oblong	square	

Shops

baker's shop	fish shop	parcel	shopkeeper
butcher's shop	flower shop	pet shop	stationer
chemist	greengrocer	price	supermarket
counter	grocer	self service	sweet shop
customer	ironmonger	store	till
department	jeweller	shoe shop	toyshop
store	newsagent		

Street and Town

archway	cover	grit	palace
bank	crane	gutter	pavement
bar	crowd	hospital	petrol pump
beacon	drain	hotel	pole
bridge	exit	houses	police station
bungalow	factory	keep left sign	post
bus stop	fete	kerb	poster
cafe	fire station	lamp post	post office
castle	flag	letter-box	prison
cathedral	flats	library	procession
chapel	gaol	lift	pub
church	garage	litter bin	public lavatory
cinema	gasworks	market	puddle
cobbles	grating	museum	queue
corner	graveyard	office	railway station

Street – continued

red lamp	shops	supermarket	town hall
road	sign	tar	traffic
road sign	slope	telegraph pole	traffic lights
ruin	slot	telephone box	turret
sack	spire	theatre	weathercock
school	statue	tower	zebra crossing
shelter			

Sweets

chocolate	liquorice	mint	toffee
gum	lollipop	smarties	

Swimming Pool

arm bands	float	life guard	shower
changing room	footbath	locker	swimming
cubicle	goggles	mask	teacher
diving board	hair dryer	pool	wire basket
flippers	lifebelt	rubber ring	wringer

Toys, Play, Entertainment

ark	chief	film	Lego
arrow	cog	football	ludo
ball	cowboy	game	magnet
balloon	cricket	goal	marble
bat	crown	golliwog	mask
battle	dagger	guard	model
bead	dice	guitar	net
block	die	gun	ogre
boat	doll	helmet	pad
bomb	doll's house	hide and seek	party
bubble	dominoes	hoop	patrol
bubble pipe	draughts	hopscotch	pedal car
camp	dressing-up	jigsaw puzzle	piggy back
cannon	clothes	kite	pilot
card	drum	knight	pirate
chess	elf	leapfrog	pistol

Toys – continued

pitch	riddle	shield	team
plan	rifle	skipping rope	teddy
propeller	robber	sledge	tennis
Punch and	rocket	slide	tent
Judy	rocking horse	soldiers	toboggan
puppet	rod	somersault	top
racquet	rugger	space	tricycle
raid	scabbard	spade	trigger
rattle	scooter	sparkler	wagon
record	set	sword	weapon
Red Indian	sheriff	tank	wig-wam

Vegetables

bean	corn on	mushroom	pumpkin
beetroot	the cob	onion	radish
cabbage	cucumber	parsley	spinach
carrot	leeks	peas	sprouts
cauliflower	lettuce	potatoes	turnip
celery	marrow		

Vehicles

ambulance	cart	mail van	taxi
barrow	coach	milk float	tractor
bicycle	dustcart	motor bike	trailer
bulldozer	fire engine	motor scooter	transporter
bus	furniture van	police car	tricycle
car	ice cream van	post office van	truck
caravan	jeep	push chair	van
carriage	lorry	tanker	wagon

Weather Words

breeze	gale	rainbow	snowball
damp	hail	raindrop	snowflake
dull	ice	shower	snowman
flood	lightning	sleet	storm
fog	mist	slush	sunshine
frost	rain	snow	

What Things Are Made Of

brass	glass	plastic	stone
brick	gold	putty	straw
canvas	iron	rubber	tin
cement	lead	satin	velvet
clay	leather	silk	wax
copper	linen	silver	wicker
cork	metal	skin	wood
cotton	mortar	slate	wool
fur	paper	steel	zinc

Wild Creatures at the Zoo

alligator	elephant	monkey	sea-lion
bear	giraffe	ostrich	snake
beast	gorilla	panda	stork
buffalo	hippo	parrot	tiger
cage	hump	pelican	trunk
camel	kangaroo	penguin	turtle
chimpanzee	keeper	polar bear	walrus
crocodile	leopard	rhino	wolf
deer	lion	seal	zoo
eagle			

Time, Days, Seasons

afternoon	day	in the morning	month
always	December	January	morning
April	diary	July	never
at once	dusk	June	New Year
August	early	last week	next week
autumn	Easter	late	night
beginning	end	later	noon
big hand	evening	little hand	November
birthday	every	March	now
calendar	February	May	o'clock
Christmas	fortnight	midday	October
clock	Friday	midnight	often
date	half past	minute	past
dawn	hour	Monday	quarter past

Time – continued

quarter to	spring	time	watch
Saturday	summer	to	Wednesday
second	Sunday	today	week
September	sunrise	tomorrow	winter
sometimes	sunset	tonight	year
soon	Thursday	Tuesday	yesterday

Numbers

one	eight	fifteen	second
two	nine	sixteen	third
three	ten	seventeen	fourth
four	eleven	eighteen	fifth
five	twelve	nineteen	sixth
six	thirteen	twenty	seventh
seven	fourteen	first	eighth etc.

Positional Words

about	behind	into	round
above	below	near	through
across	beside	next to	to
after	between	of	together
against	by	off	towards
along	down	on	under
among	for	onto	up
around	from	out	upon
at	in	outside	with
away	in front of	over	without
before	inside		

Quantifiers

all	even	lot	only
another	every	many	pair
any	extra	more	quarter
both	few	most	several
couple	first	much	single
dozen	half	no	some
each	last	odd	whole
enough	less		

Amount Words – often followed by 'of'

a bag of	a bundle of	a heap of	a pile of
a basket of	a crowd of	a load of	a plate of
a bit of	a cup of	a lump of	plenty of
a bowl of	a drop of	a mouthful of	a pot of
a box of	a glass of	a packet of	a row of
a bucket of	a group of	a pair of	a scrap of
a bunch of	a handful of	a piece of	a spoonful of

Descriptive Words

afraid	brave	dry	funny
again	bright	dull	furious
ago	broken	dumb	gay
alive	burst	eager	gentle
almost	calm	early	gigantic
alone	careful	easy	glad
already	chapped	else	golden
also	cheap	empty	good
always	chilly	engaged	greasy
annoyed	clean	excited	great
ashamed	close	even	greedy
asleep	cold	ever	handsome
awake	cool	evil	happy
back to front	crooked	faint	hard
backwards	cross	fair	high
bad	curious	fairly	horrible
bald	curly	false	hot
bare	curved	far	hungry
beautiful	dangerous	fast	icy
best	dark	fat	indoors
better	dead	fierce	inside
big	deaf	fine	inside out
bitter	dear	flat	instead
blank	deceitful	forwards	interesting
blind	deep	free	jealous
blunt	different	fresh	just
boggy	dim	frightened	keen
bored	dirty	friendly	large
bottom	disappointed	full	late

Descriptive Words – continued

lazy	pale	shallow	swift
left	past	sharp	tall
light	peaceful	shiny	tame
little	perhaps	short	tangled
long	plain	shrill	tender
lose	pleased	shrunken	terrible
lost	plump	shy	thick
lovely	polite	sideways	thirsty
low	poor	silly	tidy
lucky	pop	simple	tight
mad	pretty	slack	timid
magic	proud	slim	tiny
main	public	small	tired
mean	queer	smart	too
melted	quick	smooth	tough
middle	quiet	soft	true
middle-sized	quite	soon	ugly
miserable	rapid	sore	upset
much	rare	sorry	upside down
muddy	raw	sour	upwards
narrow	ready	south	vague
nasty	real	special	vain
naughty	rich	stale	very
nearly	right	steady	warm
neat	right side out	steep	weary
never	right way up	stiff	wet
new	ripe	still	wicked
next	rough	stout	wide
nice	royal	straight	wild
north	rude	strange	wise
now	rusty	strict	wooden
numb	sad	strong	worse
odd	safe	stupid	wrong
old	same	such	wrong side out
once	scared	sudden	yet
open	selfish	super	young
other	sensible	surprised	zig-zag
outdoors	shabby	sweet	

Less Tangible, Non-Concrete Words

age	footsteps	neighbour	someone
anybody	friend	nobody	something
anyone	fright	noise	somewhere
anything	frown	nonsense	sort
anywhere	fuss	no one	sound
bang	game	nothing	spanking
birthday	gap	nowhere	spark
blank	gift	opening	speech
breath	help	peace and	splash
bump	hole	quiet	step (a step)
christening	hurry	pest	story
corner	(in a hurry)	pet	surface
cost	idea	place	temper
crack	invitation	plan	thing
crash	itch	price	thud
danger	job	punishment	thump
disobedient	joke	question	time
dream	jolt	reflection	treasure
Easter	kiss	rest	treat
echo	knock	scream	trick
edge	lap	secret	trouble
end	look	shade	truth
everybody	(have a look)	shadow	untruth
everyone	luck	shock	visit
everything	manners	side	visitor
everywhere	mark	size	voice
expensive	matter	sleep (asleep)	weekend
fib	mess	smack	wish
fight	mistake	smell	word
fool	mouthful	smile	work
footprints	name	somebody	yawn

Action Words

*add	arrest	*bark	*beat
act	*ask	*bath	become
allow	*bake	*bathe	*bcg
argue	*balance	be	begin

(219)

Action Words – continued

behave	*chase	*cycle	*fish
believe	chat	dance	fit
*bend	cheat	dash	fix
*bite	check	decide	flap
bleed	cheer	*decorate	flash
block	chew	dial	*float
blot	chime	die	*fly
blow	chip	*dig	fold
blush	choke	dip	*follow
boil	*choose	*dive	forget
bolt	chop	do	freeze
borrow	christen	*drag	gargle
*bounce	*clap	*draw	gather
bow	clash	dream	get
bowl	clean	*dress	*get up
*break	clear	*drink	give
breathe	clear up	*drive	glad
*bring	*climb	*drop	go
*brush	clip	drown	grab
*buckle	*close	*dry	grin
*build	collect	earn	grip
*bump	*colour	*eat	grow
*buoy	*comb	escape	guard
burn	come	expect	guess
burst	*cook	expel	gulp
bury	*copy	explain	halt
*button	cough	faint	*hang
call	count	*fall	happen
can	cover	*feed	hatch
capture	crack	feel	hate
care	*crash	fetch	have
*carry	*crawl	*fight	hear
carve	*cross	fill	*help
*catch	crush	find	*hide
change	*cry	finish	hiss
charge	*cut	fire	*hit

* Illustrated by the materials listed on page 184.

Actions Words – continued

*hold	*lick	peck	rain
hoot	*lie	peel	rattle
*hop	*lift	peep	*reach
hope	like	*pick	*read
*howl	limp	*pick up	reap
*hug	listen	pinch	remember
hum	live	*plant	rescue
hunt	load	*play	rest
hurry	lock	plough	return
hurt	*look	poach	*ride
ice	lose	*point	ring
imagine	love	poison	rinse
*iron	*make	poke	rise
jerk	march	polish	roar
jig	marry	pop	roast
jog	mash	*post	rob
join	mean	pounce	rock
*jump	measure	*pour	*roll
keep	meet	practise	row
*kick	*melt	pray	rub
kill	*mend	press	*run
*kiss	might	pretend	sail
*kneel	miss	prick	save
*knit	*mix	promise	saw
*knock	move	prop	say
*knot	need	puff	scald
know	notice	*pull	scold
land	*open	punch	scramble
*laugh	pack	punish	scratch
*lay	pad	purr	scream
lead	*paddle	*push	*scribble
leak	*paint	*put	*scrub
*lean	pass	*put in	see
*leap	*paste	*put on	*sell
learn	pat	quack	send
leave	patter	quarrel	set
let	*pay	race	*sew

Action Words – continued

*shake	sneeze	study	twist
share	sniff	suck	type
shave	snore	suppose	unbolt
shine	soak	swallow	unbutton
*shiver	sob	*sweep	uncover
shoot	speak	*swim	understand
*shop	spell	*swing	undress
*shout	spend	switch	unload
show	*spill	tackle	unlock
shriek	spin	take	unpack
shrink	spit	*take out	unpin
shrug	*splash	*talk	unroll
shuffle	split	tap	untie
*shut	spoil	taste	*unwrap
sigh	spread	teach	upset
*sing	sprinkle	tease	use
sink	squash	tell	vanish
sip	squeak	thank	varnish
*sit	squeeze	think	visit
*skate	stack	throb	*wag
*ski	stagger	*throw	wait
skid	stamp	*tie	wake
*skip	*stand	tinkle	*wake up
slap	*stare	tip	*walk
*sleep	start	*toast	wander
*slide	starve	toot	want
slip	stay	toss	*wash
slit	steady	touch	*wash up
slop	steal	trap	waste
smack	steer	travel	*watch
smash	step	trip up	*wave
smell	stick	trot	wear
*smile	*stir	try	weave
*smoke	stop	tuck	*weigh
smother	stretch	*tug	welcome
smoulder	strike	*tumble	whine
snatch	stroke	turn	whisper

Action Words – continued

whistle	wipe	worry	*write
win	wish	wrap	yawn
wind	work	wring	*zip
wink			

Question Words

how?	when?	which?	why?
what?	where?	who?	

18

Widening Verbal Skills

As we see from the example of Polly at the end of the last chapter, a child who has covered the work outlined so far may understand speech so well and speak so normally that he has caught up with his contemporaries and can henceforth learn the things that they learn at a normal age. Whether or not he has done so depends upon the many factors described in Chapter 5. What is more likely is that the child will have made a great deal of progress, but will still have many things to learn and a great deal more progress to make before he has caught up with his hearing peers.

One problem is likely to be incorrect sentence formation. When a child is talking a great deal and asking many questions, parents are often concerned because word order in sentences is poor and the child makes many errors in sentence construction. 'I went to Ann house. I play she doll. I go again tomorrow. When you go Ann house?' There are difficulties with pronouns and possessive adjectives, question forms and, above all, with verb tense. There are also difficulties with apostrophe 's', negative forms, plural forms of nouns and the use of 'is' and 'are'. The cure for some of these difficulties is conversation and more conversation with other people. We all of us learn language patterns by listening to the mass of language fed to us by other people. Once a hearing-impaired child is listening and lip-reading effectively, he will correct many of his errors, though this will take time. If he is obviously struggling to couch a question in words, he should be helped by having the question written down. We say, for instance, 'He swims every day' but the associated question is '*Does* he *swim* every day?' and the negative reply 'He *doesn't swim* every day.' These variations are difficult to grasp, as are complicated questions like 'Why can't we go when you said before that we could?' They may become clearer when the visual form is seen.

Some errors of sentence formation persist because even when the child lip-reads well and listens effectively, the 's' sound is still not heard or not heard clearly and is quite difficult to see. Further, the hearing-impaired child lacks general experience of the language pattern. We do not expect a tiny hearing child to have mastered such forms as:

> He run*s* fast.
> He goe*s* to school.
> She *is* cooking.
> One flower, two flower*s*.
> Doe*s* he swim?
> Ann'*s* house.

which depend upon the correct insertion of 's', and similarly, the older deaf child lacks the experience to use them. Difficulties are added to if the child has no ability to make the 's' sound himself. If the child can hear the 's' sound at all, training the ear specifically in relation to these things may help. Make it clear that 'He go to school' is wrong and 'He goes to school' is right.

Ask the child to detect 'right' or 'wrong' when sentences are said each way:

> He go to school – wrong!
> He go to school – wrong!
> He goes to school – right!
> He go to school – wrong!
> He goes to school – right!

Children who can't hear 's', or hear it very faintly, are dependent upon the written form, since writing 's' correctly helps to get it right in speech. Trained teachers of the deaf have many techniques by which they help children with these problems, but not all hearing-impaired children are lucky enough to have this specialised help. All written work done by the child and corrected by an adult is helpful, and once the child is able to write fluently, he should write his daily diary himself, and the parent should correct his errors.

Plural forms are easier than verb forms containing 's' and it is simple to draw pictures of 'one cat', 'two cats', 'one dog', 'three dogs', etc. Philip & Tacey make some matching sets to help to teach more difficult plural forms ('one church', 'two church*es*') and irregular forms ('one mouse', 'two mice').

Certain measures can be taken to help the child to use 'his' and 'her' correctly. A boy and girl may be drawn and labelled as shown

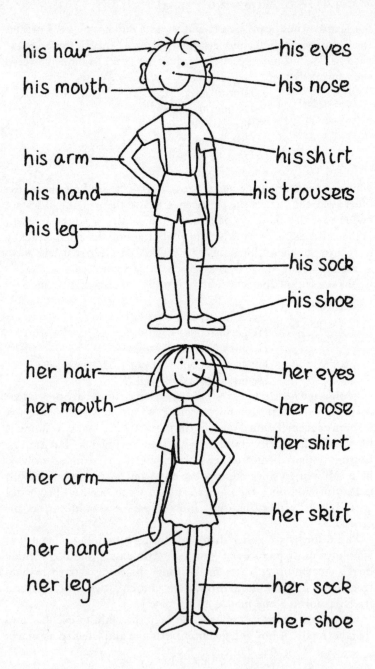

his hair — his eyes
his mouth — his nose
his arm — his shirt
his hand — his trousers
his leg
his sock
his shoe

her hair — her eyes
her mouth — her nose
her shirt
her arm
her skirt
her hand
her leg
her sock
her shoe

him

her

them

on page 226 and the child points to boy, girl and himself in turn, saying, 'his hair', 'her hair', 'my hair', etc.

Actions by boy and girl dolls introduce 'his' and 'her' into sentences. The boy can be made to scratch his head, touch his toes, clap his hands while the child says, '*He* is scratching *his* head', '*He* is touching *his* toes', etc.

The girl then does actions. Even more complicated are actions involving both dolls: for example, '*He* is treading on *her* toes', '*She* is pulling *his* hair'.

Counters may be laid on the sort of pictures drawn on this page while the child says:

'I am giving a red counter to *him*.'
'I am giving a blue counter to *her*.'
'I am giving a yellow counter to *them*.'
'I am giving a green counter to *you*.'

Then, pointing to the counters:

'This one is *his*.'
'This one is *hers*.'
'This one is *theirs*.'
'This one is *yours*.'

(227)

The irregular past tense is confusing because we ask:

> 'Did you *buy* so-and-so?'
> 'When *did* you *go*?'
> 'Where *did* you *find* it?'

and yet the replies are:

> 'I *bought* it' or 'I *didn't buy* it'
> 'I *went*' or 'I *didn't go*'
> 'I *found*' or 'I *didn't find*'

Deaf children find it easy to absorb the oft-used 'I went', 'I found', but not unnaturally then ask 'Where you found?' or 'Where did you found?' They also use negative forms such as 'I not found', 'I not go'. Sometimes the less used past tense forms elude them, so they fall back on a form used by young normal children: 'I did drink my milk' or 'I did hurt my knee.'

A list of common irregular past tense forms is given on page 229. It is helpful to make one picture card for each verb and to write a short sentence in the past tense on the back of the card:

> 'He *bent* his ruler.'
> 'She *bit* the apple.'
> 'She *blew* out her candles.'
> 'Her knee *bled*.'

A card is held up, picture towards the child and the adult says, 'Today he is bending his ruler.' The child responds, 'Yesterday he *bent* his ruler.' The adult then turns his card round so that the spoken word is reinforced by seeing the written sentence. On a second time round with the cards, the adult may ask a fake question, for example, 'Did he bend his pencil?' The child may reply with either a positive or a negative sentence as he wishes. Often he demands, after practice, to be the one to hold the card and to ask the question. Children seem to enjoy this activity or one would not burden them with it, and even if they still do not always remember to use the correct form in speech, they at least feel reassured that it is more accessible to them.*

---

* English is made more complicated by having a past participle as well as a past tense, e.g. 'I *began* to do it' (past tense), 'I have *begun* to do it' (past participle).

(228)

Past Tenses of Common Irregular Verbs

am	— was		do	— did
beat	— beat		draw	— drew
begin	— began		drink	— drank
bend	— bent		drive	— drove
bite	— bit		eat	— ate
bleed	— bled		feel	— felt
blow	— blew		fight	— fought
break	— broke		fly	— flew
bring	— brought		forget	— forgot
build	— built		freeze	— froze
buy	— bought		get	— got
catch	— caught		grow	— grew
choose	— chose		hear	— heard
come	— came		hide	— hid
creep	— crept		hurt	— hurt
cut	— cut		keep	— kept
dig	— dug			

The regular past is difficult, e.g.

> I skipp*ed*
> I hopp*ed*
> I walk*ed*
> I wash*ed*
> I play*ed*
> I look*ed*

because the vital 'ed' is not heard at all or heard very imperfectly by hearing-impaired children. Written work is again helpful and *The Hop, Skip and Jump Book* (see Appendix 3) may again be used. The adult looks at a picture with the child and asks a real or fake question using the past tense, like 'Did the dog bite the little boy?' The child may either reply, 'No, the dog *didn't bite* the little boy' or 'The dog *licked* the little boy.' Once again the child should be encouraged to become the questioner.

To encourage understanding of the future, a footnote may be added to each day's entry in the diary: 'Tomorrow I am going to Ann's house for tea. I will wear my new dress.'

The 'Read, Write and Remember' series of eight inexpensive

small books is extremely helpful, both in promoting reading comprehension and in straightening out sentence construction. Very simple pictures are shown about which questions are asked:

'Have you had a birthday cake?'
'Did it have candles on it?'
'How many candles has this cake got on it?'
'What colour are the candles on the cake?'
'Are candles made of wax?'
'Can you blow out candles?'
'How many candles are not on the cake?'
'How many candles are lit?'
'How many candles can you see altogether?'

The child must both interpret the questions and couch the replies correctly. As can be seen, there is, even in one set of questions, practice of verb tense, a negative form, singular and plural forms. If a child is too young to write fluently, the work may be done orally. Five-and-a-half-year-old Catherine, for instance, was a proficient reader but needed practice in both reading comprehension and sentence formation. Her ability to control a pencil was still (not surprisingly at her age) immature and the writing of even one answer would have taken a considerable time. 'Read, Write and Remember' was therefore done orally and, since Catherine was able to make an 's' sound, all 's' forms were beautifully said; a quite dramatic improvement of sentence construction in everyday speech resulted. An older child who is able to write more fluently may write the replies. Many types of English workbook are also very helpful at this stage. Particularly recommended are Wheaton's Workbooks in Primary English (see Appendix 4). An older child who can write loves to fill in the replies, but it is as well to rehearse these orally before writing so that material is retained. Weak spots in knowledge and comprehension become visible to adults and with ingenuity it is possible to improvise extra work on these. *Better English* by Ronald Ridout (see Appendix 4) is also useful. The Macdonald book *Sentences* which contains many questions and is intended to help the child to interpret these, to think and to answer orally, is once again helpful. Less formal than other books mentioned, it offers a quite different type of verbal experience.

I am aware that this has been a very brief glance at the difficulties in sentence formation experienced by hearing-impaired children. An entire book could easily be written only about these. However, what has been said will, I hope, serve to give parents a little insight into the source of some of the major difficulties and their possible remedies.

At this stage of language development, when the child will be speaking so much more, the difficulties mentioned in Chapter 2 become much more noticeable. The parent may notice, for instance, repeated questioning by the child about something that the parent had felt was clear, lack of imagination, lack of ability to see a word or situation in more than one way, lack of general knowledge. The following exercises are designed to help the child to think, to use language in a flexible way, or to use his imagination. From now on, it becomes increasingly difficult to separate verbal comprehension, verbal expression and use of the thought processes. Though some exercises obviously encourage one, rather than another of these things, most of them involve several processes.

Homonyms and Homophones

A homonym is a word with two different meanings, e.g.

> bark – the noise a dog makes
> bark – the outer covering of a tree

A homophone is two words that sound the same but are spelt differently and have different meanings, e.g.

> 'We will *raise* the table.'
> 'The *rays* of the sun are hot.'

Learning Development Aids make a set of homonym and homophone cards entitled 'Sound the Same'.

Developmental Learning Materials make a box each of Homonym Cards and Homophone Cards.* One card is given to the child and he is asked to think of another meaning of the word. This is, of course, much more difficult in the case of homophones, since the child cannot rely on the spelling to give him a clue. Parents may think of homonyms and homophones themselves. At this stage

---

* Several of the pairs of cards refer either to American vocabulary ('sent' and 'cent') or American pronunciation ('ant' and 'aunt') but the sets are none the less useful.

there may be no need to draw; words may simply be written on cards like this:

He *blew* out his candles   Her dress is *blue*

Hearing-impaired children think in a rigid way. They may know that an elephant has a *trunk* and that a *trunk* is a piece of luggage, but keep the two in separate compartments in their minds. This work is excellent for promoting mental flexibility and agility. A game may be played in which the adult gives verbal clues and the child guesses the answer, for example, 'I am thinking of a word that means two and a fruit' (pair and pear). If the child can give clues himself, this is excellent practice in word definition.

Describing Objects

Since hearing-impaired children find mental ordering of material difficult, they need definite guidelines to help them to describe objects at first. The following questions should be written down for the child to follow in describing an object:

What shape is it?
What size is it?
What colour is it?
What weight is it?
How does it feel?
What is it made of?
What do you do with it?

To begin with, a child may have actually to see the object he is describing and familiar objects of simple shape should be chosen (a ball, a ruler, a comb, a pen, a needle, a pencil box, an egg). As he becomes more adept, the child may be asked to describe objects without looking at them.

Word Definitions

Describing objects may help a child with word definitions, which hearing-impaired children find very difficult. A child may be asked, for instance, 'What is a table?' and be quite unable to reply. The fact that he is actually sitting at a table is no help whatsoever! Naming words are the easiest to define, and one of the simplest ways to define, if not by description, is by use, as in, 'A table is to eat off!' This involves a connection between the object and what is done with it, which is what a hearing-impaired child finds hard to make initially. To begin with, a child should be asked to define everyday objects – a chair, a bed, a dog, a cup, a comb, a garden, etc. Later he may be asked to define simple descriptive words:

> What does hot mean?
>
> What does cold mean?

'The fire is hot' is an acceptable definition. 'Hot is very warm' would be even better, but not to be expected without considerable practice. LDA's 'Description' may be used again at this stage and the child encouraged to produce two related ideas about each picture, for example:

> The man is fat; he has eaten a lot.
>
> The boy is dirty; he played in the mud.
>
> The freezer is cold; it is icy.

This again helps richness and flexibility of thought.

Categorisation

It has already been said that hearing-impaired children find this difficult, though previous training suggested in this book should make it somewhat easier. The child may be asked to think of as many things as possible in the following categories:

birds	food	seasons
body parts	fruit	shapes
boy's names	furniture	shops
buildings	garden tools	story titles
clothes	girl's names	tame animals
colours	insects	tools
days of the week	materials	vegetables
drinks	months	weather
flowers	people's jobs	wild animals

Parents may think of additional groups.

Some children enjoy the challenge of thinking of words, but if the going is slow, a limited number in any one category may be asked for. To reverse the process, the child may be asked:

> What is a dog?   (an animal)
>
> What is July?   (a month)
>
> What is a table?   (furniture)

This is a higher level of definition than by use or description, but definition by use or description is important and should be taught before description by category.

The child may also be asked how many things he can think of that:

climb	hiss	run	smoke
cut	melt	shine	spin
flash	pinch	shoot	swim
float	prick	sink	turn
fly	roll		

and how many things he can think of that are:

cold	hard	rough	sweet
crooked	high	sharp	tall
curved	hot	shiny	thick
dark	little	smooth	ugly
deep	long	soft	wet
dirty	old	stiff	wooden
flat	pretty	straight	young
funny	quick	strong	

Talking about Something Interesting

A child himself is often currently very interested in something. Sometimes interests are rather rigid so that the same topic is always raised for discussion. Other hearing-impaired children really are interested in many different things; as Felicity would volunteer at ten years old, 'I want to talk about dogs today' or 'I want to talk about the country.' If the child has no particular ideas, the adult should be ready with some topic and it helps if the real thing can be produced – a coconut, a branch of blossom, a ladybird, a Jubilee coin, any sort of animal. Adult and child should try to explore the topic verbally, the adult asking questions, encouraging the child to do so and making the conversation as interesting and lively as possible.

General Knowledge and Vocabulary

The Macdonald 'Starter Books' are full of interesting materials, well illustrated, and again lead to interesting conversation. All the books by Edwards and Gibbon in the 'Words Your Children Use' series (listed in Appendix 3) can now be read as they stand and are full of information. It is often useful at this stage to use the book in the series entitled *Listening* and to demonstrate to the child the various sounds discussed. Though one might suppose a hearing-impaired child would have no appreciation of these sounds, this is far from the case and I have never undertaken this project without finding the child fascinated by it.

Parts of Objects

As the child's language becomes more sophisticated he needs to know the names of parts of objects. The following objects and their parts can be cut out of a catalogue or easily drawn:

Coat	*Chair*	*Door*	*Book*
collar	back	frame	colour
lapel	seat	knob	title
button hole	legs	panel	pages
button		hinge	margin
sleeve			
cuff			
belt			
buckle			
pocket			

Tree	*Telephone*	*Egg*	*Orange*
leaves	receiver	shell	rind
branches	dial	white	pith
trunk	flex	yolk	pips
root			
fork			
twig			

Clock	*Window*	*Gun*	*Candle*
face	frame	handle	wick
hands	pane	trigger	flame
	catch	holster	wax
	sill	barrel	

Boat	*Lamp*	*Chest*	*Flower*
sail	bulb	drawer	petals
mast	switch	knob	centre
anchor	shade	keyhole	stem or
chain	flex	foot	stalk
rudder	plug		leaf

Hat	*Apple*	*Shoe*	*Eye*
crown	peel	tongue	lash
brim	stalk	lace	lid
band	pips	heel	white
	core	sole	iris
			pupil

Bottle	*Finger*	*Cage*
cork	nail	hook
neck	knuckle	bars
label		perch

A good exercise in comprehension is then to ask the following type of question:

'What do you call the part of the kettle that the water comes out of?'

'What do you call the yellow part of an egg?'

'What do you call the part of the telephone that you turn round with your finger?'

There is also an opportunity for riddles:

'What has legs but can't walk?'

'What has a trunk but isn't an elephant?'

'What kind of pupil doesn't go to school?'

'What has teeth but can't bite?'

'What has a foot but no toes?'

'What has a crown but isn't a king?'

'What has a tongue but can't talk?'

'What never washes its own hands and face?'

This again promotes mental flexibility – a different way of 'seeing' the same word.

Box of Mixed Objects

This is an exercise for quick comprehension and one which again encourages flexible thinking. One type of question should be unlike the next, so that the child must constantly be on the alert. A shoe box is filled with a variety of objects – long and short coloured pencils, string, thread, small toy animals, doll's furniture, doll's cutlery and crockery, bricks of various shapes, sizes and colours, toy scissors, miniature objects of all sorts. The objects are spread out on the table, not grouped or sorted in any way. The child is then asked the following type of question:

'Which is the longest thing on the table? Tell me something not on the table which is longer than that.' (Here the table will probably have to be covered with a cloth because children tend to stare hopefully at the table rather than *thinking*.)

'Find me something made of plastic. Tell me six other things, not on the table, that are made of plastic.'

'Which is thicker, cotton or string? Tell me something thicker than string.'

'Tell me something thinner than the straw.'

'Find me something you could sit on if it was real. Tell me six other things you could sit on.'

'Find the toy cat. How would she feel if she was real?'

'Touch all the green things on the table.'

'Put all the green things except the frog into the box.' (*Except* is a quite difficult idea.)

'Put all the toy furniture at the *far end* of the shoe box.'

'Show me the bed. Tell me six other things you would put in a bedroom.'

'Put two small red bricks on top of a green brick and give me a blue brick.'

'Which animals would be dangerous if they were real?'

A Further Exercise to Improve Comprehension

This exercise helps to strengthen knowledge of ordinal numbers and also the previously learned words 'top', 'bottom', 'side', 'upside down', 'next to', 'front', 'back', 'full' and 'empty'. However, this is a very difficult exercise and requires a thorough knowledge of the words before it is attempted.

Sainsbury's pack their dried herbs in transparent plastic jars.

Eight of these jars should be obtained and, if possible, the flat, cardboard holder in which they are displayed in the shop. Pictures should be stuck on some of the lids, bottoms and sides of the jars. Thus one pot may have three pictures on, some two pictures, some one and some none at all. Some of the pots are filled with buttons, rice, dried peas, etc. The pots are placed on their flat cardboard stand (which consists of four holes in the back row and four in the front) or, if there is no stand, in a back row of four and a front row of four. An order is agreed – that the first pot on the left is first, the next the second, the next the third, and the next the fourth or last. The child is then asked:

'If the first pot in the back row is full, pick it up. If it is empty, leave it where it is.'

'How many pots have pictures on the bottom as well as pictures on the top?'

'Change the second pot in the back line with the fourth pot in the front line.'

'Which picture is nearest to the picture of the cat?'

'If the third pot in the front row has a picture of a cat on top, give it to me.'

'Touch the first and third pots in each row.'

'Take out all the pots that have nothing in them.'

'Touch the pot next to the pot that has buttons inside.'

'Turn the second pot in the front row upside down.'

'How many full pots have pictures on the side?'

This is the most demanding short exercise in comprehension I have yet described.

Encouraging Imaginative Thought

It has already been said that hearing-impaired children often have great difficulty in producing imaginative material, but encouragement often produces better results.

1. The adult should present a box with a transparent lid (e.g. a notelets box) which has been filled with some colourful material such as shiny red paper. The adult should not allow the child to touch the box or to look inside but should ask who, or what, the child thinks is in there. One eight-year-old girl with severe high tone loss who had great difficulty in writing imaginative stories replied: 'A tiny little girl is in the box.' When questioned

further, she said that 'A big rough man put the little girl there –
he was going to sell her to a circus.' More questions were
needed but without leading questions, a short story full of
incident was produced resulting in a dramatic rescue and a happy
ending. The child then wrote down the story and was plainly
pleased with the result.

2. The shorter and simpler LDA sequence cards can be used to
stimulate imagination. Take, for instance, the sequence in Set 3
of the girl eating an apple and leaving the core. This may not
seem, superficially, very interesting but skilful questioning may
elicit, say, the story of a mother who bought apples for a special
occasion and forbade the girl to touch them. The girl takes an
apple and eats it. Where does she hide the core? Does the
mother find out? What does she say? There is ample scope for
expression of ideas. If the exercise is primarily intended to
evoke imaginative thought, the adult can write down the story
for the child to read back, but it is also good practice in sequencing for the child to write the story himself.

3. All acting, whether it be fairy stories, the stories in sequence
cards or a sequence concocted impromptu to demonstrate a
word or idea is, of course, very stimulating to the imagination
of the hearing-impaired child.

Nonsense Questions

Hearing-impaired children can be very slow to see a joke. This
exercise is intended as practice in comprehension and may also
cause the child amusement. The child should be asked nonsense
questions such as:

> 'Do scissors eat bread?'
> 'Does the sun wear pyjamas?'
> 'Do you sleep on the roof?'
> 'Do you sit on the ceiling?'
> 'Can you look through the wall?'
> 'Do you run on your hands?'

If the child can become the questioner, that is more good practice
in imagination.

Hearing Stories

A normal child can enjoy a story told to him without pictures before he goes to school. A hearing-impaired child is so much more dependent upon pictures than a hearing child that the ability to interpret a story without pictures is a major landmark. It demands concentration and the power to link sentences and incidents that is not demanded by short instructions of even the more complex description. Very simple stories should be chosen to begin with. Adults either possess the capacity to make up stories out of their heads or they do not. Other adults have an ability to memorise stories they have heard and read. *My Naughty Little Sister* (see Appendix 4) makes a good starting point. These stories have wide appeal, being about an erring child, and can be retold by an adult at a level appropriate to the chronological age of any particular hearing-impaired child. The story should be told slowly but steadily, as to a normal child, and very simple props used if need be. When a hearing-impaired child has been brought from understanding almost nothing to this stage, it is tremendously moving to observe his appreciation of his first whole story. At a suitable stopping point questions can be asked to see that the child is truly able to follow what is being told to him, but questions should not be allowed to spoil the story or break up its continuity.

A hearing-impaired child who can listen to a story told in this way and clamour for another has come a considerable way in understanding language and, once the process is begun, the adult can tell more stories, gradually increasing their complexity. Stories are very stimulating to the imagination and are often a source of new vocabulary and general knowledge.

Reading Stories Silently

Hearing-impaired children are frequently said to 'love books' and indeed often do so. One usually finds on questioning that they are extremely reliant upon pictures. Later on, the child may read but does not interpret the words nearly as accurately as does a hearing child. Often the child seems to have enjoyed the story yet missed salient points or even a vital central point upon which the whole story pivots.

I have mentioned building reading comprehension, and once a child can read a simple book, his parents should supervise a large part of his reading. Much vital vocabulary and knowledge comes from books and if the child does not fully understand what he reads he will be at a disadvantage in an activity that could be very helpful in his education. Since an average hearing child is about seven years old before he wishes to read for pleasure, a hearing-impaired child is likely to be older and will read books designed for younger children. An attractive book should be selected to read as it stands – *Wide-awake Jake* by Helen Young is a charming example. The child is asked to read one page *silently*. When he has finished the page, the adult asks him questions on the content and is likely to discover that the child has not understood all he has read. If this is so, the child is asked to look again and to find the answer to the question. The adult then clears up any points the child has not understood and checks to find whether the child knows the meaning of each word on the page. Even in the earlier picture books, some quite difficult vocabulary occurs. Hearing children, meeting these words again and again, learn to interpret them from contextual clues and they are helped, of course, by conversation they hear. The language framework of the hearing-impaired child is neither firm not familiar enough to enable him to do this. He simply ignores what he is unable to understand, unless it is taught directly to him. It is useless to explain a word once and hope that the child will remember it. A vocabulary book should be kept, and all unknown words entered into it. In the early stages, words may have to be illustrated but, as progress is made, one word is defined in terms of another. The example on page 242 shows a page from the vocabulary book of a partially-hearing child of seven years old.

Words in a vocabulary book must be gone over regularly – either the child is asked to name a picture or, if he is more advanced, he defines the word. Words put into the vocabulary book should be brought into everyday conversation. Once a story is worked through, with an adult, the child may take it away to read on his own and in my experience enjoys it the better for knowing more. Later he may want to tell the story in his own words, using the pictures as a guide.

The whole of this exercise is very valuable and is the means by which many words are learned. Experience is widened, the child practises word definition and he learns to study sentences carefully and so extract their full meaning. It is most important that reading is *silent* so that the child gives all his energies to the interpretation of the word. In reading aloud, a great deal of energy

- freckles

a blind person - a person who can't see
a dumb person - a person who can't talk

- the pan is boiling over

rage - anger
to shrink - to get smaller
to boast - to say "I'm good, I'm clever,
               I'm the best"
to weep - to cry
an ache - a pain
to starve - to die because you are
          hungry and haven't any food to eat
chimpanzee - a kind of monkey

is spent on clarity of articulation and expression, so that there is less attention to give to comprehension.

As reading comprehension progresses, harder books can gradually be introduced. The child should be encouraged to use a children's dictionary of appropriate level and to look up words for himself, but he will need a great deal of supervised reading practice for a considerable time. When a child reads alone, books with very simple vocabulary should be chosen. Enid Blyton books have a simple story line and very easy vocabulary. It is better that a child read and understand than attempt difficult stories beyond his comprehension. For girls the 'Milly-Molly-Mandy' series is excellent.

Some ideas for books are given in Appendix 4. These are intended as a guide to the *level* of reading required. Children, like adults, like or dislike certain books quite strongly and have strong preferences. Boys obviously do not care for Milly-Molly-Mandy as much as girls. The parent should look in bookshops to find what books at that level a boy will enjoy – there are many in the Young Puffin series.

Continuing Auditory Discrimination

When so much effort is spent in building language, it is easy to neglect continued auditory discrimination, but it is very important that this should continue. Appendix 5 contains lists of words that sound alike and a child who is working on the lines suggested in this chapter should also work regularly at discriminating between these words. The words should be written down in an exercise book kept for the purpose. For a young child, the simple familiar words should be taken from any one list and illustrated thus:

back   bat   bag

A slightly older child who is reading well will require only some words illustrated, as shown by the example at the top of the next page:

sack
sad
Sam
sat

sank (The boat sank. It went under the water.)

sash

A still older child will require no drawings but may have meanings of words he does not know written in brackets:

row
robe
road
rogue (a bad man)
roam (to wander about)
roll
rope
rose

In all age groups, the adult shields his lips and dodges about the list asking the child to point to the word said. This may seem a difficult task when the words are so alike, but in fact there are clues available that hearing people never use because they do not need to. These clues are accessible to hearing-impaired people simply because the more normal clues are, for them, missing. (Thus, for example, the 'a' sound in 'bad' is longer than the 'a' sound in 'back'.) Hearing-impaired children do not have to analyse the clues, but simply learn by listening to make use of them. One list of words is abandoned in favour of another when a child is making few or no mistakes. Listening practice of this type is hard work for a child and should be given only for five minutes at a time. The lists are, of course, good for building vocabulary.

The sort of results obtained if a child does work based upon the sort of exercises and materials described in this chapter vary a great deal. Here is the story of a child who was placed on a programme based on the techniques and materials described in Chapters 10–18.

Catherine (*Audiogram Figure 10, page 50*)

Catherine was discovered to have a hearing problem at the age of nine months and was fitted with two body-worn aids at twelve months old. When she was two, these were replaced by two body aids which were obviously more helpful to her. Catherine and her mother had received excellent help and support during several stays at the Nuffield Centre's Ealing Hostel and the parents found themselves able, during Catherine's early years, to utilise the example and advice given to them there. A peripatetic teacher of the deaf visited the home for one hour each week. None the less, when Catherine was seen for speech therapy assessment at exactly four years old, her mother felt that despite early gains Catherine was now 'not getting on further in speech development', and that she herself no longer knew how to promote progress.

At four, Catherine's understanding of speech was at the two year three months level. The child used her voice a great deal, jargonising and naming many objects since her parents had taught her to do this. She used no doing words beyond the very familiar 'go', 'break', 'cry', 'sleep', 'wash' and 'fall', nor descriptive words other than 'naughty', 'good', 'dirty' and 'broken'. She used no positional words and asked no questions. Her rare attempts to join words together consisted of linking two naming words, for example, 'baby pram' though she had been taught to use 'Please may I have – ?' The parents' chief queries were 'How can we help Catherine to understand us more? How can we help her to join words together?'

The child, who had no siblings, seemed calm and happy with adults. On the other hand she showed little initiative or imagination in play and no curiosity about her surroundings. She found concentration extremely difficult, seeming to drift into a dreamy state unless constant efforts were made to keep her involved in the task in hand. Though she enjoyed the company of other children, communication with them presented great problems and this often resulted in Catherine hitting out for no apparent reason. Explanations of why she should not do so meant nothing to her because of her poor comprehension.

Catherine was placed on a speech and language programme based upon the ideas outlined in this book. She worked with the speech therapist for one hour each week and the work was then repeated at home for about one hour each day. Both parents were supportive and conscientious in every respect. The daily work was done by Catherine's mother, but her father spent much time with her at the weekend. Catherine was also fortunate in possessing grandparents who supported the parents' efforts, even to the extent of attending speech therapy sessions. Catherine's mother found that once Catherine's speech and language programme was initiated, increased ideas for day-to-day conversation were generated. The mother also felt stimulated to produce original ideas of her own that were most helpful.

Six months after work was started, when she was four and a half years old, Catherine's comprehension had risen to three years two months. Providing her with action, descriptive and positional words had greatly increased her ability to link words and her mother noted down the following examples of spontaneous sentences:

> 'Catherine too small, please turn light on.'
> 'Don't want to get Adam.'
> 'Daddy tying his tie.'
> 'Man going back to the house.'

At this juncture, Catherine was fitted with two specific power post-aural hearing aids. Aided audiometry showed her to be more responsive to them than to her body-worn aids, and it was also noticeable that her auditory discrimination and awareness were greater during speech therapy sessions.

During her second year of speech therapy, Catherine's own sentences lengthened further: 'I fell downstairs and banged my bottom', but she still rarely asked a question, seeming persistently uninterested in her surroundings and very dreamy. Renewed efforts were made to provide stimulating work material and to set an example by constantly asking questions of Catherine. Towards the end of this year the effects at last began to show and Catherine began to ask questions of all kinds and to use speech to command and demand and even to argue. On being asked, for instance, 'Tell me something sharp,' Catherine replied, 'A book.' 'A book isn't sharp,' said her therapist. 'But the *corner* of a book *is* sharp,' rejoined Catherine.

Because of her youth, some language procedures outlined in Chapter 18 had to be modified, but by her sixth birthday Catherine could read well and, provided the reading material was simple, could answer questions about what she had read. She could give opposites of simple words and showed that she had grasped the principle of homonyms by describing correctly two kinds of 'spring' though this word had never actually been included in the set of homonyms worked upon. She was well aware of time throughout the week and the year, but could not tell the time by the clock, still orientating herself by 'after breakfast', 'before tea', 'at bedtime', etc. She showed herself able to utilise what she had been taught about describing objects when she came to her mother and said (having lost her yo-yo), 'Mummy, I've lost the purple ball with the string round it.' She also said to her speech therapist during a thunderstorm, 'I see a bright zig-zag line above the trees.'

At six years and two months, further language tests were carried out and showed the following results:

*Verbal Comprehension	5 years	2 months
*Verbal Expression	4 years	11 months
**Reading Age (word recognition)	8 years	2 months
**Reading Comprehension Age	6 years	2 months
**Word Definition Level	6 years	

* Reynell Developmental Language Scale.

** Standardised tests were used to obtain these results.

Her mother had read *My Naughty Little Sister* to Catherine just as it stood and her comments showed good understanding of the story. She now found relationships with other children much easier and was heard to say to a friend, 'The coal shed is the prison. I run away and you got (sic) to catch me. You're the policeman.'

The hitting out had ceased except on rare occasions. Despite her low level of motivation, Catherine had acquired an amount of general knowledge and surprised her therapist one day by commenting, 'Look! A chrysalis.' She had at last become far more interested in her environment. Articulation had become much clearer, there being no sounds Catherine was unable to say, but there was still a tendency to leave the endings off words, particularly 's'.

Catherine had always attended a normal school, first in the nursery class, then in a reception class and always with her peer group. Her teachers found no outstanding difficulties with her and she was one of the better readers in the class. Catherine is certainly a bright child but by no means exceptionally gifted and certainly with little early natural drive to learn. Her success came from the persistence and hard work of her parents.

Catherine's prime means of comprehending speech is through listening. She rarely watches a speaker's face and indeed had to be asked to make an effort to do so in order to improve her articulation.

Obvious areas of difficulty remain. Comprehension has still not reached its full potential. Use of verb tense is poor and also the use of 's' as a syntactical tool (i.e. Mummy's hat, he runs, three cups). There is still a great deal of abstract vocabulary to be learned.

19

Working towards Clear Speech

If parents are determined to develop their hearing-impaired child's understanding and use of spoken language, it is difficult for them to make errors that will be harmful to him. It has already been shown that, given minimal guidance, many parents are capable of training their hearing-impaired child to the point where his spoken language approaches normal.

What is much less easy is to train a hearing-impaired child to speak *clearly*. I have already said earlier that a normal child's own production of vowel and consonant sounds is monitored by his listening to them and attempting to approximate to the spoken patterns of the adults around him. Not only can the hearing-impaired child neither hear sounds distinctly, nor monitor his own productions correctly, but his incorrect production of sounds is strengthened by the faulty muscular patterns he gradually builds up and then habitually uses. Thus if, as many profoundly deaf children do, he reproduces 'Mummy' as 'Bubby', each time he says 'Bubby' the muscular sensations he receives strengthen the wrong pronunciation.

In originally planning this book, I intended to attempt to give detailed guidance about the making of each speech sound and the best ways to help a child to make sounds correctly. I realised, however, that it is impossible to teach what is a highly specialised skill, the correction of articulation, through the printed word alone, and that to attempt to do so might lead parents into errors that could be harmful to the child. It is only possible, therefore, to give broad guidelines. In cases where parents feel that their child speaks unclearly and is showing no signs of becoming clearer, the help of a qualified speech therapist should be sought.

Needless to say, the fitting of the best possible hearing aids early in life is the surest way to promote good pronunciation or articulation, since the sounds fed back to the child's ear help him to place his speech organs correctly and to control the muscles of his mouth.

(249)

Even when appropriate hearing aids are fitted at a much later age than should be the case, a marked improvement in articulation can often be observed. Equally, the removal of a hearing aid for even a short period of time will cause deterioration in articulation.

When partially-hearing children first start to speak, they often do so very unclearly and in this they are the same as many normally-hearing toddlers. Continual auditory training in connection with learning language, and of the type that utilises the minimal pairs lists, usually effects a gradual but marked improvement in the general clarity of speech. Peter, for instance, was never properly aided until he was four and a half years old. At this age he spoke little, but regular training was effective in developing speech that was, for the first six months, mostly unintelligible. By five and a half years of age, with constant listening practice but no other articulation training, Peter could pronounce all the vowels and consonant sounds of English correctly when saying single words. He showed an increasing tendency to do so when making sentences.

Obviously, since many consonants may not be heard at all whatever amplification is provided, the problem of the pronunciation of the severely or profoundly deaf child is much more difficult. None the less, correct early aiding and intensive auditory training will promote an acceptable voice and good vowel sounds which are the basis of clear speech. If they are well established, it is much easier for a speech therapist to teach articulation of consonants, and this can often be done successfully even when a child is quite old. Poor voice and vowel sounds, on the other hand, tend to be difficult if not impossible to correct in an older child. When severely or profoundly deaf children have good voice and speech sounds, it is frequently found that they have been encouraged to listen effectively.

Kate, for instance, (Audiogram Figure 11, page 51) had excellent amplification from babyhood and was trained by her mother to use it. Despite her extreme deafness, speech developed with no wrong vowels or consonants, except a rather weak 's' sound. Kate was an excellent lip-reader and must have observed to good effect the movements made by people's mouths when they spoke.

Some hearing-impaired children, particularly those who have not been aided well, develop quite early in life strange tongue and mouth posture. Pam, for instance, unaided in any way until she was four and a half, habitually had her mouth hanging open, tucked the tip of her tongue behind her bottom teeth and protruded the middle of her tongue between her teeth. Her utterances, made from this mouth posture, caused people to insist that her speech troubles lay not in hearing loss, but in 'a defective mouth'. A child should not be allowed to go through the day with his mouth hanging open. He should be trained to keep it shut, particularly if he is engrossed in television. If he seems unable to breathe freely through his nose, it should be established by medical consultation whether or not there is nasal obstruction, but if the nasal passages are clear, a finger gently placed under his chin will remind him to close his mouth unless he is speaking. An open mouth encourages slack mouth muscles and poor breathing habits, which will in turn encourage poor speech.

One general rule for saying single words is never, when it can be avoided, to allow a child to learn to say a word badly if a little perseverance will enable him to say it better. This is particularly relevant to the number of syllables a word contains. Eighteen-year-old Madge, a good lip-reader, perpetually said things like, 'My bro sent me a le this mor.' ('My brother sent me a letter this morning.') Even though her articulation was incorrect, completing each word would have made Madge far more intelligible. If a small child cannot pronounce all the sounds in a word like 'aeroplane', at least make sure he says three syllables and not one or two. Gently tapping out the correct number of syllables on the back of his hand, and asking him to do the same before he repeats the word, usually helps. Though, as has been pointed out, some time has to be given for articulation to develop through listening, some children can actually say single words much better than they usually do. For instance, a child may say 'a' for 'tap', because he hears 'a', but he may also be able to say 'tap' correctly if encouraged to do so. In instances like these, the child should be trained to learn correct pronunciation of the word along with its meaning. Some isolated mispronounced words are retained as bad habits. Seven-year-old Duncan, who spoke a lot, habitually said, 'Have you *dot* so-and-so.' When this was pointed out to his parents they said defensively, 'He can say "got" quite easily.' If a child *can* say an oft-used word such as 'got' properly, he should be asked to do so.

When a new word is introduced to a child, he should be given the opportunity to listen to it several times before he attempts to say it, and also to watch the speaker's face which should, of course, be in a good light and on a level with his own. Some children rush to 'say' before they have listened and looked sufficiently, and so copy incorrectly. It is then helpful to put a finger on the child's lips and say, 'Don't talk, listen.' It is important that the achievement of a good sound is greeted with enthusiasm by the adult. Since the child has reduced auditory feedback, he needs reinforcement by other means if he is to feel that his efforts are worthwhile.

It may be helpful to use a mirror so that the child can see what the pattern of a word looks like on his own mouth in relation to how it sounds and feels. If a mirror is used, it should be a big one such as a dressing-table mirror in which the child can see his own face and that of the adult simultaneously. He should observe the adult's mirror image when saying a word and then his own, not twist to see the 'real adult' and then his own image in the mirror. A mirror is by no means always helpful and can be confusing. The child may be distracted by background objects or features of his appearance other than his mouth and some children even seem to be made a little nervous or embarrassed by their mirror image.

Very deaf children are often helped to say certain sounds correctly by feeling escape of air or vibrations on their hand. In making the sounds 'm' and 'n', the air escapes through the nose and marked vibrations of the lips and cheek can be felt. If the young child says 'Bubby' for 'Mummy', cup his hand round the adult's cheek and chin whilst 'Mummy' is said correctly but in a slightly exaggerated way so that he receives a strong impression of vibration. He should also be asked to feel the lip vibrations. If he then feels his own cheek and lips when saying 'Mummy' he may well reproduce the vibrations and so the correct sound – which should be greeted with enthusiasm. Mark's mother reported that Mark was shown this once as a toddler and found it so striking an experience that he repeated the humming noise, holding his cheek, all day. Thenceforth 'm' was used quite easily and correctly in his speech. The consonants 'p', 'b', 't', 'd', 'k', 'g', 'f', 'v', 's', 'sh', 'ch' and 'j' are all made with more or less escape of air from the mouth and a child may be helped by feeling this on the back of his hand. Children who cannot hear an 's' sound often obligingly adopt the correct mouth position but have no idea, until they are asked to feel it, that air escapes through the teeth when 's' is said.

Final consonants, the last consonants on words, are particularly difficult to hearing-impaired children since they are heard poorly or not at all. Thus the hearing-impaired child will say, for instance, 'Pa can hop bu I hop a ri my bi,' ('Pat can't hop, but I hop and ride my bike.') Often each word can be said correctly on its own, but the final sounds are missed out when a sentence is made. Once a child is able to read, seeing how each sound looks in print and linking it to the word said makes this aspect of speech much easier. It will help to lightly underline in pencil the final consonants of each word. Short books such as the *This is my Colour, This is my Shape* series (see Appendix 2) and the invaluable 'Breakthrough' series are useful and also *The Eye Book* and *The Foot Book* from the 'Beginner Books' series (see Appendix 3). Both these books are simple and *The Foot Book* offers opportunities for sounding the important final sound 't':

> Left foot
> Left foot
> Left foot
> Right!
> Feet in the morning, feet at night.

The use of the 'Read, Write and Remember' series (see Appendix 4) takes practice in saying final sounds a stage further. The child must read such questions as 'Is one horse jumping a fence?' correctly and his answer, 'Yes, one horse is jumping a fence', comes partly from his own head as well as from the print, thus requiring correct word endings to be used in connection with his own ideas. 'Little words' such as 'is', 'has' and 'was', and plural forms and apostrophe 's' have all to be used correctly in replying to the questions in the books.

Their poor auditory memory makes the memorising of rhymes very difficult for hearing-impaired children, but when their language has developed sufficiently, it will be found that memory for rhymes has also developed and that, with some effort, the child is able to learn by heart and in some cases to say rhymes with final consonants in place. Learning by heart is, in turn, excellent training for auditory memory. The earliest rhymes to learn are not nursery rhymes which deal with unintelligible events ('The cow jumped over the moon') but rhymes accompanied by easy hand action that illustrate a simple thought. In my own personal opinion, by far the best is 'Two little dicky birds'. The adult can use sticky paper on the fore-finger nail of each hand to represent the disappearing birds and children clamour for it repeatedly – provided they do not know the secret. This and other rhymes can be found in *This Little Puffin* compiled by Elizabeth Matterson. *The Puffin Book of Verse* compiled by Eleanor Graham contains simple poetry for older children. Both are in the Young Puffin Original series.

Though some children need to 'try harder' to speak correctly, too much trying can be destructive and leads to a tense, jerky, speech pattern and also to facial grimacing. The tense child who puts too much effort into speech needs to be encouraged to relax. Similarly, children who speak very rapidly are often seen to be over-quick in all their activities and need to live their life at a more even tempo.

The foregoing represents a commonsense approach to attempting to develop clear speech in the child, and the parents would be well advised not to go beyond it in dealing with a child's articulation. Direct, uninformed advice to the child about how to make certain sounds or to place their mouths not only invariably fails, but may actually confuse the child. I have heard all the following examples of parental advice given to children about their speech. Not one is valid in scientific terms:

'When you say "k", *spit* it out.'

    (Spitting is performed by the *front* of the tongue and the lips: 'k' is made by raising the *back* of the tongue.)

'Roll your "r".'

    (There is no rolled 'r' in the English language, though there is in the Arabic languages.)

'Make "o" *in the middle* of your mouth.'

    (There are many difficulties involved in making vowel sounds, but at least one is not lopsideness!)

'Sound the "e" *on the end* when you say "cake".'

    (The 'e' on the end of 'cake' is not sounded. The final sound is the consonant 'k'.)

Bearing in mind this last example, it is helpful if parents attempt to think in terms of *sounds* not *letters*, e.g. it was pointed out in connection with the phonetic chart on page 44 that though we write 'cow' and 'key', we sound only one 'k' sound.

An 's' sound may be spelled 'c' or 'ce', e.g. 'circus', 'face', 'lace', 'ice'. 'Sugar' though spelled with an 's' is pronounced 'shugar'.

'Jar' and 'jam' are written with 'j', but 'ginger' which contains the same sound as 'jar' and 'jam' is written with 'g'.

'J' at the end of a word is often spelled 'ge' as in 'page' or 'dge' as in 'fudge'.

'Ph' is sounded 'f' as in 'photo'.

Double letters are not sounded twice, e.g. 'bell', 'hopping', 'off'.

'Ck' at the end of a word is sounded once, e.g. 'back', 'sack'. Many words end with a silent 'e', e.g. 'cake', 'cape', 'ate', 'made'. It is particularly important to remember this when underlining final consonants in a reading book.

Children would be greatly helped if adults would forget how words are spelled and think of how they sound.

Lastly, a child is often enabled to say a seemingly long and difficult word if it can be split into syllables, e.g.

> teh – li – fohn   (telephone)
> ga – rahj – man   (garageman)
> po – lees – man   (policeman)
> di – vi – shun   (division)
> foh – toh – grahf   (photograph)
> kyou – kum – ber   (cucumber)

In the case of small children, the adult should ask the child to repeat one syllable at a time. After several repetitions, the child can usually make a much better approximation than previously. If the older child is a good reader, he will usually be quick to appreciate the sort of homemade phonetic system given above if each syllable is pointed out to him as the word is said. A syllable should always begin with a consonant where possible, e.g. not gar-ahj-man but ga-rahj-man, not tehl-i-fohn but teh-li-fohn.

Finally, once again, if your child is beginning to understand speech well and to speak a lot himself, but is not improving in clarity, do seek professional help from a qualified speech therapist. Information can be obtained from The College of Speech Therapists, Harold Poster House, 6 Lechmore Road, London NW2 5BU, Telephone: 01-459 8521.

20

Some Final Points

The procedures described in this book are intended to help parents to teach a hearing-impaired child the bases of communication and no claim is made that the child's speech will be normal as a result. In cases of those like David and Polly, where speech became normal as a result of the work carried out, their parents did not then feel their job was over. A child with a partial hearing loss will need, throughout his childhood, extra supervision, extra understanding, and often extra help. A child with a severe deafness will need a great deal of constant on-going teaching if he is to acquire the knowledge of the world and skills for living that most of us take for granted. Figures of speech such as 'in hot water', 'open-mouthed', 'up in the clouds' constantly used in the speech of normal adults and usually acquired naturally at adolescence, remain a mystery to deaf people so, to some extent, cutting them off from other people. The reading of government brochures and the filling in of forms, as a deaf person grows older, present a problem because of lack of vocabulary. Words with two meanings that we take for granted lurk on every side to catch out the un-initiated deaf person. One profoundly deaf girl of eighteen who superficially spoke well, was taken to view an empty Magistrate's Court. Looking at the seat labelled 'Press' she commented, 'But I don't see the bell!' Much that we take for granted must be deliberately and painstakingly taught to a deaf person or he will never know it.

The amount of time and effort that has to be put in by parents to achieve basic, childhood speech bears direct relation to whether or not there was an early start in aiding and teaching. A child who is speaking a little at three years old, and whose parents are working hard to help him, may well communicate adequately by the time he is seven – though plenty of problems and plenty of learning stretch beyond that. A child who has learned little or nothing by seven years old has already lost years of his childhood in which valuable school learning, based on language, should have been taking place. He is most unlikely to have the time available during the rest of his childhood, both to learn to communicate in spoken language and to catch up what he has lost academically.

This opens up the question of schooling and the reader will notice that I have said so far little about the type of education received by the children I have mentioned. A few of these children attended schools for the deaf and one or two were taught at home. Mostly, they attended schools for normal children, state or private, or partially-hearing units. A partially-hearing unit (PHU) was originally intended to be for partially-hearing children, but many units do accept children with more severe degrees of hearing loss.

The advantage of a partially-hearing unit is that, since it is situated in a state school for normal children, the hearing-impaired child should be able to spend part of his school day with his normally-hearing peers. He thus hears normal speech. Some of the best results I have achieved have been in cases where the staff of a partially-hearing unit, which should number at least one trained teacher of the deaf, have been responsible for grounding a child in reading, writing and arithmetic whilst the speech therapist and parents formed a team for the purpose of developing the child's spoken language. All the adults worked closely together. Children who achieved normality within this framework were found after a time not to need attendance at the unit, and were able to manage in a class of normal children.

Some parents have, sometimes mistakenly, a horror of special education and insist upon placing their child in a school for normal children. Whether or not this works depends a great deal upon the motives that lead the parent to choose normal schooling. Do they really believe in the value of keeping their child with hearing children, or do they wish to pretend that he has no problem? Much also depends upon the attitude of the teachers at a school for normal children. Some accept the hearing-impaired child, realising full well that they have taken on an arduous and demanding job. Such teachers ask to be briefed, before the hearing-impaired child comes to school, on his particular difficulties in speech, education and peer relationships and are willing to work closely with specially trained personnel. Sometimes hearing-impaired children are accepted by schools for normal children willingly, but in

(257)

ignorance. Teachers may have no idea of the nature of the problem they have taken on, and no inkling of the restrictions of comprehension, vocabulary and general knowledge. They believe that a loud voice will overcome most problems and are even surprised at the child's defective speech. Having discovered a little of the true situation, many schools none the less stand by the child and try their best to help him.*

Schools to beware of are those in which the teachers ask for no information, but insist that they understand the problem and need no guidance. They are used, they say, to educating all sorts of difficult children and cannot believe that a hearing-impaired child is 'any different'. These teachers do not wish to learn about the hearing-impaired child, or really to help him, but only to prove how knowledgeable they are. In some cases I have known young hearing-impaired children actually being given French lessons before they have mastered their own language, and other teaching methods have been hopelessly inappropriate.

At the same time, it would be less than truthful to pretend that all partially-hearing units or schools for the deaf and partially deaf are equally good. Many are excellent, but some do not welcome additional help in developing a child's speech, and at the same time are inadequate in their own ability to teach speech and language. The child is then trapped in a situation in which he is unlikely to learn to speak or even to have enough language to prepare him for the 'education' he is apparently to receive. While some units work hard to encourage the hearing-impaired child to integrate with his normal peers, others have a possessive attitude either to the child's mixing with normal children or ever being able to leave the unit.

Parents of a hearing-impaired child must decide for themselves just what type of education will best help their child. A great deal

* I would here like to pay tribute to the many schools for normal children known to me who have accepted the challenge of receiving a hearing-impaired child and particularly those who have educated a carefully spaced series of hearing-impaired children and so learned how to deal with their problems. I will refrain from enlarging upon the ignorance and prejudice against hearing impairment occasionally met with in schools where good help could and should have been given to children with well developed powers of communication but was in fact denied them.

depends upon his age and his stage of language development at that age. If a child of five or six has already progressed substantially in his understanding of speech, and speaks intelligibly himself, has started to read and is socially well-adjusted, then he should be placed in a normal school, particularly if he is bright and, of course, well supported by his parents. If he is communicating little, is socially disruptive or an unwilling learner, an oral school for the deaf or a partially-hearing unit will be a more suitable placement. Parents must consider, before they insist upon normal schooling, just what is involved. The child may feel inadequate and unhappy because he cannot join in with class work. A teacher with a class of normal children cannot be expected to devote herself exclusively to the handicapped member of the class, who thus fails to learn in many areas. In cases like this, attendance at normal school is a pretence, based usually upon the blind determination of the parents that their child 'is the same as everyone else'. Such parents should remind themselves of what good special education may have to offer – specially trained staff, amplifying equipment and a small number of children in a group.

I have come across a number of severely deaf children who have not learned either to understand speech or to join words together by the age of seven, eight or nine. With good hearing aids and massive language teaching, such children can often learn to talk to some extent, which gives their parents the desire to educate them as normally as possible. It is usually much more sensible to retain such children in special education, since there is little hope of their coping in a school for normal children. A big effort should be made to provide them with normal companions outside school hours and to continue to develop language at home.

If parents decide to attempt to place their hearing-impaired child in a school for normal children, they should look for a school with small classes where the teachers are truly sympathetic to the hearing-impaired child and welcome his presence in the school. It is never a good idea to try to coerce a school into accepting a child it does not really wish to educate. The parents should be completely frank about their child's level of hearing loss, his comprehension, his difficulties in expressing himself and any social difficulties. They should look for teachers who will listen to an explanation of the problem, learn to read an audiogram, and who are willing to understand the implications of childhood hearing loss. The child should always be seated in the front of the classroom near his teacher – not an easy matter once children get to the stage where teachers and rooms change for various subjects.

In one really excellent junior school, a head teacher of many years' experience said honestly that she had never in her teaching career had anything to do with hearing-impaired children and that it had taken her a long time to understand the one entrusted to her. Needless to say, with such an honest attitude, an excellent contribution was made to the child taken on by this school.

A teacher should be able to make a simple check as to whether hearing aids are working, and should be given a supply of fresh batteries in case of need.

Personally, I would like to see much greater flexibility in the attitude to teaching hearing-impaired children and a departure from the idea that once a child is in a school he must stay there. David, for instance (see page 157 and Audiogram Figure 13) started his educational career in an oral school for the deaf (not the partially deaf) where he was taught to listen well and to use a basic noun vocabulary. He also learned to work hard. He removed to a partially-hearing unit at four and, at five years nine months, was able to enter a normal state infant school with no PHU attached. This sort of movement that meets a child's current needs is excellent, but not always easy to obtain. It would also be pleasant if more independent schools would be willing to accept one or two suitable hearing-impaired children rather than regard them as a strange species. (On the other hand, there is no reason why a school should accept such a child unless his parents are making a genuine effort steadily to improve his understanding and speech.)

Parents who place their hearing-impaired child in a normal school must be prepared to give him much more help with his school work than they would give a normal child and to co-operate with his teachers in finding out just what teaching methods are being used. It is unwise, for instance, to try to help the child with maths unless the exact methods used at school are understood, and also the type of vocabulary used by the teacher (times, multiply; sharing, dividing; taking away, subtracting; equals, makes). If a book is being read aloud to the class, the hearing-impaired child will probably have great difficulty in following it; if he is told the story at home and acquainted with the characters and plot, he may manage much better.

The parent must be prepared to supervise homework and to tell his teacher if the child is in real difficulties. While it may be legitimate to say to a normally-hearing child, 'It's your work, get on with it,' it is unrealistic to adopt this attitude to a hearing-impaired child who is likely to need help with his work over a great number of years.

The hearing-impaired child in a normal school is likely to become extremely tired at times. Where schools for handicapped children tend to have shorter hours and allowance is made for the fatigue of constant listening and lip-reading, no such allowances can be made in schools for normal children. On the other hand, if a hearing-impaired child *can* manage in a normal school, he has taken an enormous step in learning to adjust to normal society.

However good a school and whatever kind it is, for normal or for hearing-impaired children, the parents should realise that the responsibility for teaching their child to talk and to increase his knowledge and understanding lies primarily with themselves. As one mother of a successful, hearing-impaired child said, 'People can help you, but they can't do it for you. You have to teach your child yourself.'

Appendix 1

Toys for Very Young Children

Galt

Board books – indestructible books with clear, everyday pictures
Picture tiles – each tile divides into four pieces which can be
  pieced together
Plain wooden bricks
Posting box
Wooden musical box with handle
'See Inside' jigsaw puzzles: See Inside the Shops
                            See Inside the Farm
                            See Inside the Cars

Abbatt Toys

(Obtainable from Educational Supply Association by mail order
  but are stocked at other shops)
Giant Picture Snap
Giant Picture Lotto
Posting box
Pop-up cones – press a lever and a tier of cones pops up
Baby jigsaws – four or five big jigsaw pieces make a common
  object
Colour picture puzzles – two pieces make a common object

Kiddicraft

Kiddicraft stacking beakers
Kiddicraft stacking baskets
Kiddicraft Billy and his Seven Barrels – seven barrels one inside
  another
Kiddicraft puzzles
Also:
Victory Play and Learn Tray – each object can be taken out of the
  tray

Appendix 2

Materials and Books suitable for use with the techniques described in Chapters 10-14

The toys, equipment and books listed are intended as helpful suggestions and are not all essential to teaching a hearing-impaired child. A limited amount of equipment is vital, and books, toys and equipment that I have used repeatedly have been marked *. It is not therefore suggested that any parent attempt to obtain all the items listed. A piece of equipment tailor-made for a child's particular need by his parents is often superior to an expensive one bought without sufficient thought. The symbol ** denotes books which are also suitable as material with pictures to ask questions about and the symbol R denotes material also suitable for developing early reading. Some items may be available from the Toy Libraries Association, Seabrooke House, Wyllotts Manor, Darkes Lane, Herts. It may also be possible to borrow from relatives and friends.

The items listed are not by any means the only useful ones. They are simply items that have been useful to me in my years of teaching hearing-impaired children. Parents will find other books and equipment for themselves.

Some items, particularly toys, are expensive and parents are advised to ask toyshop personnel to allow them to examine, say, the contents of a lotto set very carefully before purchasing it, to make sure that it meets the language need of the particular child for whom it is being bought.

As far as I have been able to ascertain, toys are obtainable and books in print at the time of writing. Some books that suddenly go out of print are reprinted, but reprinting can take a considerable time. As far as possible widely popular, well-known and established sets of books have been recommended, partly for that reason.

Mail Order Firms

Educational Supply Association, Pinnacles, PO Box 22, Harlow, Essex. (Make a postal and packing charge on all orders under £15 in value.)

Learning Development Aids, Park Works, Norwich Rd, Wisbech, Cambs. PE13 2AX. (Make a postal and packing charge on all orders under £7 in value.)

Philip & Tacey Ltd, North Way, Walworth Industrial Estate, Andover, Hampshire SP10 5BA (Tel. Andover 61171). (Do not accept orders under a minimum amount. Parents are advised to ascertain this amount before attempting to order.)

Taskmaster Ltd, Morris Road, Clarendon Park, Leicester LE2 6BR. (Make a delivery charge on small orders.) Taskmaster produces the 'Developmental Learning Materials' range.

Galt toys are obtainable from Galt stocklists, a list of whom can be obtained from James Galt & Co. Ltd, Cheadle, Cheshire N127 6B.

Books not specifically mentioned as being supplied by one of the four mail order firms listed above may be obtained from an ordinary children's bookshop.

The usefulness of any and every sort of catalogue—mail order, gift, gardening—and magazines as a source of pictures cannot be overstressed.

Gummed picture stamps, large, with perforated edges, produced by Philip & Tacey are extremely useful basic equipment since the pictures can be torn off and they cover many of the aspects of living dealt with throughout this book. The packets recommended from the Philip & Tacey range are as follows:

    *Work and Play Vocabulary Picture stamps
    *Early Word Picture and Word stamps
    *Reading-and-Doing Picture gummed stamps
    *Richmond Phonogram Picture and Word gummed stamps
    *Groundwork Coloured gummed stamps
    *Things-We-Do Pictorial gummed stamps
    *Let's Go Shopping stamps
    *Gonville Associational Picture and Vocabulary sheets

Where these stamps have been found particularly applicable to a certain topic, they will be mentioned again in the equipment list.

Naming Words – Materials related to work in Chapter 10
Pictures

> 100 black and white pictures (line drawings) for use with the John Horniman School Language Scheme. Obtainable from the Invalid Children's Aid Association, 126 Buckingham Palace Road, London SW1 9SB.

Games

> *Animal Lotto – Galt
> *Picture Lotto – Galt
> *Picture Word Lotto (with name cards) – Galt
> *Remember, Remember (a pairs game) – Galt
> *Picture Dominoes – Galt
> Find It – Galt
> Animal Sixes (a dice game) – Galt
> *Tummy Ache (particularly useful for learning food and objects on the meal table) – Kiddicraft
> *Pairs – Spear's Games
> Jumbo Dominoes – Spear's Games
> Pairs Game – Educational Supply Association
> *Animal Dominoes – Educational Supply Association
> The House That Jack Built – Spear's Games
> Uniset House – Bambola Toys (Galt stocklists)

Jigsaw Puzzles

> Farm Animal Puzzle – Galt
> Boy and Girl Puzzle – Galt
> Victory Alphabet Play Tray
> Perception Puzzle Inset Board – Developmental Learning Materials

Books

> *A Ladybird First Picture Book*
> *A Ladybird Second Picture Book*
> *A Ladybird Third Picture Book*
> *A Ladybird Fourth Picture Book*
> *A Ladybird Fifth Picture Book*
> *Picture Dictionary* by Richard Hefter, Picture Lions

Action Words – Materials related to work in Chapter 11
Gummed Stamps

> *Things-We-Do Pictorial gummed stamps – Philip & Tacey

*Gonville Associational Picture and Vocabulary sheets – Philip & Tacey

Picture Cards

*Action Cards, Sets 1 and 2 – Learning Development Aids
*Photographic Action Cards – Learning Development Aids

Books

Silly Billy by Ruth Ainsworth and Ronald Ridout, Purnell Bancroft

A Pram and a Bicycle by Ruth Ainsworth and Ronald Ridout, Purnell Bancroft

Places by J. D. Bevington, a 'Turn and Learn' book, Hamlyn

Going Out by Lesley Anne Ivory, a 'Head Start' book, Burke

Playing by Lesley Anne Ivory, a 'Head Start' book, Burke

At Home by Lesley Anne Ivory, a 'Head Start' book, Burke

Positional Words – Materials related to work in Chapter 12

Cards

Spatial Relationships-Concept Cards – Learning Development Aids

R Positional Word and Picture Matching Cards – Philip & Tacey

Books

R*Bears in the Night* by Stan and Jan Berenstain, William Collins and Picture Lions

R*Where Shall I Hide?* by June Melser, a 'Read it Yourself' book, Methuen Educational

R*Rosie's Walk* by Pat Hutchins, Bodley Head and Picture Puffins

R*Buster is Lost* by Helen Solomon, Macmillan Educational

Descriptive Words – Materials related to work in Chapter 13

COLOUR

Games

*Assorted Round Counters – Educational Supply Association

Books about Colour

R *Real Things Colour Book* by F. T. Fife, Philip & Tacey

What Colour Is It? by Eileen Ryder, a 'Head Start' book, Burke

R 'This is my Colour' series by Derek and Lucy Thackray (6 books), George Philip Alexander

SHAPES
Games
*Geometric Tracer (Catalogue No. 7007) – Educational Supply
    Association
Shapes Game – Galt
Shapes Puzzles – Taskmaster
*Dimensional Puzzle – Baby Relax
*Shape-fitting Cube by Magneto – F. Bing & Co.
Books about Shape
R 'This is my Shape' series by Derek and Lucy Thackray
    (6 books), George Philip Alexander

OTHER DESCRIPTIVE MATERIAL
Cards
*Description – Learning Development Aids
Books
R*What is Big?* a 'Read It Yourself' book, Reed Education
R*What is Little?* a 'Read It Yourself' book, Reed Education
R*This and That* by Joyce Mildred Morris, 'Language in
    Action' series, Macmillan Educational
R Macdonald Opposite Books
    Big and Little
    Fast and Slow
    Front and Back
    Noisy and Quiet
    Old and New
Counting by L. Bradbury, Ladybird
Understanding Numbers by Joseph McNally and William
    Murray, Ladybird
Words We Need for Numbers by Joseph McNally and William
    Murray, Ladybird
More Words for Numbers by Joseph McNally and William
    Murray, Ladybird

BOOKS FOR TELLING
A STORY FROM PICTURES
R The Gay Way Introductory Series by E. R. Boyce, Macmillan
    Cat and Dog
    The Red Pig

Pig, Pots and Pans
Who is it?
The Fat Pig
The Red Lorry
The Red Fox
A House to Live in

These are introductory reading books but make good story-telling material.

R*Puddles by Fisher Hynds and John McKensie, Blackie

**R*Cat and Rat by Donald Moyle and Eileen Sykes, Talk-a-rounders series, Holmes McDougall

**R*Breakthrough to Literacy books, Longman

Yellow Series	*A Fish Book*
	The Cat, the Bird and the Tree
	*I Fell Over
	A Rainy Day
Red Series	*The Lost Girl
	The Loose Tooth
Blue Series	**Tom's Accident*
	Fire!

**Who Knows the Little Man?* by Walberga Attenberger, Hart-Davis Educational

LONGER STORIES

* **Topsy and Tim Books by Jean and Gareth Adamson, Blackie

Topsy and Tim's Monday Book	
,,	*Tuesday Book*
,,	*Wednesday Book*
,,	*Thursday Book*
,,	*Friday Book*
,,	*Saturday Book*
,,	*Sunday Book*
,,	*Birthday Party*
,,	*Paddling Pool*
,,	*Snowy Day*
Topsy and Tim	*Go Fishing*
,,	*at the Football Match*
,,	*Go on Holiday*
,,	*Go to Hospital*

Topsy and Tim at School
      ,,   *Go Sailing*
**The Story of Little Black Sambo* by Helen Bannerman, Chatto & Windus
Jesus is Born British & Foreign Bible Society
* **Thumbs Up by Helen Solomon, 'Language in Action' series, Macmillan Educational
***Mr Huff, Puff and Gruff* by E. T. Reed, 'Language in Action' series, Macmillan Educational
The Story of Miss Moppet by Beatrice Potter, Frederick Warne
The Story of a Fierce, Bad Rabbit by Beatrice Potter, Frederick Warne
Rose in the River by Ann Thwaite, A Stepping Stone Book, Brockhampton Press
**Harry the Dirty Dog* by Gene Zion, Bodley Head and Picture Puffins
Ladybird Easy Reading Books by Vera Southgate
  **Goldilocks and the Three Bears*
  **The Three Little Pigs* (Omit the detail about the third pig tricking the wolf in various ways – move straight on to the chimney incident.)
  The Gingerbread Boy
  The Sly Fox and the Little Red Hen
  **The Three Billy Goats Gruff*
  The Enormous Turnip
  **Little Red Riding Hood*

BOOKS THAT CAN BE READ TO THE CHILD AS THEY STAND

R**Inside, Outside, Upside Down* by Stan and Jan Berenstain, William Collins
R 'Little Book' series by John Burningham, Jonathan Cape
  The Friend
  The Snow
  The Rabbit
  *The Dog
  The Cupboard
  *The Blanket
  The School

R The Ronald Ridout Reading Scheme, Purnell

*'Books for me to Begin in' series *I Can See*
What Can I See?
I Can Hear
I Can Smell
Look at Me
Look, Listen and Smell

Red Series   The *House of Hay* by Ruth Ainsworth and Ronald Ridout

Green Series   *What Can You Hear?* by Ruth Ainsworth and Ronald Ridout
Susan's House by Ruth Ainsworth and Ronald Ridout

Yellow Series *David's Picture* by Ruth Ainsworth and Ronald Ridout

R* The 'Gay Colour Books' series, books 1–16, published by E. J. Arnold

R* 'Read it Yourself' books by June Melser, Methuen Educational

Set A   1. *What is little?*
2. *What is big?*
3. *What goes fast?*
4. *What comes down?*
5. *What can jump?*
6. *What goes up?*
7. *What can fly?*
8. *What goes round and round?*

Set B   1. *What I like*
2. *What I like to play*
3. *Where shall I hide?*
4. *Where do you live?*
5. *Which are you?*
6. *What I can do*
7. *Yes or No?*
8. *Where do you go?*

BOOKS WITH PICTURES TO ASK QUESTIONS ABOUT

'Language in Action' series by Joyce Mildred Morris, Macmillan Educational

Cat and Mouse
Tim and Tom
A Dog and His Bone
Hugo and his Grandma by Catherine Storr, Dinosaur Publications
The Wind Blew by Pat Hutchins, Bodley Head and Picture Puffins
All those books in the previous reading lists marked **

SEQUENCE CARDS

Picture Story Cards for use with the John Horniman School Language Scheme, obtainable from the Invalid Children's Aid Association, 126 Buckingham Palace Road, London SW1 9SB.

Appendix 3

Materials and Books suitable for use
with the techniques described
in Chapters 16-17

COVERING MANY TOPICS
> *Word Book* by Richard Hefter, William Collins and Picture Lions
> R My Picture Word Games – Galt
> Picture Line Books – sold only in a set of six books: *The Street*, *The River*, *The Farm*, *The Zoo*, *The Funfair*, *The Market*, Philograph Publications (only obtainable by mail order from Philip & Tacey)

The following headings are listed according to the order in which they are mentioned in Chapters 16–17

BOOKS THAT HELP TO DEVELOP
READING SKILLS
> 'Through the Rainbow' series by Elizabeth S. Bradburne, Schofield and Sims
> Ladybird 'Key Words' Reading Scheme up to 6a and 6b
> Ladybird 'Read it Yourself' series

> *Reading Level 2 – up to 'Key Words' book 2c
> *Goldilocks and the Three Bears* by Fran Hunia
> *The Three Billy Goats Gruff* by Fran Hunia
> *Sly Fox and the Little Red Hen* by Fran Hunia
> *The Elves and the Shoemaker* by Fran Hunia

> *Reading Level 3 – up to 'Key Words' book 3c
> *Three Little Pigs* by Fran Hunia
> *Little Red Riding Hood* by Fran Hunia
> *Puss in Boots* by Fran Hunia
> *Dick Whittington and his Cat* by Fran Hunia

> *Especially useful.
> R Also suitable for developing early reading.

*Reading Level 4 – up to 'Key Words' book 4c
   Gingerbread Boy by Fran Hunia
   Jack and the Beanstalk by Fran Hunia
   Cinderella by Fran Hunia
   Snow White and the Seven Dwarfs by Fran Hunia
'Can You Do This?' Books by Jenny Taylor and Terry
Ingleby, Longman

Set 1	*I Can Play*	Set 2	*I Can Ride*
	I Can Dig		*I Can Carry*
	I Can Help		*I Can Eat*
	I Can Write		*I Can Pull*

The 'Laugh and Learn' series by Terry Hall, George Philip
   Alexander
'My Work Books' by Mollie Clarke, Books 1-4, A. Wheaton
   & Co. Ltd.

THE STREET, PEOPLE AND VEHICLES
What are They? by Ruth Ainsworth and Ronald Ridout, a
   'Book for Me to Read', Purnell Bancroft
'Words Your Children Use' books by R. P. A. Edwards and
   V. Gibbon, Burke
   Travelling by Land
   People We Meet
   *Buildings
In the Town, 'Create a Story', a flip-over book, Kiddicraft

THE SHOPS
 R*Shopping with Mother*, Ladybird

THE FARM, COUNTRYSIDE,
BIRDS AND ANIMALS
Topsy and Tim on the Farm by Jean and Gareth Adamson,
   Blackie
Tame Animals by R. P. A. Edwards and V. Gibbon, a 'Words
Your Children Use' book, Burke
Seaside and Country by R. P. A. Edwards and V. Gibbon, a
   'Words Your Children Use' book, Burke

R**Who Lives Here?* by Eileen Ryder, a 'Head Start' book, Burke
R*The Farm by M. E. Gagg, Ladybird
*In the Country, 'Create a Story', a flip-over book, Kiddicraft
*On the Farm, 'Create a Story', a flip-over book, Kiddicraft
*Eggs, 'Starter Books', Macdonald
*Milk, 'Starter Books', Macdonald
Uniset Farm – Bambola Toys (Galt stocklists)

GARDENS

Garden Bird Lotto – Spear's Games
**Gardens and Flowers* by R. P. A. Edwards and V. Gibbon, a 'Words Your Children Use' book, Burke

THE ZOO

Topsy and Tim at the Zoo by Jean and Gareth Adamson, Blackie
R*The Zoo by M. E. Gagg, Ladybird
Uniset Zoo – Bambola Toys (Galt stocklists)
Who's at the Zoo? by Eileen Ryder, a 'Head Start' book, Burke
*At the Zoo, 'Create a Story', a flip-over book, Kiddicraft

THE SEASIDE

Topsy and Tim at the Seaside by Jean and Gareth Adamson, Blackie
**Seaside and Country* by R. P. A. Edwards and V. Gibbon, a 'Words Your Children Use' book, Burke
Seashore, 'Starter Books', Macdonald
*At the Seaside, 'Create a Story', a flip-over book, Kiddicraft
The Beach, a Kiddicraft jigsaw puzzle

RAILWAYS AND STATIONS

**Travelling by Land* by R. P. A. Edwards and V. Gibbon, a 'Words Your Children Use' book, Burke
The Little Red Engine Goes to Market by Diana Ross, Faber & Faber

SWIMMING POOL

Topsy and Tim Learn to Swim by Jean and Gareth Adamson, Blackie

THE WEATHER AND SEASONS

Weather by R. P. A. Edwards and V. Gibbon, a 'Words Your Children Use' book, Burke

Topsy and Tim's Snowy Day by Jean and Gareth Adamson, Blackie

Topsy and Tim's Foggy Day by Jean and Gareth Adamson, Blackie

Topsy and Tim's Monday Book by Jean and Gareth Adamson, Blackie

Topsy and Tim's Paddling Pool by Jean and Gareth Adamson Blackie

Rain, 'Starter Books', Macdonald

About the Seasons by A. Blackwood, a Beanstalk Book, Nelson Young World

OTHER BOOKS TO HELP
WITH WORD LISTS

Drinks, Food and Meals

Eating and Drinking by R. P. A. Edwards and V. Gibbon, a 'Words Your Children Use' book, Burke

An ABC for Hungry Boys and Girls, a 'Breakthrough' book, Longman

Inside the House and Outside the House

About the House, a 'Breakthrough' book, Longman

At Home with the Family by R. P. A. Edwards and V. Gibbon, a 'Words Your Children Use' book, Burke

Machines and Gadgets, by R. P. A. Edwards and V. Gibbon, a 'Words Your Children Use' book, Burke

In the Home, 'Create a Story', a flip-over book, Kiddicraft

Uniset Kitchen – Bambola Toys (Galt stocklists)

Uniset House – Bambola Toys (Galt stocklists)

R *About the House* by F. T. Fife, a 'Real Things' book, Philip & Tacey

Clothes

Uniset Girls' Clothes – Bambola Toys (Galt stocklists)

Myself and My Clothes by R. P. A. Edwards and V. Gibbon, a 'Words Your Children Use' book, Burke

Sea and Air Travel
    **Travelling by Sea and Air* by R. P. A. Edwards and V. Gibbon,
    a 'Words Your Children Use' book, Burke
    *Uniset Airport – Bambola Toys (Galt stocklists)

Toys and Games
    *Toys and Games by R. P. A. Edwards and V. Gibbon, a
    'Words Your Children Use' book, Burke

Circus and Fairground
    Topsy and Tim at the Circus by Jean and Gareth Adamson,
    Blackie
    Uniset Circus – Bambola Toys (Galt stocklists)
    *At the Circus, 'Create a Story', a flip-over book, Kiddicraft

School
    School by R. P. A. Edwards and V. Gibbon, a 'Words
    Your Children Use' book, Burke
    *Going to School, 'Create a Story', a flip-over book, Kiddicraft

What Things Are Made Of
    **What Are Things Made Of* by R. P. A. Edwards and V.
    Gibbon, a 'Words Your Children Use' book, Burke

Action Words
    **The Hop, Skip and Jump Book* by Jack Kent, William Collins
    and Picture Lions
    Busy Days by J. D. Bevington, a 'Turn and Learn' book,
    Hamlyn

Descriptive Words
    *Opposites by R. P. A. Edwards and V. Gibbon, a 'Words Your
    Children Use' book, Burke
    Top and Bottom, a 'Macdonald Opposites' book, Macdonald

Positional Words
    Spatial Relationships-Concept Cards, Learning Development
    Aids
  R Position Words Strip Books (set of four books: A, B, C, D),
    Philip & Tacey
    Places by J. D. Bevington, a 'Turn and Learn' book, Hamlyn
  R**Andrew's Engine* by Ruth Ainsworth and Ronald Ridout, a
    'Book for Me to Read', Purnell Bancroft
    Hunt the Thimble by Ruth Ainsworth and Ronald Ridout, a
    'Book for Me to Read', Purnell Bancroft

Round and Round, an 'Althea's Brightstar Book', Souvenir
Press

Why? – Because
'Why – Because' cards – Learning Development Aids

When? – Time
*Toy Clock – Spear's Games
When? by R. P. A. Edwards and V. Gibbon, a 'Words Your
Children Use' book, Burke
At Night by Lesley Anne Ivory, a 'Head Start' book, Burke

STORY BOOKS FOR THE ADULT TO TELL A STORY FROM

The Berenstain Bears' New Baby by Stan and Jan Berenstain,
Picture Lions
The Trouble with Jack by Shirley Hughes, William Collins
and Picture Lions
The Tiger Who Came to Tea by Judith Kerr, William Collins
and Picture Lions
Harry by the Sea by Gene Zion, Bodley Head and Picture
Puffins
No Roses for Harry! by Gene Zion, Bodley Head and Picture
Puffins
Sylvester and the Magic Pebble by William Steig, Abelard
Schuman and Picture Lions
Wide-awake Jake by Helen Young, William Collins and
Picture Lions

FOR READING THE WHOLE BOOK ALOUD TO THE CHILD

R *Tim's Kite* by Ruth Ainsworth and Ronald Ridout, a 'Book
for Me to Read', Purnell Bancroft
A House for a Mouse by Ruth Ainsworth and Ronald Ridout,
a 'Book for Me to Read', Purnell Bancroft
The Very Hungry Caterpillar by Eric Carle, Hamish Hamilton
and Picture Puffins
Are You My Mother? by P. D. Eastman, a 'Beginner Book',
William Collins

Julius by Sid Hoff, World's Work

Sammy the Seal by Sid Hoff, World's Work

Hurry! Hurry! by Edith Thatcher Hurd, an 'I Can Read It Myself' book, World's Work

Stop! Stop! by Edith Thatcher Hurd, an 'I Can Read It Myself' book, World's Work and other books in the 'I Can Read It Myself' series

Shirley Sharpeyes by Frances Knowles and Brian Thompson, a 'Breakthrough' book, Longman

Who's Scared of the Dark? by Frances Knowles and Brian Thompson, a 'Breakthrough' book, Longman

R *The Eye Book* by Theo Le Sieg, a 'Beginner Book', William Collins

A Lion in the Meadow by Margaret Mahy, Dent and Picture Puffins

R *The Ear Book* by Al Perkins, a 'Beginner Book', William Collins

R**Go, Dog, Go* by P. D. Eastman, a 'Beginner Book', William Collins

Rabbit is Hungry by Helen Piers, Methuen

Run, Rabbit Run! by Helen Piers, Methuen

Rabbit Digs a Burrow by Helen Piers, Methuen

The Kitten Who Couldn't Get Down by Helen Piers, Methuen

Hugo and his Grandmother by Catherine Storr, an 'Althea's Dinosaur' book, Souvenir Press

The Elephant and the Bad Baby by Elfrida Vipont and Raymond Briggs, Hamish Hamilton and Picture Puffins

Egrin and the Painted Wizard by Amanda Walsh, Picture Puffins

R *The Foot Book* by Dr Seuss, a 'Beginner Book', William Collins

Mr Rabbit and the Lovely Present by Charlotte Zolotow, Bodley Head and Picture Puffins

Ladybird Easy Reading Books, Grades I and II by Vera Southgate, Ladybird – some children may comprehend Grade III

PAIRS OF CARDS TO ENCOURAGE SENTENCE CONSTRUCTION

Motor Expressive Language Cards, Sets I and II – Developmental Learning Materials

Things That Go Together – Learning Development Aids

What Goes With What? puzzle dominoes – Abbatt Toys

SEQUENCE CARDS

Sequential Picture Cards, Sets I, II and III – Developmental Learning Materials

Sequential Thinking-Concept Cards, Sets 1–5 – Learning Development Aids

Look, Think and Write by F. H. M. Meade and F. Kerry, Chambers

DETECTION OF ABSURDITIES

What's Wrong? Cards, Sets I and II – Learning Development Aids

Macdonald 'Zero' Books
  In the Kitchen
  On the Beach
  At the Zoo
  In the Garden
  In the Park
  In the Shops

PROBLEM SOLVING

What Would You Do? Cards – Learning Development Aids

Appendix 4

Materials and Books suitable for use with the techniques described in Chapter 18

R 'Motspur Singulars-and-Plurals' cards – Philip & Tacey

R*'Read, Write and Remember' (books 1–8) by Constance Milburn, Blackie

R*_Better English: New Primary Course_ (books 1–2) by Ronald Ridout, Ginn

R _Sentences_, Macdonald
Workbooks in Primary English by O. M. Gregory, A. Wheaton & Co. Ltd.

*'Sounds the Same' cards – Learning Development Aids
Homonym cards – Developmental Learning Materials
Homophone cards – Developmental Learning Materials

R*'Starter Books' series, Macdonald (There are about 50 books in the series, each one on a separate topic.)
Things People Often Say by R. P. A. Edwards and V. Gibbon, Burke

R*_Listening_ by R. P. A. Edwards and V. Gibbon, Burke
My Naughty Little Sister by Dorothy Edwards, Young Puffin

For early silent reading supervised by an adult
Paul, the Hero of the Fire by Edward Ardizzone, Longman Young Books and Picture Puffins
Jim and the Beanstalk by Raymond Briggs, Longman Young Books and Picture Puffins
Mrs Pepperpot's Busy Day by Bjorn Berg, Longman Young Books and Picture Puffins
Humbert by John Burningham, Jonathan Cape and Picture Puffins

* Especially useful.
R Also suitable for developing early reading.

The Happy Lion by Louise Fatio, Bodley Head and Picture Puffins

The Trouble with Jack by Shirley Hughes, Bodley Head and Picture Lions

The *Captain Pugwash* books by John Ryan, Bodley Head and Picture Puffins

Grandfather Ben by Eva Scherbarth, Blackie and Piccolo Picture Books

Wide-awake Jake by Helen Young and Jenny Williams, Collins and Picture Lions

Harry by the Sea by Gene Zion, Bodley Head and Picture Puffins

No Roses for Harry by Gene Zion, Bodley Head and Picture Puffins

Ladybird Easy Reading Books by Vera Southgate

More difficult

The Berenstain Bears' New Baby by Stan and Jan Berenstain, Picture Lions

The Book of Giant Stories by David Harrison, Jonathan Cape and Piccolo Picture Books

Sylvester and the Magic Pebble by William Steig, Abelard Schuman and Picture Lions

First stories with few or no pictures for children to read to themselves
For girls:

The 'Milly Molly Mandy' books by Joyce Brisley, Harrap and Picture Puffins

My Naughty Little Sister by Dorothy Edwards, Methuen and Picture Puffins

My Naughty Little Sister's Friends by Dorothy Edwards, Methuen and Picture Puffins

The Adventures of Galldora by Modwena Sedgwick, Picture Puffins

For boys:

The Bus Under the Leaves by Margaret Mahy, Dent and Picture Puffins

Bad Boys ed. Eileen H. Colwell, Longman Young Books and Young Puffin Books

The Sawdust Secret by Jean Wills, Hamish Hamilton and Picture Puffins

For boys and girls:
> *Stories for Under Fives, Stories for Five Year Olds, Stories for Six Year Olds, Stories for Seven Year Olds, Stories for Eight Year Olds* ed. Sara and Stephen Corrin, Faber & Faber and Young Puffin Books
>
> *A Gift from Winklesea* by Helen Cresswell, Brockhampton Press and Young Puffin Books

These books have simple vocabulary and it is suggested that parents look at the word level and try to find other books of a similar level their children may like.

Dictionaries

Various children's dictionaries are available – some picture dictionaries entertain rather than inform. For serious study the *Oxford Children's Dictionary* in colour can be used from eight years old upwards. Also recommended are Chamber's *Young Set Dictionaries* (Dictionaries One, Two, Three and Four) by Brown, Dowing and Sceats.

A book to help with spelling rules
> *Alpha to Omega* by Bevé Hornsby and Frula Shear, Heinemann Educational Books

Poetry books
> *This Little Puffin* ed. Elizabeth M. Matterson, Puffin
> *The Puffin Book of Verse* ed. Eleanor Graham, Puffin
> *Bedtime Rhymes* by Audrey Daly, Ladybird

Appendix 5

Groups of Similar-Sounding Words
for use in Auditory Discrimination Work

The lists have no pretensions to be exhaustive and many other permutations exist. The following words have been chosen because they are frequently used in everyday speech.

back	mad	egg	led	web
bad	mac	edge	leg	well
badge	man	end	ledge	when
bat	map		less	west
band	mat		let	wet
	match		lend	went
	smack		lent	sweat
			sledge	swell
can	pack	fed	men	if
cap	pan	fell	mess	ill
cat	pad	fetch	met	in
catch	pat			is
camp	patch			it
	pant			itch
	spat			
had	rag	head	peg	big
has	ram	hedge	pen	bill
hat	ran	hen	pet	bin
have	rash	held	peck	bit
ham				build
hand				brick
hang				

lamb	sack	jet	tell	dig
lash	sad	check	ten	dim
latch	sat	chess	tent	dip
lap	sash			dish
slap				ditch
fig	mill	tick	fog	rob
fin	mist	tin	fox	rod
fit	miss	tip	font	rock
fix		till	frog	wrong
fizz		trick	frock	
fish			from	
fill			frost	
frill			flock	
chill	pick	wig	log	sob
chin	pig	will	lock	sock
chip	pill	win	lot	song
chimp	pip	with	long	salt
	pit	wind	lost	
	pitch	twin	slot	
	spill	twist		
	spit	twig		
hid	rib	odd	knob	was
hill	rid	of	knock	what
him	rip	off	knot	wash
hip	rich	on		watch
hit				want
hiss				wasp
				swan
lid	sick	cock	pop	bud
lick	sill	cop	pot	bun
lip	sip	cot	pond	bus
live	sit	cross		but
link	sing	clock		buzz
slid		clog		bump
slim				bunk
slip				

cub	mud	could	park	key
cuff	muff	cook	palm	keel
come	mug	crook	part	keep
cup	must		past	
cut			path	
			plant	
			spark	

dug	rub	put	shark	feed
duck	rough	pull	sharp	feel
dull	run	puss	shan't	feet
dumb	rush	push		field
done	rung			
dump	rust			
dove				
dust				
dusk				

hug	suck	half	eat	lead
hum	sum	hard	each	leaf
hut	sun	harm	east	leek
hush	such	heart		lean
hutch	sunk	hearth		least
hunt				

luck	book	laugh	beak	she
love	bull	large	beef	sheep
lump	bush	last	beam	sheet
			beat	shield
			bee	
			beach	

cheek	tea	four	rude	ache
cheap	team	fork	roof	age
cheat	tease	form	room	eight
cheese	teach	fort	root	
	teeth	fourth	rule	

need kneel neat	weed wheel wheat weave	paw pork port porch sport	two toot tooth	cage cake came cane cape case cave
pea peel peep peach	board ball bought bald	war walk warm worn	gale game gate gave	
seek seed seal seem seen seat	core caught cord cork call corn	who hoof hoot whose	were word work worm worse	hay hail hate
lay lake lane late	rake rage rail rain race	lie life like lime line light	ride rhyme rice right rise rind	dough dose don't
mole moat most	shake shade shape	say safe sail same	my mine might mice mind	sigh side size sign
go goal goes goat gold	no note nose snow	may make made mail mate maze	take tale tame tape taste	knife nine nice night

tie	hole	row	pay	fine
tide	home	road	paid	fight
tile	hope	roll	page	five
time	hose	rope	pail	find
type	hold	rose	paint	
tight				
pie	why	low	sew	
pile	wide	load	sole	
pine	wife	loaf	soap	
pipe	while	slow	soak	
pint	wine		sold	
spine	wipe			
	white			
	wise			
	wind			
	wild			

Appendix 6

Word Lists

The following word lists contain the naming, doing, descriptive and positional words listed throughout this book. They represent an attempt to guide parents as to what has been found from experience can be absorbed by hearing-impaired children. Where there is more than one meaning of a word, e.g. 'watch' (a timepiece) and 'watch' (look at) the word is listed once only in the alphabetical list. Words that have been dealt with in Chapters 10–14 are marked *

about	aid	answer
above	aircraft	ant
absent	airport	any
accident	airport control	anybody
ache	tower	anyone
acorn	alarm	anything
acrobat	alive	anywhere
across	*all	*apple
act	alligator	apple pie
actor	allow	apricot
actress	almost	April
add	alone	apron
adder	along	archer
address	already	archway
aerodrome	also	argue
*aeroplane	always	arithmetic
afraid	*ambulance	ark
*after	anchor	*arm
afternoon	angel	arm bands
*again	ankle	armchair
against	annoyed	around
age	anorak	arrest
ago	*another	arrow

art
ash
ashamed
ashtray
*ask
*asleep
aspirin
*at
atlas
at once
attention
attic
August
awake
away
axe
*baby
bachelor
*back
*back to front
backwards
bacon
*bad
*baddie
badge
badger
*bag
bake
baked beans
baker
baker's shop
balance
bald
*ball
*balloon
ballpoint
*banana
band
bandstand

*bang
banister
bank
bar
barbecue
*bare
barge
bark
barley
barn
barrel
barrier
barrow
*basement
*basin
*basket
*bat
*bath
bathe
bathmat
*bathroom
batter
battery
battle
bay
*be
beach
beacon
bead
beak
bean
*bear
beard
beast
beat
beautiful
become
*bed
bedcover

*bedroom
*bee
beef
beefburger
beehive
beer
beetle
beetroot
before
*beg
beggar
begin
beginning
behave
behind
believe
*bell
bellows
below
*belt
bench
*bend
*beside
best
*better
between
bib
*bicycle (or bike)
*big
big hand
    (of the clock)
big toe
big wheel
    (at the fair)
bill
bills
bin
*bird
birdbath

*birthday
*biscuit
bit of, a
bite
bitter
blackberry
*blackboard
blank
*blanket
bleed
blind
blind man
blister
block
*blood
blossom
blot
blouse
*blow
bluebell
bluebottle
blue tit
blunt
blush
board
*boat
bog
boggy
boil
bolt
bomb
bone
bonfire
bonnet
*book
*bookcase (or
  bookshelf)
*boot
bootees

border
bored
borrow
*both
*bottle
*bottom
bounce
*bow
*bowl
bowling green
bowtie
*box
box office
*boy
boy scout
bracelet
brain
brake
branch
brass
*brave
*bread
*break
breakers
*breakfast
breakwater
breath
breathe
breed
breeze
*brick
bricklayer
bride
bridegroom
bridesmaid
*bridge
*bright
*bring
*broken

brook
broom
*brother
bruise
*brush
*bubble
bubble pipe
*bucket
buckle
bud
budgerigar
buffalo
buffers
bugle
*build
builder
*bulb
bull
bulldozer
*bump
bumper
bumper car
bun
bunch of, a
bundle of, a
bungalow
bunk
buoy
burglar
*burn
burst
bury
*bus
bush
bus stop
but
butcher
butcher's shop
*butter

buttercup
*butterfly
*button
buy
buzz
*by
cabbage
cabin
cafe
cage
*cake
calendar
calf
*call
calm
*camel
*camera
camp
can
canal
canary
*candle
candlestick
candy floss
cane
cannon
canoe
canvas
*cap
cape
captain
capture
*car
caravan
*card
cardboard
cardigan
care
careful

cargo
carol
carol singers
carpenter
*carpet
carpet sweeper
carriage
carrot
*carry
carry cot
cart
carve
*case
cashier
casserole
castle
*cat
*catch
caterpillar
cathedral
cauliflower
cave
ceiling
celery
cellar
cement
*cereal
chain
*chair
*chalk
champion
change
changing room
channel
chapel
chapped
charge
chart
*chase

chatter
chauffeur
cheap
cheat
check
cheek
cheer
*cheese
cheese spread
chemist
cheque book
cherry
chess
chest
chew
*chick
*chicken
chicken-pox
chief
child
*children
chilly
chime
*chimney
chimpanzee
chin
china
chip
chirp
chisel
*chocolate
chocolate pudding
choke
choose
*chop
christen
christening
*Christmas
Christmas cake

Christmas card
Christmas crackers
Christmas present
Christmas pudding
Christmas
    stocking
*Christmas tree
*church
churn
cigar
*cigarette
cinema
*circle
clap
clash
class
claw
clay
*clean
cleaning
clear
clear up
cliff
*climb
clip
cloak
cloakroom
*clock
clog
close
*cloth
*clothes
*cloud
*clown
coach
*coat
cobbles
cobweb
*Coca-Cola

*cock
cocoa
coconut
*coffee
coffee-pot
cog
*cold
*collar
collect
*colour
*comb
*come
comic
compartment
concert
conjurer
conker
*cook
*cooker
cool
coop
copper
copy
cord
core
cork
corn
*cornflakes
corn on the cob
*corner
corridor
cost
*cot
cottage
cotton
cough
could
count
counter

couple
cousin
*cover
*cow
*cowboy
cowshed
crab
crack
*cradle
crane
crash
*crawl
crayon
*cream
cricket
crisps
*crocodile
crocus
crook
*crooked
*cross
crossbar
crossroads
crow
crowd
crowd of, a
*crown
crumb
crumpet
crush
crust
crutch
*cry
cub
cubicle
cuckoo
cucumber
cuff
*cup

*cupboard
curious
curl
*curly
curtain
*curved
*cushion
custard
customer
*cut
cycling
*Daddy
daffodil
dagger
daisy
damp
dance
dandelion
danger
dangerous
*dark
dash
date
dates
daughter
dawn
*day
*dead
deaf
dear
deceitful
December
decide
deck
deckchair
decorate
decorations
*deep
deer

dentist
department store
*desk
devil
dial
*diamond
diary
dice
dictation
*die
diesel engine
*different
*dig
dim
dimple
dining room
*dinner
dip
dirt
*dirty
disappointed
discover
dish
disobedient
ditch
dive
diving board
division
*do
dock
*doctor
*dog
dog dirt
*doll
doll's house
dolphin
dominoes
*donkey
*door

door knob
dose
dot
dough
doughnut
dove
*down
*downstairs
dozen
drag
dragon
dragonfly
drain
draining board
drainpipe
drake
draughts
*draw
*drawer
drawing pin
dream
*dress
*dressing-gown
dressing-table
dressing-up
    clothes
*drink
drinking fountain
*drive
driver
*drop
drop of, a
drown
*drum
*dry
*duck
duckling
dull
dumb

dump
dumpling
dungarees
dusk
dust
dustcart
duster
dustman
dustpan
*duvet
dwarf
dye
each
eager
eagle
*ear
early
earn
earth
east
Easter
easy
*eat
echo
edge
*egg
eggcup
eight
eighteen
eighteenth
eighth
elastic
elbow
electric cooker
electric engine
electricity
*elephant
elevenses
elf

*else
embankment
*empty
*end
engaged
engine
engine driver
enough
envelope
escape
even
evening
ever
every
everybody
everyone
everything
everywhere
evil
except
excited
exercise
exit
expect
expel
expensive
explain
express
extra
*eye
eyebrow
*face
factory
fade
faint
fair
fairly
*fairy
fairy godmother

*fall
false
fan
*far
fare
farm
farmer
farmhouse
*fast
*fat
*father
Father Christmas
fawn
*feather
February
*feed
feel
*feet
*fence
fetch
fete
*few
fib
*field
fierce
fifth
fifteen
fifteenth
fig
*fight
figure
*fill
film
fin
*find
fine
*finger
finish
*fire

*fire engine
fireplace
fire station
first
*fish
fish finger
fish shop
fisherman
fishing line
fishing rod
fit
*five
fix
fizz
*flag
flap
flash
flat
flats
flea
fleece
flesh
flippers
float
flock
flood
*floor
flour
*flower
flower bed
flower shop
*fly
foal
foam
fog
fold
follow
fool
*foot

football
footbath
footbridge
footprint
footstep
*for
force
forehead
forest
forge
forget
*fork
form
fort
fortnight
fortune teller
forwards
fountain
*four
fourteen
fourteenth
fourth
*fox
frame
freckles
free
freeze
fresh
Friday
*friend
friendly
*fridge
fright
*frightened
frill
fringe
frock
*frog
*from

frost
frown
frying pan
*full
funnel
*funny
fur
furious
furniture van
fuss
gale
*game
gaol
gap
gape
garage
garageman
*garden
gargle
gas
gas works
*gate
gather
gay
gear
gentle
germ
*ge
*get up
ghost
ghost house
giant
gift
gigantic
gipsy
giraffe
*girl
girl guide
*give

glad
*glass
*glasses
glider
globe
*glove
*glue
gnome
*go
goal
*goat
goblin
goggles
gold
golden
goldfish
golliwog
*good
*goodbye
good morning
*goodnight
goods train
goose
gooseberry
gorilla
gown
grab
grace
*grandma
*grandpa
grapefruit
grapes
*grass
grasshopper
grating
graveyard
gravy
greasy
great

greedy
green flag
greengrocer
greenhouse
greet
grin
grip
grit
grocer
ground
group of, a
*grow
grown up
guard
guard's van
*guess
guide
guinea-pig
guitar
gull
gulp
gum
gums
*gun
gutter
hack
hail
*hair
hairdryer
hairdresser
half
*half-moon
half past
halt
ham
hamburger
hammer
hammock
hamster

*hand
handbag
handbrake
*handkerchief
*handle
handlebars
handsome
handwork
hang
hanger
happen
*happy
harbour
*hard
hare
harm
*hat
hatch
hate
*have
hay
haystack
*head
headache
headlamp
headmaster
headmistress
heap of, a
*hear
*hearing aid
*heart
hearth
*heater
*heavy
*hedge
hedgehog
heel
helicopter
*hello

helmet
*help
helter skelter
hem
*hen
henhouse
herd
hiccups
*hide
hide and seek
*high
high heels
*hill
him
hip
hippo
hiss
*hit
hive
hoard
hockey
*hold
*hole
holiday
holly
*home
*honey
hood
hoof
hook
*hoop
hoopla
hoot
*hop
hope
hopscotch
horn
horrible
*horse

horseshoe
hose
hosepipe
*hospital
*hot
hot dog
hotel
hot-water
  bottle
hour
*house
hovercraft
how
howl
*hug
hum
hump
*hungry
hunt
*hurry
hurry, in a
hurt
husband
hush
hut
hutch
hymn
*ice
*ice cream
ice cream van
icing
icy
idea
if
ill
imagine
*I'm sorry
*in
indoors

infection
in front of
injection
ink
*inside
*inside out
instead
interesting
*into
invitation
*iron
ironing board
ironmonger
island
it
itch
ivy
jab
jacket
*jam
jam tarts
January
jar
jaw
jealous
jeans
jeep
jetty
jelly fish
jerk
jersey
jet
jetty
jeweller
jig
jigsaw puzzle
job
jockey
jog

join
joint
joke
jolt
journey
*juice
*jug
juggler
July
*jump
*jumper
June
just
kangaroo
keel
keen
keep
keeper
'keep left' sign
kennel
kerb
ketchup
*kettle
*key
*kick
kid
*kill
kilt
*king
kipper
*kiss
*kitchen
*kite
*kitten
*knee
*kneel
*knife
knight
knit

knob
*knock
knocker
knot
*know
knuckle
lace
ladder
*lady
*ladybird
lake
lamb
*lamp
lamp post
land
landing
lane
*lap
lard
large
lash
last
last week
latch
*late
*later
*laugh
lavender
lawn
lawn-mower
*lay
lazy
lead
*leaf
leak
lean
leap
leaptrog
learn

*least
leather
leave
ledge
leeks
*left
left luggage office
*leg
Lego
*lemon
lemonade
lemon juice
lend
length
leopard
less
lesson
let
*letter
*letter-box
letters
lettuce
level crossing
library
lick
*lid
lie
lifebelt
lifeboat
lifeguard
lift
*light
lighter
*lighthouse
lightning
*like
lime juice
limp
limpet

line
linen
link
lino
*lion
lion tamer
*lip
lipstick
liquorice
list
*listen
litter
litter basket
litter bin
*little
little hand
  (of the clock)
little toe
live
liver
*living-room
load
load of, a
loaf
lobster
*lock
locker
loft
log
*lollipop
lollipop man
*long
*loo
*look
look, have a
loop
*lorry
lose
*lost

*lot
*lots of
love
lovely
low
luck
lucky
ludo
luggage
luggage rack
luggage van
lump
lump of, a
*lunch
*mac
mad
magic
*maggot
magician
magnet
mail
mail bag
mail van
main
*make
*man
manners
mantelpiece
manure
many
map
*marble
March
mare
margarine
*mark
market
marmalade
marrow

marry
marsh
mash
mask
master
*mat
*matches
maths
matter
mattress
May
meadow
mean
measles
*meat
medal
medicine
meet
melon
*melt
melted
*men
*mend
meringue
mermaid
*mess
message
metal
mice
midday
middle
middle-sized
midge
midnight
might
*milk
milk float
*milkman
mince

mince pies
mind
mine
mint
minus
*minute
*mirror
miserable
miss
mist
mistake
mistletoe
mittens
*mix
mixer
moat
model
mole
Monday
*money
*monkey
monster
month
*moon
mop
*more
*morning
mortar
moss
*most
moth
*mother
*motor bike
motor scooter
mould
moult
mountain
*mouse
moustache

*mouth
mouthful
*move
much
*mud
muddy
muff
muffin
*mug
*Mummy
mumps
muscle
museum
mushroom
music
must
mutton
my
*nail
nailbrush
*name
napkin
nappy
narrow
nasty
nature
*naughty
*near
nearly
neat
neck
need
*needle
neighbour
*nest
*net
nettle
never
*new

New Year
newsagent
newspaper
newspaper stall
*next
next to
nib
*nice
*night
*nightdress (or
    nightie)
nine
nineteen
nineteenth
ninth
*no
nobody
*noise
*noisy
nonsense
noodles
noon
no one
north
*nose
note
nothing
notice
nought
November
now
nowhere
numb
*number
nun
*nurse
*nut
oars
oats

*oblong
ocean
o'clock
October
octopus
odd
of
*off
office
often
ogre
oil
*old
omelet
*on
*once
one
onion
only
*onto
*open
opening
operation
*orange
orange juice
orchard
order
ostrich
*other
otter
*out
outdoors
*outside
*oval
oven
*over
overall
overhead wires
*owl

*pack
packet of, a
pad
paddle
paddle boat
padlock
page
pageant
*pain
*paint
painter
pair
pair of, a
palace
pale
palm
pancakes
panda
pant
*pants
*paper
paper boy
paper chain
parachute
parcel
*park
park keeper
parrot
parsley
parson
part
parting
party
pass
passage
passenger
past
paste
pastry

pasture
*pat
*patch
*path
patient
patrol
patter
pattern
*pavement
paw
pay
peace and quiet
peaceful
peach
peacock
peak
*pear
*peas
pebble
peck
pedal
pedal car
peel
peep
peg
pelican
*pen
*pencil
penguin
*people
pepper
perhaps
pest
pet
pet shop
petrol pump
petticoat
phlegm
photograph

piano
*pick
pick up
picnic
*picture
pie
piece of, a
pier
*pig
pigeon
piggy back
pigsty
pile of, a
pill
*pillow
pilot
*pin
pinafore
pinafore dress
pinch
pine
pineapple
pint
pip
*pipe
pipes
pirate
pistol
pit
pitch
place
place mat
plain
plan
*plant
*plaster
plastic
*plate
*play

playground
playroom
playtime
*please
pleased
pleat
plenty of
plimsolls
plot
plough
plug
plum
plum pudding
plumber
plump
plus
poach
*pocket
poem
*point
points
poison
poke
poker
polar bear
pole
police car
*policeman
police station
polish
polite
pom-pom
*pond
pony
pony tail
pool
*poor
*pop
poppy

porch
pore
pork
porridge
port
porter
*pos
postcard
poster
*postman
post office
post office van
pot
potatoes
*pottie
pouch
pounce
*pour
*powder
practise
*pram
pray
press
*pretend
*pretty
price
prick
prince
princess
prison
private
prize
procession
promise
prop
propeller
proud
prune
prunes

pub
public
public lavatory
pudding
*puddle
puff
*pull
pullover
pulse
pump
pumpkin
punch
Punch and Judy
punish
punishment
pupil
*puppet
puppy
purr
*purse
pus
*push
pushchair
puss
*put
put in
put on
putty
*pyjamas
quack
quarrel
quarter
quarter past
quarter to
quay
*queen
queer
question
queue

*quick
*quiet
*quite
*rabbit
race
rack
racquet
radiator
radio
radish
raft
rag
rage
raid
rail
railings
railway line
railway station
*rain
rainbow
raincoat
raindrop
rake
ram
rapid
rare
rash
raspberry
rat
rattle
ravioli
raw
*reach
*read
reading book
*ready
*real
reap
recite

*record
recorder
record player
red flag
red lamp
Red Indian
reed
reflection
register
reindeer
*remember
report
rescue
rest
return
rhino
rhubarb
rhyme
rib
ribbon
ribena
rice
rice pudding
rich
rid
riddle
*ride
ridge
rifle
rigging
*right
*right side up
*right way up
rind
*ring
ring master
rinse
rip
ripe

rise
risk
river
*road
road sign
roar
roast
rob
robber
robin
rock
rockery
rocket
rocking horse
rod
*roll
roller
rolling pin
*roof
*room
root
*rope
rose
*rough
*round
*roundabout
row
row of, a
rowing boat
royal
rub
rubber
rubber ring
rubbish
rude
*rug
rugger
ruin
rule

ruler
*run
runway
rush
rusk
rustle
rusty
sack
*sad
saddle
saddle bag
safe
safety belt
safety net
sag
*sail
sailor
salad
salmon
*salt
*same
*sand
sand castle
sandals
sandpie
sandpit
*sandwich
*Santa Claus
sardines
sash
satchel
satin
Saturday
*saucepan
saucer
*sausage
save
*saw
sawdust

say
scab
scabbard
scaffolding
scald
scale
scalp
scar
scarecrow
scared
scarf
scent
*school
*scissors
scold
scooter
scramble
scrap of, a
scratch
scream
screw
screwdriver
scribble
scrub
scrubbing brush
*sea
*seal
sea-lion
seat
seaweed
second
secret
*see
seed
seem
*see-saw
selfish
self service
sell

*sellotape
*send
sensible
September
serve
set
several
*sew
sewing machine
shabby
shade
shadow
*shake
shallow
*shampoo
shape
share
shark
*sharp
shave
shawl
she
shed
*sheep
sheepdog
*sheet
shelf
*shell
shelter
shepherd
shepherd's pie
sheriff
shield
*shine
*shiny
*ship
*shirt
shiver
shoal

shock
*shoe
shoe shop
*shoot
*shop
shopkeeper
shore
*short
shortbread
shorts
shoulder
shout
*show
shower
shred
shriek
shrill
shrimp
shrink
shrub
shrug
shrunken
shudder
shuffle
*shut
shy
sick
side
sideways
siding
sigh
sign
sign post
signal
signal box
silk
sill
*silly
silver

simple
sing
single
*sink
sip
sir
*sister
*sit
sitting-room
size
*skate
skeleton
ski
skid
skin
*skip
skipping rope
skirt
skull
*sky
slack
slap
slate
sledge
*sleep
sleeper
sleet
sleeve
*slide
slim
sling
slip
*slipper
slit
slop
slope
slot
slot machine
slow

slug
slush
*smack
*small
smart
*smarties
smash
smell
*smile
*smoke
*smooth
smother
smoulder
snack
*snail
*snake
snatch
sneeze
sniff
snore
snout
*snow
snowball
snowdrop
snowflake
snowman
soak
*soap
soar
sob
*sock
socket
*sofa
*soft
soil
*soldier
sole
solve
some

somebody
someone
somersault
something
sometimes
somewhere
son
song
soon
sorcerer
*sore
*sorry
sort
sound
*soup
sour
south
sow
space
*spade
spaghetti
spanking
spark
sparkler
sparrow
speak
special
speech
spell
spelling
spend
*spider
spill
spin
spinach
spin dryer
spine
spire
spit

*splash
splint
splinter
split
spoil
spokes
*sponge
*spoon
spot
spout
sprain
spray
spread
spring
sprinkle
sprinkler
sprouts
*square
squash
squeak
squeeze
squirrel
stable
stack
stage
stagger
*stairs
stale
stall
*stamp
*stand
*star
stare
starfish
start
starve
station
station clock
stationer

(306)

station master
statue
stay
steady
steak
steal
steam
steamer
steel
steep
steer
steering wheel
step
step, a
steps
stethoscope
stew
*stick
stiff
stile
*still
stilts
sting
stir
stirrup
stitches
stocking
stomach
*stone
stool
*stop
stork
storm
*story
stout
stove
*straight
strange
strap

straw
strawberry
stream
*stretch
strict
stride
strike
string
stripe
*stroke
*strong
strong man
stud
studio
study
stump
stupid
submarine
subway
such
*suck
sudden
*sugar
suit
suitcase
sum
summer
*sun
Sunday
sunrise
sunset
sunshine
sun suit
super
supermarket
*supper
suppose
surface
surgery

surname
surprised
swallow
swan
swarm
sweat
*sweater
*sweep
sweeper
*sweet
sweet shop
swell
swelling
swift
*swim
swim suit
swimming teacher
*swing
swiss roll
*switch
*sword
syrup
tab
*table
tablecloth
tack
tackle
tag
*tail
tail light
tailor
*take
take out
*talk
*tall
tambourine
tame
tangerine
tangled

tank	theatre	time
tanker	thick	timetable
*tap	thief	timid
tape	thigh	tin
tape measure	thimble	tinkle
tape recorder	thing	tin-opener
tar	*think	tiny
tart	third	tip
tartan	thirteen	*tired
tassel	thirteenth	*tissue
taste	thirsty	*to
taxi	thistle	toad
*tea	thread	toadstool
teach	threaten	toast
*teacher	*three	tobacco
team	throat	toboggan
*teapot	throb	today
tease	through	toddler
teaspoon	*throw	*toe
*teddy	thrush	toffee
*teeth	thud	toffee apple
telegraph pole	*thumb	together
*telephone	Thursday	*toilet
telephone box	tick	*tomato
*television	ticket	*tomorrow
*tell	ticket collector	tongue
temper	ticket office	tonight
ten	tide	tonsil
tender	tidy	*too
tennis	*tie	toot
tennis court	tiger	*tooth
*tent	tight	*tooth-brush
term	tightrope	tooth mug
terrace	tightrope walker	*top
terrible	*tights	torch
test	tile	tortoise
tether	tiles	toss
*thank	till	total
thatch	tilt	touch

tough
towards
*towel
towel rail
tower
town hall
*toy
toy shop
track
*tractor
traffic
traffic lights
traffic warden
trailer
*train
tramp
transporter
trap
trapeze
travel
trawler
*tray
treacle
treasure
treat
*tree
trench
*triangle
trick
tricycle
trifle
trigger
trip
trip up
troll
trolley
trot
trouble
trough

*trousers
trowel
truck
true
trumpet
trunk
trunks
truth
*try
T-shirt
tub
tube of
   toothpaste
tuck
Tuesday
tulip
tumble
*tummy
tummy-ache
tune
tunic
tunnel
turf
turkey
*turn
turnip
turntable
turret
turtle
twig
twin
twist
*two
type
tyre
*ugly
*umbrella
unbolt
unbutton

uncle
uncover
*under
understand
undress
unicorn
unload
unlock
unpack
unpin
unroll
untie
untruth
unwrap
*up
upon
upset
*upstairs
*upside down
upwards
use
vacuum
vague
valley
vain
*van
vanish
varnish
vase
veal
veil
vein
velvet
verse
*very
vessel
*vest
vice
view

village
vinegar
violin
viper
visit
visitor
vixen
voice
voyage
wag
wagon
wail
waist
waistcoat
*wait
waiter
*wake
*wake up
*walk
*wall
wallet
wallpaper
walrus
wand
wander
*want
wardrobe
*warm
*wash
wash basin
*washing-machine
*wash up
wasp
waste
*watch
*water
waterfall
*watering can
water lily

*wave
wax
waxworks
weapon
*wear
weary
weathercock
weave
web
wedding cake
Wednesday
weed
week
weekend
week (last)
week (next)
weigh
welcome
well
west
*wet
*whale
wharf
what
wheat
*wheel
*wheelbarrow
when
where
which
while
whine
whisker
whisper
whistle
white
who
whole
whose

why
*wicked
wicker
wide
widow
width
wife
wig
wigwam
wild
win
*wind
*windmill
*window
window cleaner
window-sill
windscreen
wine
wing
wink
winking light
wipe
wipers
  (windscreen)
wire basket
wise
*wish
witch
witch's broom
*with
without
wizard
wolf
*woman
*wood
wooden
wool
word
*work

workman

world

*worm

worry

worse

*wrap

wreck

wring

wringer

wrinkle

wrist

*write

*wrong

wrong side out

yacht

yard

yawn

year

*yesterday

yet

yogurt

Yorkshire pudding

young

*zebra

zebra crossing

zig-zag

zinc

zip

*zoo

REFERENCES

BERRY, M. F. (1969) *Language Disorders in Children*, Appleton-Century-Crofts, Educational Division Meredith Corporation, 440 Park Avenue South, New York, USA.

Birth Impairments (1978) Office of Health Economics, London.

BLOOM, F. (1963) *Our Deaf Children*, Gresham Books, London.

BURNS, W. (1973 sec. edition) *Noise and Man*, John Murray, London.

CLEGG, D. (1953) *The Listening Eye*, Royal National Institute for the Deaf.

CONRAD, R. (1976) Research carried out on behalf of the Department of Experimental Psychology, University of Oxford and reported to the Royal National Institute for the Deaf Conference.

COOPER, J., MOODLY, M., REYNELL, J. (1978) *Helping Language Development*, A developmental programme for children with early language handicaps. Edward Arnold, London.

DALE, D. M. C. (1962) *Applied Audiology for Children*, Charles C. Thomas, Springfield, Illinois, USA.

DALE, D. M. C. (1967) *Deaf Children at Home and at School*, University of London Press.

DALE, D. M. C. *Deaf Children and their Hearing Aids*, Deaf Children's Society publication, London.

EDWARDS, R. P. A. and GIBBON, V. (1964) *Words Your Children Use*, Burke, London.

EWING, I. R. and EWING, A.W.G. (1947) *Opportunity and the Deaf Child*, University of London Press.

EWING, I. R. and EWING, A. W. G. (1958) *New Opportunities for Deaf Children*, University of London Press.

GESELL, A. (1971 paperback) *The First Five Years of Life*, Methuen, London.

GIMSON, A. C. (1970 sec. edition) *An Introduction to the Pronunciation of English*, Edward Arnold, London.

GREENE, M. (1964 sec. edition) *The Voice and its Disorders*, Pitman Medical Publishing Co. Ltd, London.

GREGORY, S. (1976) *The Deaf Child and his Family*, George Allen & Unwin, London.

REFERENCES

HARRIS G. M. (1971) *Language for the Pre-School Deaf Child*, Grune & Stratton, New York, USA.

IVES, L. A. (1967) *Deafness and the Development of Intelligence*, British Journal of Disorders of Communication Vol. 2, No. 2.

IVIMEY, G. (1976) *The Written Syntax of an English Deaf Child: an exploration of method*, British Journal of Disorders of Communication, Vol. 11, No. 2.

JEANS, J. (1968) *Science and Music*, Dover Publications Inc., New York (London: Constable).

JEFREE, D. and MCCONKEY, R. (1976) *Let Me Speak*, Human Horizons Series, Souvenir Press, London.

JOHN TRACEY Clinic Correspondence Course for Parents of Pre-School Deaf Children, John Tracey Clinic, 806 West Adams Boulevard, Los Angeles, California 90007, USA.

JONES, G. R., HEMPSTOCK, K. T. L., MULHOLLAND, K. A. and STOLT, M. A. (1965) *Acoustics*, English University Press, Hodder & Stoughton, London.

MCIVER, ANGUS *First Aid in English*, Robert Gibson & Sons, Glasgow.

MCCORMICK, B. (1975) *A Parents' Guide*, National Deaf Children's Society, London.

MYKLEBUST, H. R. (1964) *The Psychology of Deafness*, (sec. edition), Grune & Stratton, New York, USA.

REYNELL, J. (1977) Reynell Developmental Language Scales, NFER Publishing Co. Ltd, Windsor.

SMITH, F. and MILLER, G. A. (1966) *The Genesis of Language*, The MIT Press, Cambridge, Massachusetts and London.

TERMINOLOGY FOR SPEECH PATHOLOGY (1959) authorised by the College of Speech Therapists, Harold Poster House, 6 Lechmere Road, London NW2 5BU.

VALENTINE, C. W. (1950 fourth edition) *Intelligence Tests for Children*, Methuen, London.

WEPMAN, J. M. and HASS W. (1969) *A Spoken Word Count*. Language Research Association, Chicago, USA.

WHETNALL, E. and FRY, D. (1964) *The Deaf Child*, William Heinemann Medical Books Ltd, London.

INDEX